Yoga and the Sacred Fire

Self-Realization and Planetary Transformation

By David Frawley

LOTUS

Cover & Page Design/Layout: Paul Bond, Art & Soul Design
Illustrations: Hinduism Today Magazine
Copy Editing: Betheyla Anuradha
Dr. Frawley's Portrait: Sujata Bansal

First Edition, 2004
    Printed in the United States of America
    Yoga and the Sacred Fire: Self-Realization and Planetary Transformation
ISBN: 0-940985-75-6
Library of Congress Control Number: 2004093483

Published by:
Lotus Press
P.O. Box 325
Twin Lakes, Wisconsin 53181 USA
web: www.lotuspress.com
e-mail: lotuspress@lotuspress.com
800-824-6396

Table of Contents

Foreword

We live at a critical time in history, with the uncertainties of war, physical insecurity, and job loss. Technology has shrunk the world, creating new challenges and opportunities, and we are at the threshold of the age of knowledge. But although science has explained most of the outer world, it still lacks the answer to the mystery of the spirit. Meanwhile, out of the necessity to conform to the rhythms of machines that surround us, our lives have become mechanical, causing alienation and despair.

In our hearts we are convinced of a higher truth, but there is a disconnect between this promise of knowledge and the humdrum reality of our everyday lives. It is this disharmony that is making us increasingly ill. We are falling prey to new diseases, physically and psychologically. These are signals to us: stop a minute and look around, take charge of your life, know yourself, seek the mystery of your being.

This is where Yoga comes in, because it is the discipline that puts us in touch with our spirit. Many readers perhaps take Yoga to mean physical exercises (*asanas*) but that is only a small part of it. The *asanas* and the mastery of the body is preparation for the mastery of the mind. The objective of Yoga is the union of the body and the spirit — freedom, compassion and harmony.

Yoga is part of the larger tradition of the *Veda* that is concerned with self-knowledge. The *Vedas* — probably the most ancient books of our species which have been preserved — tell us that ignorance is behind the belief that we are only our physical selves, when in fact we are spiritual beings capable of experiencing the most wonderful happiness that is not limited by time or space.

The *Vedas* tell of deep connections linking the outer and the inner worlds and all beings. We are part of the web of creation not only in the biological sense, but in a deeper spiritual sense. We are here for a specific reason; each one of us has unique destiny. It is when we fail to reach our promise that we suffer from physical and mental pain.

There is an old struggle between faith and knowledge. Faith is a counterfoil to the idea of gnosis, which is that knowledge is possible through the psychological functions of thinking, sensation, and feeling. Certainly, Yoga also requires faith. But it is not the faith of dogma, but rather the faith in the certainty of self-transformation, the proof of which the Yogic practitioner finds in daily life.

The conscious mind is like the tip of the iceberg; below it lies the unconscious mind which is infinitely more complex. The conscious mind is the rational self and the unconscious mind is the irrational self. According to Yoga, the mind is like an inverted tree: the conscious mind has access to just the flowers and the leaves but beyond it lies the mighty trunk and it extends as far as one can imagine.

The struggle between the conscious and the unconscious, or knowledge and faith, has taken many forms. Gnosticism, or the search for such higher knowledge, went into decline in the West long ago, but modern science has adopted many key elements of it, and now Yoga brings it back in all its glory and power for the benefit of modern man.

Yogic postures are depicted on the third millennium BC seals of India and the even older art indicates meditational experience. The *Rig Veda,* the oldest Vedic text, speaking of the visions (*dhi*) of harmony stretched on the loom of cosmic existence, compares this task to harnessing of the plow (*yuga*), first introducing the term yoga. The mind is seen to act as the flutterings of a bird, suggesting its union in the heart with the divine. The *Rig Veda* asserts that the universe is stationed within the heart, promising knowledge if one looks within.

The goal of Yoga is self-transformation and transcendence, achieved by joining the body and mind to the spirit within. This is an interiorization of the Vedic ritual that is more commonly done externally. Since the mind is not a vessel to be filled, but rather a flame to be lit, Vedic ritual consists of those practices that help light this fire. Yogic practices, which are like movement and meditation rituals, similarly help light our inner fire.

By the time of the *Bhagavad Gita*, the most popular text of Yoga, the teachings are already very ancient. Other early texts that describe Yoga are the *Katha*, the *Shvetashvatara*, and the *Maitrayaniya Upanishads*, and the classic *Yoga Sutras* of Patanjali which came a bit later.

History informs us that Mitanni kings worshiping the *Vedas* flourished in West Asia before the rise of the Judeo-Christian tradition. Many see the Pharaoh Akhenaten as the first monotheist; it is less known that his queen Tadukhipa was the daughter of the Mitanni king Tushratta (Dasharatha) with possible connections to Vedic India. Akhenaten's worship of the sun disc is similar to the veneration of the sun disc in the Vedic tradition. The sun here represents the inner fire of the mind in its fully awakened condition. Called Agni in the *Rig Veda*, this fire is also given the name Yahvah in that text drawing yet more interesting parallels to the early phase of western religions.

David Frawley's *Yoga and the Sacred Fire* breaks fresh ground by considering Yoga and Agni, the Vedic sacred fire, together and connecting this understanding to mystical and native spiritual traditions worldwide. Calling us to reclaim our sacred fires and use them to build a consciousness friendly future for the planet, it charts a yogic course beyond our present planetary crisis that is in harmony with the vision of the most ancient seers and sages.

Doing this allows Frawley to build bridges between diverse traditions and show the path to the most secret intuitions of spiritual experience. He presents his material in a very engaging style, emphasizing universal themes, and drawing upon the wisdom of different cultures, showing also their Vedic connections in the idea of an ancient and eternal global spirituality of light. An especially delightful aspect of the book are its many autobiographical notes drawn from the author's own spiritual journey.

Frawley is one of the preeminent interpreters of Vedic wisdom of our times. I have known him for close to fifteen years and I marvel at his energy and his dedication to make Vedic knowledge accessible to the general public. This book presents the Yoga of the Sacred Fire not only in the recesses of our heart but also in the world around us. It attempts to raise the sacred fire into a universal metaphor for our spiritual aspiration as a species. It offers insights at many levels that are invaluable to the Yogic practitioner and to any seeker of the mystery of consciousness. This is a key primer of spirituality. It shows a way to personal enlightenment and wisdom, and it indicates how it can be done with grace, and compassion for all beings.

Subhash Kak

Delaune Distinguished Professor
Louisiana State University, Baton Rouge
March 2004

Author's Preface

Yoga in its true essence is about an internal fire, called *Agni* in Sanskrit. It is not simply an exercise system, a therapy, a philosophy or even a system of meditation. Yoga is about an inner transformation at the deepest core of the mind and heart, which depends upon fire not as a material force but as a spiritual being and an inner guide.

This 'fire of Yoga' is not a mere human invention but a force both of nature and of the spirit — a power of higher evolution hidden within us that can take us beyond the human to the Divine. It is a manifestation of the cosmic fire through which the universe is created and from which its development occurs on all levels from matter to mind.

This book is about Yoga and Agni both relative to individual spiritual practice and the evolution of the universe, which are interrelated. It is about our spiritual history as a soul and creative power in the cosmos. Yet, most importantly, it examines our current evolutionary crisis as a species. Our current global difficulty is above all a crisis in consciousness that has arisen from neglecting the soul and the sacred presence within and around us. To deal with it properly requires a new inner fire to lead us back into the light. Whatever else we may do today, we cannot ignore the planetary situation that grows more dangerous every year as our current civilization continues to spin out of harmony and threaten the very fabric of life.

To overcome this crisis, we must recall, re-invoke if you will, what is not only the most ancient theme of the yogic spirituality of India, but perhaps of the entire world — the sacred fire. The sacred fire, or Agni, represents both the sacred nature of the universe and of our own soul — the fire hidden in our own bodies and minds, which is our individual portion of the Divine. Our soul is not just an abstract entity but an inner fire connected to all the forces of the universe that we can use to change the nature of our reality from darkness to light, from ignorance to enlightenment. This labor of the soul is the practice of Yoga, which is our reintegration into the unitary light of consciousness that is our true being.

While the main insights I am proposing are based on India's ancient Yoga and Vedanta tradition, I have tried to make them relevant to our greater spiritual urge as a species that has taken on many names and forms. This inner heritage of light remains in the heart of every person. It is the legacy of the spiritual humanity from which we have perhaps not so much progressed as fallen. We must now labor hard and long to turn our fall into the means of a new ascension. We must once more light the sacred fire within ourselves and within our societies.

Over the past three decades, I have done extensive work with the profound spiritual and healing traditions of India, the country that has often been called 'the spiritual motherland of the planet'. This has resulted in over twenty books on Yoga, Ayurveda, Tantra, Veda and Vedanta that have examined these systems in detail and helped trained practitioners within them. I have also seen how Yoga has been, if not misrepresented, at least only superficially presented in the West, in which its deeper transformative principles and practices easily get lost in purely physical or personal concerns.

The greater Yoga tradition is one of God-realization and Self-realization, not simply as an individual practice, but as the goal of all life and creation. This yogic view of the universe is crucial for understanding our species and for dealing with our global crisis. The book aims at such a broader presentation of Yoga as an evolutionary process occurring not only in human beings but in all of nature.

Today many people on the spiritual path get lost in what could be called the 'psychology of spirituality', which remains if not a fixation on the personal self, at least one on the human self in which the greater issues of the planet are easily obscured. The book aims at the 'cosmology of spirituality', the basis of which is the universal Self that is present in all nature extending beyond time and space as pure Being-Consciousness-Bliss. Our true Self is the universal being reflected in all existence — not our psychological self that is little more than a social mirage. Self-realization requires going beyond the psychological self, not simply in trying to unravel all of its details.

I have covered a lot of ground along the way. A number of the themes and chapter subjects could be entire books in their own right. Such a panoramic approach is meant to put us in touch with the greater universe of consciousness, so that we can enter into that inner reality where there is true freedom and understanding. Hopefully, I have opened some doors and spread some light, but the vistas revealed by the fire of Yoga go far beyond what anyone could put into words. When one returns to that flame, all that is inessential gets burned away.

David Frawley (Vamadeva Shastri)

Santa Fe, New Mexico
September 2003

Format

The *Prologue* provides the background for the book through the author's story of his discovery of the *Vedas* and of Agni, the Sacred Fire.

Part I, *The Soul and the Sacred Fire,* is an introduction to the Sacred Fire and its cosmic connections, showing consciousness as the basis of all light, energy and matter in the universe, which is mirrored in the soul and its powers of mind, life and body.

Part II, *The Journey of the Soul through the Kingdoms of Nature,* describes the journey of the soul, symbolically the Sacred Fire, through the mineral, plant, animal realms and the different types of fire that it develops along the way as part of its evolutionary growth.

Part III, *Human Evolution and the Fire of Yoga,* examines the human being, our place in nature and the path of Yoga as a means of facilitating both our ordinary well-being and our higher evolutionary potential as a species.

Part IV, *A Call for a New Sacred Fire,* examines the current global situation as an evolutionary crisis that arises from the neglect of the soul. It proposes a new Sacred Fire, symbolic of a new consciousness, as the solution.

Part V, *Planetary Yoga and the Planetary Flame,* introduces a new planetary approach to Yoga as a means of dealing with this evolutionary crisis and using it as a tool for inner awakening.

Part VI, *Appendices*: More technical comments and references can be found in the endnotes, while books that provide more detail on the topics covered are listed in the Bibliography. A Glossary provides an explanation of the Sanskrit terms used. The Sanskrit translations from the *Vedas* and *Upanishads* are the author's.

=== Dedication ===

To the keepers of the sacred flame
in all lands and cultures and in all ages —
our elders in the Fire.

To the many forms of the Sacred Fire on Earth,
in Heaven and beyond — in the rocks, plants,
animals, humans, devas and all beings.

To the ancient Fire Religion of Enlightenment,
the eternal religion of humanity —
may it arise again in myriad forms and faces!

To the great Yogis who have maintained the fire
of Yoga that connects us with our true Self
that is the Self of the entire universe.

In these crucial times we are each urgently called upon to
become elders, midwifing a new planetary culture, weaving
together, as prophesized, the sky wisdoms with the earth
wisdoms. In this dharmic soul endeavor, David Frawley's
latest book appears as a particularly luminous flame, a gen-
erous-hearted gift of a modern rishi to and from the great
Sacred Fire that lives in all that is.

Duncan Campbell,
host of *Living Dialogues with Duncan Campbell*
on public television, radio, and the Internet

"In this unique and beautiful book, David Frawley brings to the modern mind the archetypal wisdom of the ages. Through the fire of his intellect, Vamadeva illuminates our path to healing and transformation."

David Simon, M.D.,
author *Vital Energy*

"The fire which burns in Vamadeva Shastri's book is, like man, both material and divine, immanent and transcendent. That fire, like man, is and contains the force of the universe which drives both change within us and evolution in the world outside. That fire is a bridge between the sacred and the profane, a bridge from this world to the world of the Gods, a bridge, if we use it, between the precarious place humanity now finds itself and the place we all yearn to be. Vamadeva Shastri takes us to the far side of that bridge, where God, soul and world are one.

This book is a journey of ideas and intuitions which draw deeply on the native wisdom found in all cultures, a book that speaks of lofty philosophical issues and everyday encounters with nature in almost every sentence. Vamadeva Shastri offers the gift of seeing anew the world around us, including plants, animals, foods and medicines — of hoping again that the world may be well ten thousand years from now, of learning once more that we are intertwined with the whole of existence and urgently need to change our relationship with nature.

Having this voice only makes us eager to ask Agni, the Divine Fire, for ten thousand more like him, for then the true form of Vedic wisdom would blossom again, as it must."

Paramacharya Palaniswami,
Hinduism Today magazine, Editor-in-Chief

Prologue

Discovering the Sacred Fire

Fire fascinates all of us, whether it is the fireplace of our living rooms on secluded winter nights, or an open campfire in the wilderness during the midst of summer. We all sense in fire something sacred beyond the merely human, a secret messenger and an ancient friend. Looking into the eyes of the fire we find a doorway into the inner world of the heart, where the unknown spreads its wings into eternity. The world opens up beyond the boundaries of our senses and we contact an all-pervasive light flooding our minds.

Fire always struck me with such an aura of mystery and magic, not simply as an outer force in nature but as an archetypal power in the psyche. After all, what is more primal than fire? Fire had a poetic and mystical reality, an inner signification for the life of the soul. Fire, lightning, the sun, the dawn, day and night — these common forms of light are the original images of our soul drawn from our experience in nature. Yet they have an inner meaning as well, reflecting our soul's development as it grows in light and truth from a mere spark to a great luminary of its own.

These many faces of light are also the images of ancient spirituality, indigenous religions and the oldest rituals of our species. They reflect not merely an awe of the great forces of nature but an intuition of a deeper consciousness working through nature, an inner fire and light that is more powerful than anything that we can observe in the visible world.

Examining poetry, philosophy and mysticism worldwide — particularly the deeper teachings of India's Yoga tradition — I gradually discovered that they were all based on different forms of fire. Some of these fires or flames appeared to be only metaphors. However, looking deeply, I found that even in metaphor the fire as a spiritual principle is known to us at a heart level, even if we may deny it with the intellect.

Fire represents the inner light that exists within the very Earth on which we live and contains the key to our own transformation. An early poem of mine reflects this inspiration:

> *The inner Fire*
> *Is the true light of awareness*
> *Supreme beyond all darkness*
> *It burns forever*
> *In the stillness of the Earth*
> *The subterranean sun*
> *Of a crystalline sky*

I was also an avid reader of ancient history and felt that there was a common spiritual culture behind the sacred symbols of the ancient world, the foremost of which was fire.[1] Eventually I came to recognize an ancient fire religion that probably underlies all the religions of the world and is the foundation of our spiritual striving as a species. This religion of fire is part of the worship of the Sun or the heavenly fire. It is the religion of light and enlightenment.

If we examine our global spiritual heritage, we see that the worship of the Sun, Fire and Lightning — the three dynamic powers of light in Heaven, Earth and the atmosphere — pervaded the ancient world from Mexico and Peru to Egypt, Sumeria, Persia, India and China, even to ancient Europe of the Greeks, Romans and Celts. The Sun

God, the Thunder or Lightning God and the Fire God are found universally, being obvious to anyone who gazes upon the light. Their worship — already sophisticated and worldwide at the dawn of what we call civilization — may reflect a deeper spiritual wisdom from even older and greater civilizations, the existence of which our historians still prefer to ignore.[2]

We can easily understand these three forces through how the light of Heaven (the Sun) takes shape through the clouds (lightning) and condenses as material forms on Earth (fire), producing what we know as life. Yet these aspects of light are not merely outer powers. They are energies of our own soul, powers of mind (sun), vital force (lightning) and body (fire). Working with these powers of light inwardly is the basis of many mystical and meditation practices, such as we see in the greater science of Yoga. The outer forms of light in the world of nature are expressions of the inner light of consciousness, which is the highest truth.

Awakening to the Ancient Vedic Vision

My main connection to this ancient fire religion came through the *Vedas*, the oldest scriptures of India and of the Yoga tradition, which have remarkably preserved their fire mantras — their chants to the great Fire God *Agni* — since long before the time of the Buddha. The *Vedas* represent an ancient fire teaching, not only as ritual but also as the practice of meditation, which is a methodology for working with our inner fire of awareness.

The *Vedas* are said to be the original teachings of the ancient Himalayan seers or 'Rishis', great yogis and mystics who lived at the dawn of this cycle of civilization many thousands of years ago after a great flood.[3] The Rishis were spiritual beings born directly from the sacred fire, reflecting that they went beyond their ordinary humanity to the universal light. They perceived the Vedic mantras inherent in the cosmic mind, which is why the Vedic teaching is said to be eternal and universal.

Most notable are seven great Rishis connected to the stars of the Big Dipper as cosmic forces.[4] They were said to be companions of the first man called *Manu* and to be the original great spiritual masters behind all spiritual traditions. Yet beyond their merely human forms, the Rishis were said to participate in the creation of life along with God or the supreme Divine, as cosmic creators in their own right. Many ancient traditions, including the Sumerian and the Chinese, speak of such seven great sages, suggesting that this Rishi tradition was once global.[5] It is bound up with our oldest myths of origins and the earliest memories of our species.

The *Vedas* present a massive corpus of fire worship — both in terms of outer rituals and inner yogic practices — such as probably once existed throughout the ancient world, but whose texts in other cultures were largely lost over the long course of time. Most notable is the *Rig Veda*, the oldest Vedic text and perhaps oldest book in the world, which among its thousand hymns contains over two hundred cryptic hymns to the sacred fire. Most of the inspiration for my writings derives from the *Rig Veda*, which has been my favorite book and constant companion for over thirty years.

From my first encounter with them, I approached the *Vedas* not as a mere scholar or academician, a westerner looking from the outside as it were, but as one for whom the tradition resonated with his own being and was part of his own inner heritage. I had no family or educational background that would explain my initial interest, much less long term work in a field as remote from modern America as the ancient Hindu *Vedas*. I was the second of ten children in a Wisconsin family and educated in Catholic schools until we settled down in Denver when I was about ten.

However, like many young people in the late nineteen sixties, I took an interest in eastern spirituality as part of the counterculture movement of the times. But I was not content merely to follow popular trends. Something drew me to the older Vedic vision behind the modern physically based Yoga that was gradually emerging at the time.

The work of the great modern Indian seer and yogi, Sri Aurobindo (1872-1950), opened the door to the Vedic world for me in 1971 when I first came upon his Vedic writings. Reading his translations of Vedic hymns to the Dawn, I experienced a kind of Vedic epiphany — a vision of a continuous spiral of luminous dawns as a dance of the Goddess from the heart of creation, ascending all the levels and stairs of existence to supernal realms of consciousness beyond time and space.

Based on that inspiration I gradually taught myself Vedic Sanskrit — something almost unheard of and I would probably have never attempted to do if I had stopped to really think about the scope of the task I was taking upon myself. I soon began translating Vedic hymns, finding in them the deepest issues of spirituality, psychology, philosophy and culture. Meanwhile, in my outer life I began working with plants and herbs, which went along well with these ancient poems and mantras born of nature. I continued this Vedic research with little outside help or recognition for several years.

The anonymous situation of my Vedic work changed in 1979 when I met M.P. Pandit, the secretary of the Sri Aurobindo Ashram, one of the largest Yoga and Vedic centers in India. Pandit, the author of nearly a hundred books, including several on the *Vedas*, was on a tour to the US in San Francisco, not far from Mendocino County where I was living at the time. I visited with him and showed him my Vedic translations, explaining that they reflected my own inspiration, that I had no educational background in the field and was wondering whether what I was doing had any value at all. Looking with his penetrating eyes that reflected long periods of meditation, he replied that such a direct approach to the *Vedas* allowed me to avoid the great mistakes scholars typically make, which had kept the wisdom of these ancient texts lost in obscurity through all these years.[6]

Pandit awakened me to what he called my 'Vedic mission' and continued to encourage me in it until his death in 1994. As soon as he returned to India, he began serializing my Vedic writings through various Sri Aurobindo ashram journals and later helped me publish my first books on the subject.[7]

Given my lack of any Vedic background in this life, Pandit suggested that my work was a continuation of a past life effort. I also had various experiences, particularly in India, which confirmed this, with Vedic chants and fire offerings that reflected deep memories within me. Vedic texts were something familiar to me, like the mountains and the clouds, not something foreign or ancient. They made more sense to me than our modern shopping malls and the rest of our commercial culture that seem quite alien to the soul.

For me karma and rebirth are part of life, not mere theories or speculations. Our present life can or should be the continuation of the spiritual practice and work of the last. The knowledge of the soul has the power to transcend death. I think we can all draw upon the past life knowledge if we look deep enough inside to contact our soul's seeking of the eternal that is our real purpose for being here.

I took on this Vedic mission as my own and have continued in it ever since. It eventually led to my recognition as a Vedic teacher in India, a surprising turn of events for an American youth who started his Vedic work before having even left the United States. I was given the name Vamadeva Shastri after the great Vedic seer Vamadeva in 1991 and was officially made into a Pandit[8] in a special ceremony in India in 1995. The *Vedas* became the basis of my own thought and the sacred fire, the light in which I understand myself.

Symbolic Poetry and the Vedic Mantra

As a great poet and philosopher, Sri Aurobindo's Vedic interpretations have a depth and insight that allows the *Vedas* to come to life for the receptive reader. As an aspiring young poet and yogi, I could appreciate his vision of the Vedic dawn as the awakening of our soul's aspiration from life to life, or the Vedic fire as the Divine will to transformation within us.

My entrance into the Vedic world came at this poetic level. The ground for it had been prepared by an examination of the mystical, symbolic and imagistic poetry of the West. French symbolist poets like Rimbaud, Mallarme and Bonnefoy, as well as the German mystical poet Rilke, showed me a deeper usage of language in which the word, the image and the idea could be woven together to intimate a higher reality far beyond the ordinary world. A series of poems came to me in a flash of inspiration immediately preceding my first efforts to translate the *Vedas* in 1978. The first began with these verses:

> *Light breaks on the unceasing shore*
> *The day descends upon the wind*
> *And again you touch the Earth and hold the sky*
> *We will sing of the ancient nights*
>
> *We will invoke luminous dawns in far-off skies*
> *You will awaken to your hidden heart*
> *Your forgotten home*
> *Your dark eyes will see deeply*
> *Drink rapturously the ascending wave*
> *The returning chant*

What we discover in ancient teachings like the *Vedas*, *I Ching* or *Egyptian Book of the Dead* is more like such symbolist poetry than any philosophy or theology. Yet it is a poetry that expresses itself through the forces of nature, not merely through human thoughts and emotions. It is not simply reflecting but actually speaking with the voice of nature through the cosmic language of light. The *Vedas* present a meta-language of nature that can function as an analogue for all forms of knowledge in the universe from science to metaphysics, something that reminded me of the Glass Bead Game in Herman Hesse's novel *Magister Ludi*, in which enlightened individuals played with the essence of all knowledge. That many scholars have confused the Vedic language with primitive poetry only shows how removed we are from the language of life, in which the images of nature are the revelation of our own soul.

Following the Vedic light, I gradually passed into the Vedic world and made it my own. I left our present civilizational mindset for an older, more primal and yet more transcendent vision. It was like traveling back in time, crossing into a previous world-age thousands of years ago. My being was recast in a different type of culture, almost becoming a different person in the process. Sometimes this was a bit frightening — a kind of death of the ego, but it was also a great adventure that brought many unexpected insights and inspirations.

Eventually I learned to hear the Vedic voice directly, its song of the ascension of the light that is the very rhythm of life. The Vedic deities began to reveal themselves as both the spirit behind the forces of nature and the secret powers of our own psyche. It became clear that the awesome and magical universe of consciousness in which we really live is much better portrayed in such ancient mantras than in our too abstract scientific discourse that only touches the surface of the boundless world.

Vedic teachings began to speak to me through the world of nature, no longer being limited to any particular texts. They helped me read the language of nature as a living language of the soul. The entire universe became revealed as a world of light and consciousness, reflecting an unlimited wisdom and bliss far beyond our human fears and desires.

Agni, the Vedic Fire God

The Vedic deity of the sacred fire called *Agni* or the 'inner guide' came to function as the high priest of this inner transformation. That fire deep within us always leads us forward in our journey and quest in life. Agni represents the soul hidden in the body, the secret intelligence of God latent in the material world, like fire hidden in wood. This inner fire is the ancient teacher, the original guru of the yogic path who abides within us.

Agni is the Divine Child or child of immortality for whom is all this creation, the Divine Self immanent in all creatures. It is our own inner core of knowledge, delight and aspiration for the supreme that leads us forward from birth to birth, helping us overcome all obstacles and turn all sorrow into joy. Discovering that inner flame, one finds a doorway to inner worlds that lie far beyond the outer world of human strife and suffering. One leaves the constriction of the physical body for realms of freedom in pure mind and unbounded awareness.

Once awakened within our hearts, this flame of consciousness expands to pervade the entire universe, which is its home. Agni is said to manifest all the Gods and Goddesses, meaning that the fire of the soul reveals all the powers of cosmic consciousness. Agni as the spiritually awakened soul brings the great godheads and cosmic powers of truth and dharma, so that we can understand the nature of reality, which is eternal. This light of the soul within us can illumine all of existence, unraveling all the mysteries of time and space to what endures beyond both birth and death.

As my Vedic studies progressed, I began to understand this inner fire as the basis for all the forces of matter, energy and mind both externally and internally, as well as the spirit that transcends all forms. I began to discover myself within this ancient Fire God that is the secret flame shining everywhere around and within us. If this book has any real value, it is because that child of fire has hopefully found a voice within it.

Yoga and Ayurveda:
Vedic Medicine and Meditation

My Vedic work developed from a study of Yoga, which I was drawn to not so much as a physical discipline but as a path of Self-realization. In this regard, I also studied the philosophy and psychology of Yoga, particularly through the great teachings of Vedanta from the *Upanishads* and *Bhagavad Gita* to the works of modern Yoga-Vedanta teachers like Ramakrishna and Vivekananda.[9] The yogic view of the Self or Atman as the supreme reality came to dominate my world-view.

I experimented with various yogic practices of pranayama (breathing exercises), mantra and meditation that resulted in the awakening of the yogic fire or *Kundalini* within me. I remember my first such efforts, breathing deeply, looking intently within, repeating certain mantras, wanting to take a leap of consciousness beyond the mind. The internal light that these practices created was quite profound, unlike anything I had experienced or even expected. The sense of the immortal Self as the inner fire arose within me.

I came to realize that the system of Yoga was a practical application of the ancient fire wisdom. Yoga is the very methodology of light, a seeking to integrate the powers of light within — our breath, senses and mind. It works not through mere ideas or beliefs but through precise methods to harness higher energy sources inside ourselves. Through a consistent practice of Yoga we can experience the insights of all the great philosophical and religious teachings of the world as our own inner awareness; we can go beyond their words and concepts to the real fire of which these are but sparks.

Yoga in turn led me to Ayurvedic medicine, India's great natural healing tradition and sister science to Yoga, what could be called 'yogic medicine'. Ayurveda is Vedic 'fire medicine', reflecting the healing power of fire (Agni) in many forms from digestion and respiration to perception and awareness. Through Ayurveda one can work with this universal power of fire at the most fundamental level of health. This provides the practical foundation from which we can probe into inner forms of fire as breath, mind and consciousness.

Ayurveda helped me understand how fire energizes our bodies and minds and is the key to our well-being on all levels. The herbal side of Ayurveda was most interesting. It brought me in contact with the healing fires of the Earth that reside in the plants. Practicing Ayurveda helped me understand how fire works as an energetic force within our bodies, adding a living and concrete dimension to my previous poetic and philosophical approaches to it.

The Sacred Universe

Just as the *Vedas* reflect the revelation of the Divine in nature, yogic wisdom is a doorway to the greater universe of consciousness that both embraces and transcends all forms. It is not a matter of merely one tradition or discipline or another. That is why the Yoga tradition always teaches, "Truth is One, but the paths are many." This understanding goes back to the *Rig Veda* which states, "That which is the One Truth, the seers teach in manifold ways."[10] In this tradition, God is first of all our friend and beloved companion, our co-traveler on the sacred journey, who leads us along our appropriate path.

The sacred fire exists in all life as the light that sustains everything. It cannot be reduced to any particular religion, philosophy or spiritual path; though it can work through many of these as well. We must remember that only what is sanctified in our own inner fire becomes real food for our souls, whatever name we may choose to call it. The fire of the soul is the power that gives life to all forms, starting with our own bodies.

The sacred fire is ultimately the universe itself, defining all processes of matter, energy and mind that exist anywhere in time and space. This cosmic fire underlies our own life processes of eating, breathing, sensing, feeling, knowing and being aware. It is the true speaker, seer, knower and doer within us, of which our current human personalities are but a reflection or a shadow. All that we see is the sacred fire in its various incarnations, starting with ourselves.

I have visited many temples and churches but find a greater sense of the sacred in the world of nature away from any human constructions. Most places that are truly sacred reflect the power of nature more than any mere human activity. I have always felt a certain presence in the world of nature, a spirit within all her animate and inanimate forms. I felt the trees as alive and aware even when I was a child. Their energy reaches out to us whenever we look at them. They lead our awareness upwards through their trunks and branches into the heavens beyond. This was no fantasy, but a fact of experience. It was self-evident. I could sense the immanent Divinity of the *Upanishads*, the Self that is in nature:

> *To the Deity who dwells in the fire and in the waters, who has entered into the entire universe, who is in the plants and in the trees, to that God we offer our humble surrender.* [11]

After all, everything *is* and Being is aware. Being is pure presence beyond limitation that carries and connects all forms into the infinite and eternal — the supreme Brahman of Vedantic thought. We can contact this essence of being in our own being, in our deeper hearts and minds, if we would but put our arrogance of knowing aside and look at the world without any demands or preconceptions.

The substratum of our experience is the sense of a sacred existence holding all things from within, but reaching beyond all boundaries, transcending time and space into the unbounded unknown. *Being is present in all things like an inextinguishable fire.* And that Being is conscious and pure, untainted by our human concerns and prejudices, calmly accepting all things in its infinite fullness and peace.

I could feel that Being even in inanimate objects, in the metal of cars reflecting the streetlights, in the stones of buildings, or the pavement of the road, looking at me, talking to me like another form of myself, drawing me to move beyond this world. Being remains in all of its serene beauty like a light behind our lives, particularly when we are quiet enough to hear its silent voice. Being is hidden in all things at their silent core. But we need an awareness that can penetrate behind the glitter of outer forms in order to contact it. Otherwise we easily overlook it and missing it lose our simplest most direct and natural connection to the Divine.

Native Traditions and the Sacred Fire

There is a Native American side about this teaching of the sacred fire as well. I have lived in Santa Fe, New Mexico, the land of the Pueblo Indians, for about twenty years, going into the nearby mountains and desert on a regular basis. My main treks have been in the Sangre De Cristo range close to Santa Fe, in the foothills of which my house is located, which have wonderful high mountains reaching above tree line. However, over the last few years I felt a special pull from the rocks of the Jemez Mountains on the other side of the Rio Grande River, from a region that was the heartland of the old Pueblo Indian culture.

The Jemez Mountains are the handiwork of great ancient volcanoes, containing the Valle Grande, a large mountain valley that is the largest volcanic caldera, or crater, in the world. I felt a spirit, perhaps the voice of an old native teacher, drawing me to the Earth in that realm of the fire rocks. This led me to an examination of geology from a Vedic point of view and a discovery of the volcanic fire, the Earth fire that is the basis of all land on the planet. The fire from within the Earth reached out to me as another form of the sacred fire. It helped me understand the fire wisdom in the land and rock on which I live. That volcanic fire, like an ancient God wishing to speak again, has aided in this book and contributed to its message.

Curiously this same Jemez Mountain region of New Mexico is the home to Los Alamos laboratories where the nuclear bomb was first invented. It is a strange irony that such a realm of the sacred fire was the very place where modern man developed perhaps the most unsacred fire ever to be released upon the planet.

The rocks and the land have their spirits and their voices that native peoples can still access. Today they are calling out to us, urging us to reconnect to our soul and reclaim our sacred fire that remains in the care of Mother Earth. Much of the world soul, including the spirits of our ancestors and gurus, has retired into the rocks and mountains as our civilization has banished the sacred from its domain. These people of the rocks are seeking to emerge again from the stone into which they withdrew long ago, bringing back all the powers of the Earth to restore the sacred order of the universe in our human realm. They represent our own souls that we have neglected and cast into obscurity, which are now crying to be restored to life.

I had not always connected native and tribal forms of spirituality with the yogic traditions that appear more philosophically and psychologically complex. However, my recent travels to India helped me bring the two together. I visited the northeast of the country (greater Assam) for the first time in early 2002. I had a rare opportunity to visit the tribal people of Arunachal Pradesh, the easternmost Himalayas in India, and the Khasi and Jayanta hills of Meghalaya to the south above Bangladesh. Later the same year I participated in a conference in Assam that featured leaders from all the main tribal groups of the region.

Various tribal cultures remain in these areas, continuing their ancient ways with not only similar customs and dress but with similar facial features as Native Americans. Clearly they are kindred souls on the other side of the planet. I became involved with efforts to help preserve such native cultures, which even in that remote part of the world are under siege by the forces of modern civilization (many it seems emanating from the United States).

Such contacts with native traditions helped me understand the Vedic as perhaps the world's best preserved ancient native tradition and Yoga as a manifestation of our global native or Earth heritage. The *Vedas* provide a link between tribal practices like fire worship and the great meditational systems of Yoga and eastern philosophy that rest upon an inner fire. The sacred is usually more obvious to those who live close to the Earth. It arises from life and from the land, not from ideas, beliefs or dogmas.

Something of my own Irish ancestry also enters into this seeking for the sacred fire, from the ancient Celts and their sacred fire, bards and sages. I have also begun exploring this connection in recent years, including working with various Celtic teachers and groups in North America. Such older European traditions like that of the Druids show that a yogic path of experiential spirituality once existed in the West and never entirely disappeared.

Ancient tribal fires still remain burning deep within us and can be brought once more to life. They represent an older core of our European heritage than our current materialistic culture, remaining hidden in seed form in our blood and in our genes. This is perhaps why so many people in the West are attracted to eastern spiritual teachings. These are not really foreign to us but reflect a forgotten cultural heritage of our own that we are now seeking to reclaim.

The sacred fire remains our ancestor, guide and oldest and most trustworthy friend, wherever we may take birth and whatever culture we may follow. Let us once more look with the eyes of fire and recognize the sacred flame in its many forms, shapes and colors, following its many movements through the universe and the Earth on which we reside and, above all, within ourselves.

I

The Soul and the Sacred Fire

CHAPTER ONE

Ancient Remembrances

Metaphor, like myth, reflects an inner reality that can be more significant than anything we can perceive externally. When we speak of something being 'like fire', we may be expressing a deeper truth — intimating the Cosmic Fire that is the basis of the entire universe. All human languages have phrases like the 'fire of love', the 'fire of anger', the 'fire of truth' or the 'fire of desire'. Clearly, our strongest feelings are like fire. This is because our core feeling nature, our soul, is an inner fire — a power, a passion and a transforming force.

This language of fire provides a key to the meaning of our lives. Both the world of nature and the Godhead behind it reflect awesome fires. Their lights teach us in many forms from when we rise in the morning to when we fall asleep at night. We live in a reality defined by light both outwardly and inwardly, from the stars to our deeper consciousness beyond the mind.

There abides deep within our hearts an inextinguishable flame of Divine light, love and life that never goes out through all our varied experiences, whether we are young or old, healthy or sick, happy or sad. I think at one time or another we have all sensed that immortal flame deep within us, providing inspiration, insight and motivation, particularly when we need it the most in times of crisis or difficulty. This spiritual flame of the heart is struggling to emerge from this world of darkness, seeking the light from which it has come. Its development is the very purpose of our existence.

Our soul journeys along with us through our life's pilgrimage of birth, growth, decay and death as we seek meaning, happiness and identity in a strange and uncertain world. It represents our deeper identity through the entire process of rebirth, from life to life, as we traverse the world of nature back to the Godhead that is our true home. The soul leads us in this cosmic dance of consciousness, of which our current life is but a step, a moment, a sojourn or perhaps a deviation.

Rediscovering the Soul

'Soul' is a commonly used, if not overly used term, but nevertheless retains an aura and a mystery that commands our attention. The idea of the soul causes us to consider the spiritual roots from which we have come. It raises the question of something within ourselves beyond the body and the senses, where we are connected to the infinite and the eternal, something that one could call God.

I would like to use the soul in the sense of the sacred fire within us, the immortal part of our nature that is our inner guide and true Self. I believe this is the original meaning of the term in ancient religions and in the minds and hearts of all true mystics and sages. Certainly this is its implication in the Yoga tradition that identifies the Jiva or reincarnating-soul with Agni or the inner fire.[12] It is perhaps because of this understanding of 'spirituality as fire' that the Yoga tradition has proved so enduring and why it has always emphasized inner energy practices over any external philosophy or dogma.

The soul is the eternal or timeless part of ourselves that belongs not to the outer human world but to nature and to God. It has evolved through the eons in the world of nature, providing a capacity far beyond our current birth, education or circumstances. The soul, therefore, is not the human part of our nature but that within us which transcends and underlies the human, making the human possible but also showing us a way beyond its limitations.

For this reason, our soul is happier in nature than in society, which is why we all experience joy and inspiration in being outdoors. There is something free and untamed about the soul. It is like a wild animal that runs away if we try to catch it. There is something tempestuous or even cataclysmic about the soul's manifestation. As we approach this unknown core of our psyche, we find it resembles a primal force of nature like forest fire, a hurricane or volcano. It can be frightening for our outer ego to get too close to our true soul, which can efface our human personality into the cosmic. We all have had such encounters with our soul that have caused us to reexamine our lives and put our lives in order, though we may not have understood what they were.

The Loss of the Soul

The soul is the main part of our nature that we have forgotten in the modern world, trapped as we are in appearances, prices and quantities. We are wandering inwardly blind in a high tech world of mass marketing that has lost all semblance to the real world of nature. Most of our current problems — from individual psychological problems to global political concerns — derive from this 'loss of the soul'.

We have little left that is sacred or priceless in our lives. The mundane, secular and superficial has swamped the deeper meaning of what we do. We are caught in glittering appearances with nothing enduring that cannot be either named or sold. Our identity no longer reflects our connection with the universe, but has become a mere commodity in the marketplace, a resume that can be filed away and forgotten. One is reminded of the words of the nineteenth century Romantic poet Wordsworth, whose statements are even more relevant today:

> The world is too much with us; late and soon,
> Getting and spending, we lay waste our powers:
> Little we see in Nature that is ours;
> We have given our hearts away, a sordid boon![13]

Yet even most of our efforts to reclaim the soul today, whether through religion, psychology, the new science or much of New Age thought, generally fail. This is because they don't go to the real essence of the soul — the pure consciousness at our core — but view the soul as the property of a religion or a philosophy, or merely some aspect of inspiration or creativity within us. In fact, most of the current literature available about the soul is not about our real soul or eternal being but only about aspects of our being slightly more internal than the ego, but still not reaching our universal essence. The result is that for all the recent talk about the soul, our culture and many of our lives continue to drift in a soulless direction.

The Soul and the Sacred Fire

The soul is like the sacred fire, a power of wonder, awe and magic. No, *the soul is the sacred fire,* not only within us but also within all of nature. The soul is the fire that gives warmth both to our world and to our hearts. It lights up both the heavens and the earths. It is the color that glistens in the plants and in the stars. It is the power of transformation, the perpetual wave that is ever renewing all life from within.

Fire is the principle of light that has entered into matter and remains latent with it. Matter, we could say, is a slow burning fire that contains the potential for even greater combustion as it returns to its source. The soul is hidden in the material of our body like fire is hidden in its fuel. It is there in a latent form, but we must work and create friction in order to bring it out. We must dive deep within ourselves, moving from our personal desires to our soul aspirations that transcend wants and circumstances.

In spiritual matters, metaphor — particularly that drawn from the world of nature — is often a better teacher than words of an abstract or logical type. This is the value of poetry, myth and legend over philosophy, dialectic or debate. Such a symbolic language — the language of fire and light — is the language both of nature and of the soul. We must learn to talk and dialogue with the soul in this universal language of light.

We must learn to listen to the voice of the soul, which is the voice in the wilderness proclaiming the miracles of the universe that are all around us. This voice of the soul has nothing to do with preaching or with any overt teaching. To hear it requires that we become silent within, letting the Word of the Godhead speak through all creation.

Messages from Our Ancestors

The great spiritual teachings of the ancient world — deriving from an era before our consciousness became dominated by the rational mind — speak primarily in terms of symbols. Vedic sages articulated this approach stating that 'the Gods love the mysterious and dislike the obvious'.[14] The wise often avoid stating anything directly because most people are unprepared to see the truth. The wise prefer to intimate the truth for real seekers whose minds are receptive, rather than trying to broadcast it to those who are not really interested.[15] Their goal is to stimulate our own insight and experience, not merely to pass on a belief or idea as final.

Spiritual truth transcends mere words. Whatever is put into words immediately becomes profane, a commodity capable of manipulation and distortion. Truth is not the evident form, but the hidden fire. We cannot find truth in outer forms any more than we can see fire in wood that has not been enkindled.

For the ancient sages the soul was the sacred fire. No philosophy was necessary to explain its self-evident effulgence. They lit its flames on their altars and in their hearts as the Divine consciousness coming forth from the material world. Through it, they achieved a state of consciousness far beyond our current idea of intelligence defined by the scientific mind and its emulation of external reality. Through it they touched the cosmic mind of which our human mind is but a spark.

The sacred fire was their main tool of communication with both inner and outer worlds, through which they could contact channels of universal thought and energy as easily as we can tune into our different broadcasting stations. Meditating on the sacred fire linked them with the sacred order of life, which they called 'sacrifice' owing its interdependence.[16] They became a sacrifice, as it were, offering their lives to the cosmic fire. Their human personality was exchanged for a sacred role as guardians of the light.

Native and tribal peoples today remain closely connected to the sacred fire. They perform regular rituals to honor the sacred link with the universe that fire represents, much like the ancients once did all over the world. They sustain the bond of the sacred fire in an age that has forgotten the luminous origins of life.

Such fire rituals are called yajnas (pronounced 'yagyas') in the Vedic tradition. There are daily, monthly and seasonal fire rituals for keeping us in harmony with the cosmic movement of the light. There are special fire rituals for specific purposes, like the achievement of personal goals such as prosperity or spiritual goals such as the reduction of negative karmas. There are broad social fire rituals for universal peace and the general well-being of the world. Some yajnas are specifically astrological in nature. Many Hindu temples still perform such fire rituals, particularly in South India. Certain modern Hindu movements like the *Arya Samaj* and *Gayatri Pariwar* emphasize them as part of daily practices for everyone.

When we participate in such special or sacred fires, particularly at key transitional points of sunrise and sunset, full moon nights or the solstices, we enter into the universal order of light. We become part of the day, the month and the year. The universe begins to stir inside us and work its magic of growth and change. Time becomes a process of transformation, nourishing our inner light and ripening our souls.

The Ancient Global Fire Religion

Our human species is a species defined by the discovery of fire. Fire, we could say, was the first teacher of our species through whom we learned our main arts, crafts and sciences. The sacred fire was the basis of the first human culture, which was the culture of fire.

The religion of fire was our first religion from the days the cavemen built their first fires and felt the great mystery of life. The fire was our first guru in the infancy of our species from which we learned the secrets of light and consciousness. The sacred fire, we could say, is the spiritual ancestor of all people of all races and continents. The religion of fire remains our natural religion — the very basis of our aspiration as a species to find the light.

The great ancient fire religions of India, Persia, Ireland, Greece, China, Israel and Mexico are but different facets of a universal and eternal fire teaching. These religions of light arose organically before any particular organized religion or code of belief was defined. They projected the religious urge at the start of our civilizations, setting in motion our spiritual aspiration as a species that remains our inner sustaining force. The *Rig Veda*,[17] perhaps the oldest book in the world, begins with the image of the fire sacrifice:

> *I worship the Sacred Fire (Agni) that is chief priest, the deity of the sacrifice, who works according to the seasons, the invoker, best to grant the treasure.*
>
> *The Sacred Fire honored by the ancient sages is invoked again by the new. For us he manifests all the Gods.*
>
> *To you, O Fire, day by day, by dawn and by dusk we come bearing our offering of surrender, the king of the sa-*

*cred rite, the guardian of truth, flourishing in his own na-
ture.*[18]

The *Rig Veda* explains this inner fire or Agni as the principle
of light in nature and in our own souls:

> *Thou, O Fire, shining forth throughout the days, from the
> waters, from the stones, from the forests and from the
> herbs, thou O Lord of souls are ever born pure!*[19]
>
> *O Fire, whom the waters, the mountains and the forests
> carry as the child of truth, you are enkindled with force by
> men on the summit of the Earth. You have filled with your
> radiance both the worlds and stream with smoke in
> Heaven.*[20]

A related ancient text, the *Atharva Veda*, states the all-per-
vasiveness of the Divine fire principle in its Hymn to the
Earth:

> *There is a Divine fire in the Earth and in the plants. The
> Waters carry the fire and the same fire dwells in the rocks.
> There is a fire within human beings, within the cows and
> the horses are sacred fires.*
>
> *The Divine fire shines from heaven as the Sun. The
> Divine fire extends the wide atmosphere through the wind.
> Mortals enkindle the Fire that carries their prayers, which
> loves clarity.*[21]

Such statements became the foundation of the Hindu religion, what is called 'Sanatana Dharma', the eternal dharma
or eternal tradition of truth.[22] Out of it came Buddhist,
Jain and Sikh traditions that similarly reflect a vision of
enlightenment as the supreme goal of life.

Yet not only the Hindu but also the Zoroastrian religion
— whose vision of the universe as a play of light and darkness had a strong impact on both Judaism and early Christianity — was centered on the sacred fire. The ancient Per-
sians, who had a language and religion close to the Vedic,
built fire temples on their mountaintops and echoed similar thoughts in their most ancient scripture, the *Zend
Avesta*:

We worship the Fire, the son of God, the holy lord of the ritual order. And we worship all the Fires and the mountain that holds the light. And we worship every holy celestial spirit and every holy earthly spirit.[23]

The most holy site of the ancient Greeks, the temple of Delphi, had a place for 'the Central Fire behind the universe' at the apex of its famous pyramidal symbol designed by Pythagoras himself.[24] The great Greek pre-Socratic philosopher Heraclitus created an entire sacred philosophy of fire. The Romans also had their sacred fires, as did all the ancient Europeans. Fire was the ancient Celtic God of wisdom. A Druidic poet states:

I am the God who fashions fire in the mind. Who save I knows the secrets of the stone door?[25]

The Lithuanians probably best preserved their ancient European pagan religion based on fire and continue such practices today as their Romuva religion is undergoing a great revival.[26] Their language is the closest to Vedic Sanskrit of any languages today and reflects how closely these ancient cultures were connected.

The *Egyptian Book of the Dead* identifies Osiris, the God of the soul who symbolizes death and resurrection, with fire:

I am the great One, the son of the great One. I am Fire, the son of Fire. I have made myself whole and sound. I have become young once more. I am Osiris, the Lord of Eternity.[27]

The Bible refers to the many fire offerings given to the Lord at the great temple in Jerusalem that was the center of Jewish religious life. Moses received the Ten Commandments from God who spoke to him in the form of a burning bush — clearly another symbol of the cosmic fire that has always been God's main vehicle of expression. The Holy Spirit appeared on the heads of the disciples of Jesus in the form of a flame, reflecting a similar imagery.

The *I Ching*, the oldest book of China, also recognizes the spiritual symbolism of Fire. This became the basis of the understanding of fire both in Taoism and in traditional Chinese medicine:[28]

> THE IMAGE OF FIRE: *Thus the great man, by perpetuating this brightness, illumines the four corners of the world.*[29]

It also speaks of the *ting* or fire caldron into which offerings are made to the Lord of Heaven.[30]

Native Americans have their sweat lodges and kivas based on the sacred fire around which they perform regular chants and rituals. The Mayas and Incas had their great ceremonial fires in their many temples and pyramids. The Cherokees, a great and ancient tribe, speak of the earthen mound (hill or mountain) where the Great Spirit gave them their first fire, establishing them as a people.[31]

These are but a few examples of the many that can be found in all cultures. To deal with them would require an entire book in its own right. The universality of our ancient fire religion is easy to see if we but look with open minds. Unfortunately, those of us caught in the mindset of modern western civilization often regard fire worship as primitive, as mere 'nature worship'. But for the ancients their experience of the Divine was real and concrete, which is why they used the dramatic image of fire. They were reading the book of nature, which is the real scripture or Divine Word written in the language of light. We must recognize this experience of consciousness behind the image of the sacred fire to really appreciate both ancient and native traditions.

While we like to associate the origins of civilization with more material inventions of writing and the first cities, it may more appropriately reside in this ancient fire religion, perhaps even in India, the civilization that has best preserved it. As Graham Hancock notes in his *Underworld: Flooded Kingdoms of the Ice Age*:

But India, with its vibrant spiritual culture, its armies of ragged pilgrims and its remarkable Vedas *raises the possibility that the real origins of civilization could be very different — not driven by economics but by the spiritual quest that all true ascetics of India still pursue with the utmost dedication.*[32]

Hancock's idea echoes the insights of Sri Yukteswar, the guru of Paramahansa Yogananda, one of the great teachers who brought Yoga to the West in the twentieth century. According to Yukteswar, Vedic India and humanity as a whole reached its highest level of civilization before 6700 BCE by following the science of Yoga.[33]

Early humanity learned that by making offerings to God through the medium of fire we could purify our hearts and bring noble aspirations into the world. It discovered that the same fire existed within our hearts as our own soul or sacred spirit. The influence of these ancient fires remains and can come forth again. Just as we cannot deny our family, we cannot deny the fire that is our ancestor across all boundaries of religion, race or culture.

The sacred fire is our father and mother, our grandfather and grandmother, our brother, sister and friend. Yet it is also our child, the fruit of our labor and aspiration that we must cherish and nourish. The sacred fire remains our future goal as well as our deepest root. This ancestral fire of the ancient world remains the foundational creative fire of the worlds yet to be born.

Native and ancient traditions along with meditation-based eastern teachings like the Hindu, Tibetan and Taoist show us how spirituality must be linked with the whole of nature in order to be authentic. This is reflected in the science of Yoga that shows us how to harness the forces of body, breath, sound and consciousness for inner transformation. True spirituality works through the nature within us (our soul) according to its connections with the nature around us (the spirit), using not just the external forms of nature but also the inner consciousness behind it.

It is crucial today that we restore this older natural form

of spirituality that is not mere nature worship but using nature as an experiential path to the transcendent. Seeing how native spirituality interfaces with yogic traditions and traditional systems of medicine (like Chinese medicine or Ayurveda) can help us do this. Through the soul's connection to the sacred fire we can discover a spiritual life that goes beyond mere belief to a real experience of the cosmic — beyond the mere verbal shadow to the living light.

The Descent of the Soul

Our birth is but a sleep and a forgetting:
The Soul that rises with us, our life's Star,
Hath had elsewhere its setting,
And cometh from afar:
Not in entire forgetfulness,
And not in utter nakedness,
But trailing clouds of glory do we come
From God, who is our home.[34]

Wordsworth's verses reflect our experience in childhood during which we fall from the innocence of the soul into the complications, if not corruption of the adult world. This descent of the soul also occurs every day as we fall from the peace of our connection to the Divine in the state of deep sleep to the turbulence of our waking lives. We are a light and a flame that has traveled far — that has descended far from luminous heavens of pure consciousness down to this earthly travail of tears, toil and trauma. We are like children cast out of heaven, sparks of the fire that yearn for the warmth and light of their long lost home.

Yet our birth is also a Divine mission to bring a higher light into the world. We retain a cord within us that we can follow back to our original light. This core soul fire remains in our hearts but its many branches, its streams to enlighten the world, have been extinguished by ego-fires of greed, ambition and domination. We must raise up the fire of the soul to consume these lesser fires and bring back the Divine light into the world.

It is crucial today that we relight our ancestral sacred fires to reclaim our spiritual heritage as a species and renew our link with the sacred universe. Such a return to origins is the necessary foundation to build a true spiritual civilization, a new humanity in tune with the entire universe. Our future as a species rests upon the return of the sacred fire as the beacon of a new humanity at one with nature yet capable of moving to the stars!

Our heritage is that of fire. But what type of fire will be our legacy — that of aggression, conflict and war, or that of love, beauty and truth? This depends upon the fire that we build our lives around and whether it is sacred or unsacred. Which fire will you choose? Our destiny will be that of our flame.

CHAPTER TWO

Light as Consciousness

The beauty of light pervades the universe on all levels from the glow of spiral galaxies in boundless space to colorful sunsets on Earth. It is an awesome presence that all of us are still humbled before. Light is the ultimate force in the cosmos from which all other forces derive. It is the most evident factor of our existence, bringing into manifestation all that is.

Light defines both time and space. We could say that time is the movement of light. It is defined by the revolutions of the Sun and Moon and other heavenly bodies. Similarly, space is light's field of expansion, the domain that its radiance reveals.

Light is probably our main definition of God. It is one that can be accepted by all religious and spiritual groups despite their many differences of belief and practice. Even the English word Divine, which is based on the Latin Deus, in related Indo-European languages like Deva (Sanskrit) or Theos (Greek) means a 'being of light' or 'shining one'. In the Biblical account in Genesis, in the beginning was Light.

Yet light can indicate the truth that we are seeking in any domain of life, like art, science or law. Seeking knowledge in any form is a seeking of the light. Expressing beauty in any form is an expression of the light. We are all looking for light in one way or another. We are all striving to remain true to our light, however we may formulate it. Though we may not define this light in the same way, it remains our motivating force and guiding star.

A wonderful prayer in the *Upanishads* eloquently sums up our soul's striving; showing how light, truth and immortality are inherently connected:

> *From non-being lead us to being.*
> *From darkness lead us to light.*
> *From death lead us to immortality.*[35]

We arise from the darkness of ignorance and seek the light of truth. Yet there remains a great mystery to light. Though light reveals all things, what is it that reveals light? Where does light come from and how are we connected to it? Light is the mystery of our lives that begins when we are born, open our eyes and first gaze upon the world. Light is also our main experience in death when we leave this mortal realm for the great unknown. Those who have had near death experiences refer to a powerful white light that appears to guide them on their journey beyond this world. We live and die, grow and strive, know and forget in the mystery of light.

The realm of heaven to which religions aspire is generally envisioned as a higher realm of light beyond this earthly travail. We intuitively feel that we will return to such a radiant realm after death if we are good and true to our hearts. We live in a world defined by light that rules us from above, of which we are perhaps only its shadows below.

Yet light is not simply a transcendent reality; it exists as a general potential in all things. It is hidden in all material forms from a piece of wood down to the very core of the Earth in the form of fire. Even objects that are not themselves luminous, like rocks, exist through and are revealed by light.

Light works within us as our own bodily powers of life, perception and awareness. Our physiology and psychology is governed by light, fire and warmth. Even darkness is something we can recognize only because of the perceptive light of the mind. Above, below, within and without, we see only light with light.

Light as the Sole Element

Light is the dominant force, the main element and sole substance in the universe, out of which all things are fashioned. The ancient sages from Greece to India recognized five great elements as earth, water, fire, air and ether.[36] These are not different chemicals but states of matter as solid, liquid, radiant, gaseous and etheric — the layers or strata of existence from the most dense to the most subtle.

Yet all five elements are really forms of fire and light. In terms of fire: earth and water (solid and liquid matter) provide the fuel for fire like wood or oil and could also be said to be fire in its latent or hidden form. Air is the energy that comes forth from fire, which includes smoke. Space is the field of illumination created by fire. In terms of light: Earth is shadow. Water is reflected light like that of the Moon. Air is the electrical form of light like lightning. Ether is clear light. Note that our seeing depends upon space for objects to be revealed.

Our bodies are defined by these same five elements — the earth of our flesh, the water of our blood, the fire of our digestive system, the air of our nervous system and the ether of our minds. These also contain fire and heat from the work power of our muscles, to our blood that is warm and red, to the electrical impulses that move through our nerves, to our minds that take in light through the senses. We are concentrated forms of light seeking to unfold from a dark or latent state in the finite to a bright or realized condition in the infinite.

The Great Equation of Light and Consciousness

Light is the universal constant, the ultimate substance from which all things arise and into which they can all be converted. We can express this in a simple equation that could be called the 'great equation of light and consciousness'. This is the basic formula behind all the forces in the universe.

Matter = Energy = Light = Life = Mind = Consciousness

Modern science has proved the equivalence of matter, energy and light. This is most evident in Einstein's famous formula that energy equals matter times the speed of light squared ($E = MC^2$). The speed of light is the main constant in the physical universe that upholds all physical laws. However, this equation is incomplete. It considers only the outer world of physics, not the inner world of the psyche. It deals with the outer light, not with the inner light. On an inner level, light is also life, mind and consciousness, which all reflect processes of combustion, illumination and perception.

In the view of Yoga, the great spiritual science of the East, life evolves out of matter because it is already inherent within matter. One cannot produce oil from sand but only from a seed that contains oil latent within it. So too, life can only come out of light if it is already present within light in a seed form.

Life evolves from matter through the instrumentality of light. It is the plant's ability to convert sunlight into biochemical energy or 'life-light' that allows for life to develop on Earth. This means that life is also an evolution of light. Light causes the universe to evolve not only on a material level but also on a biological level. Light is a form of life just as life is a form of light.

Breath, the basis of our life-force, is another kind of light or combustible energy. *You can try a simple experiment in order to experience this for yourself.*

Sit calmly and relaxed. Close your eyes and breathe rapidly in and out without pause through your nostrils for a few minutes. Then stop breathing, gently press your fingers to your eyelids and turn your gaze within. You will naturally see light. This is the fire of the breath within you.

Just as life is inherent in matter, so mind is inherent in life. Life evolves into mind through another transformation of light. The mind is an internal instrument of light through its processes of perception, recognition and reflection. Our minds naturally seek a greater light to expand their powers of knowing.

Our senses are the mind's different tools of light. Their function is perception or illumination of various types. Most obvious is the eye that takes in visible light, but all the senses work to perceive different aspects of existence. In addition to these outer senses, we have inner senses, inner eyes and ears that can sense subtle realities of cosmic light and sound. Ultimately, it is the mind's eye that enables us to perceive anything.

Consciousness itself, the power behind the mind, is the ultimate power of light. The light of consciousness, what is called *Chidjyoti* in Sanskrit, like a mirror illumines all the objects of the mind and senses. This immutable light of the soul does not go out or change despite all the fluctuations of body, mind and senses. The soul's awareness is the origin and support of all other forms and manifestations of light. You can contact that inner light through the witness consciousness within you, the part of your awareness that is capable of observing the movements of the mind. *Remember first the light through which you see; then nothing you observe can ever overcome you.*

According to Yoga philosophy: life, mind and consciousness are different frequencies of light. They are inner powers of light, just as matter and energy are outer powers of light. The entire universe, animate and inanimate, is a tapestry of light, an overflowing of the ocean of light into both inner and outer dimensions.

- Matter is light in its shadow form.
- Energy is light in action, its lightning or electrical form.
- Life is light in its bioelectrical form, its vital energy form.
- Mind is light as the power of perception.
- Consciousness is light as pure awareness.

Light evolves into life, mind and consciousness just as the seed of a tree evolves into its trunk, branches and leaves. Yet it would be more accurate to look at this process in reverse. It is conscious or inner light that takes the form of mind, life and light as outer forms of expression.

The problem is that we look upon light only as a material force, not as a power of consciousness. We fail to touch the real presence of light except when we perceive great natural beauty or feel deep inner inspiration. We do not live in the light of consciousness but in the shadows of the senses and the reactions of the mind. We perceive external objects but miss the inner light through which they exist. We fail to recognize the light of consciousness or the spirit through which they shine.

Mystics and yogis, however, are aware of the sacred nature of light, which makes their world full of wonder and delight. According to them, light is a universal force of consciousness. The different forms of light from fire to the stars are Divine powers, the great Gods and Goddesses of the conscious universe. It was these cosmic powers of light that the ancients saw in nature, reflected in all forms and systems of the living world and which made their lives a thing of worship.[37]

Inherent in light, even at a physical level, are all the powers of the mind and the senses in seed form. *This means that when we see light, the light also sees us.* Light sees, hears, feels and knows as it spreads from the stars to all corners of the universe. It is the very presence of God. When we merge into light, which is our true home, we gain the ability to know all things from within. We once more become pure light beyond all sorrow.

Cosmic Light and the Individualization of the Soul

Light is not just a general force in the universe; it has a special capacity to individualize itself, to form various discrete or independent centers. Light is not simply a wave motion but is composed of individual particles as well. This means that the light of consciousness exists both as a universal principle and as different particles or entities, which are individual souls. Each one of us is a unique center of conscious light, a point of light that can express and manifest the entire universe of light.

Light gets projected into the field of matter on Earth in the form of the soul or individualized light ray. This unit of light develops into plant, animal and human creatures, creating the body and endowing it with consciousness. The soul or inner light, which is like a point-flame, generates all of nature's evolutionary transformations.

Forget for a moment your bodily image. Look at yourself as a small sphere of light that can assume any form, which is at home anywhere in the universe and is akin to all creatures. This is a better indication of your true reality than your current physical appearance. Recognize yourself as a point of conscious light that can reveal the truth of all that you see, just as a lamp can light up any room.

The soul, we could say, is the 'quantum' form of the light of consciousness, a particle capable of transcending the ordinary laws of physics and working beyond the limitations of time and space. The soul is the ultimate particle or 'atom of light' that contains the blueprint of the entire universe. The universal being becomes individualized through the soul, which then must seek to return to its universal form. This is the universal breath, the 'breath of light', which is the movement from the universal to the individual and then from the individual back to the universal again.

Enlightenment and the Alchemy of Light

Ancient alchemists worked to turn lead into gold, which was to turn heavy and base metal into metallic light. The great psychologist Carl Jung explained this alchemical process as a metaphor for transforming the dark matter of the unconscious into the pure gold of the integrated self — for turning our own internal darkness into light.[38]

The universe reflects an alchemical process of transforming matter into consciousness, which we could call the 'alchemy of light'. From mineral to plant, to animal, human and then to enlightened sage is a progressive evolution of the light of consciousness. This ability to extract consciousness from matter is the internal alchemy of light. Our lives are part of this churning process, to bring the light out of darkness, to bring our soul out of our bodily density and inertia.

Through the inner light of awareness we can discover light, truth and beauty in all things, which is to return the world to God without any loss of diversity. All life is moving towards this alchemical transformation of consciousness.

The process of evolution does not end with the human mind as we know it. The mind too must evolve further to its source — which is pure consciousness or pure light transcending all material forms. We must move beyond our current dualistic thought-based intellect, trapped as it is in likes and dislikes, attractions and repulsions, opinions and prejudices to a greater unitary awareness. This pure light of universal consciousness is what great yogis and mystics have always sought to realize through their meditation practices.

The universe is evolving toward enlightenment as its true goal. Our role as a species is to bring the evolutionary process to its decisive phase in which we consciously seek enlightenment, so that the plenary light of pure consciousness can come forth out of the half-light of the mind. This search for enlightenment is our real contribution to the evolutionary movement.

CHAPTER THREE

The Purusha
Principle of Yoga:
The Cosmic
Person of Light

Imagine for a moment — as in the Isaac Azimov movie and science fiction novel *Fantastic Voyage* — that you are reduced in size to a miniscule level, placed inside a human body in a microscopic vessel and begin to travel through it. You would see blood and fluid, perhaps noting larger tissues and organs. You might consider that a blood vessel was simply a river or that the cells in the body were creatures in their own right, with tissues and organs as lands and mountains. Confronted by the diversity of forms inside the organism, you would not perceive the overall organism. You would not even imagine that these apparently different entities were part of a single person with its own consciousness who could travel at will, carrying them along as part of his own greater individuality.

We are in the same position as individuals in the conscious universe. We do not perceive the greater cosmic being but only the smaller objects or entities within it, the forms and creatures of our external environment. As creatures ourselves, we look at the universe from the inside like mere cells in a greater organism. We miss the overall being, the Divinity that exists at a vaster level than all we perceive. We exaggerate our own independence and importance, thinking that we are real in our own rights rather than just small parts of a totality that extends far beyond us.

However, those who live in harmony with nature, from animals to tribal peoples, to those who practice deep meditation, are aware that they are part of a greater cosmic organism, that they are cells in the body of God. In this regard they have much to teach us about the real structure of the universe, in which everything is part of a greater whole that is alive and aware.

Man and the Universe or Man as the Universe

Western civilization has generally looked upon the human being as existing apart from nature, with nature existing mainly for our own benefit. Western science regards humans as the only real intelligent life form on the planet. Its model of intelligent life on other worlds consists of technologically developed humanoids like us. It sees little wrong with disrupting or damaging nature as long as some progress for our species may come of it.

Dominant western religions have generally portrayed the human being as God's chosen creature, the pinnacle of nature, given dominion over all the Earth. They view the soul as belonging only to humans and not to animals or plants, which do not possess any capacity for salvation or eternal life. While notable exceptions can be found in both science and religion — and while true science and religion may stand apart from them — such anthropocentric beliefs have created the main thrust of our current civilization.

Our social and political orders follow the same impetus. For our urban development we are willing to eliminate not only individual species that are a nuisance to us, but entire ecosystems that may get in our way. We lay waste to the resources of the planet, both living and non-living, as if all planetary rights belonged to our species alone. However carelessly we act, we seem to regard ourselves as the only real feeling entity in the world. Nature just provides the raw material for our human projects — rocks that yield minerals, trees that are a source of wood, animals for food and so on. Other creatures seldom count, being fit for whatever purpose we deem convenient.

This predominant thrust of western civilization, and modern civilization based upon it, can be defined according to the image of 'man against nature'. The result of this civilization is the growing devastation of our planet. We are proud of our material progress and forget that it has occurred only at the expense of numerous other creatures, great and small. We have created a culture of exploitation in which not only plants and animals but also human beings are quickly consumed and discarded.

On the other hand, in Eastern and native traditions, the human being is often presented as an insignificant part of the greater universe that could probably do well enough without us. The human is merely another creature, one among many in the boundless universe, like the small figure of a man placed in a vast panorama of a Chinese landscape painting. Nature is the reality and we humans are at best a small part of nature, at worst something unnatural and out of place in a universe that transcends our creaturely arrogance. This is the image of 'nature transcending man'. While this view is closer to the truth, there is an important evolutionary potential for our species that we should not overlook while recognizing it.

A third view exists that can integrate humanity and nature in a way that affords greater meaning to both. There is an underlying unity of the human being and the universe, not simply relative to material factors, but in terms of consciousness itself. The human being at a soul level reflects the entire universe, while the universe itself is the Supreme Person or conscious being. It is not an issue of man ruling over nature or nature ruling over man. The same Self and sense of personhood underlies both the human being and the greater universe. We are the world, not in our current limited state of mind but in our true nature and higher potential for enlightenment.

The Cosmic Person of Consciousness and Light

One could say that the essence of our humanity is that we are 'sentient' beings, conscious entities possessed of feelings and capable of suffering. We cannot accept that human beings are enslaved, experimented on, used for food, killed or tortured or any other such demeaning actions that we might allow for animals. It offends our sensibilities when we see a human being treated as a mere thing or 'object'. We respect our dignity and inviolability as a conscious 'subject'. This is because we recognize existence of a consciousness principle in the human person.

We see the human as an independent being, possessing free will and entitled to his or her own life and happiness. We feel that humans should be treated fairly and allowed to live as they see fit, which we refer to as 'human rights' in our various law codes. There is nothing inherently wrong with this line of thought except that it does not go far enough. Our mistake is thinking that such a consciousness principle and the rights that go along with it are unique to our species and do not belong to the rest of the universe.

Consciousness is not something that our species owns. It is as universal as light. Some form of consciousness or feeling exists in all beings down to the rocks. However, once we recognize the all-pervasive nature of consciousness then we must treat all creatures 'humanely' — with a similar care and regard that we would afford a fellow human being. The same consciousness principle that makes us feel human is a universal principle that fills the world with light and allows other creatures to live and move as well.

The universe itself is a person, though without the limitations and prejudices of our human personality. This is what the science of Yoga calls the 'Purusha'. The Purusha, meaning a person or conscious being, is a Sanskrit term for the Cosmic Being behind the universe, the spirit within all things. The entire universe is a manifestation of the Cosmic Person. This Cosmic Person endows every creature with personhood or a sense of self, not only humans but also animals and ultimately all of nature.

The goal of classical Yoga — as defined in the *Yoga Sutras* of Patanjali, the prime ancient textbook of Yoga — is the realization of the Purusha or cosmic being as our true Self.[39] This is a different definition than most people today consider, with the physical image of yoga that has become popular in our culture, but it is the actual foundation of the Yoga tradition. The Purusha or true Self is the ultimate goal of all Vedic practices and all Vedantic philosophy, examination and inquiry. Yoga is a path of Self-realization in the deeper sense of this Cosmic Self, not simply knowing our human self but realizing the entire universe within our own minds and hearts.[40] Our true Self is the universal Self or Purusha that exists within all nature.[41] The greater concern of Yoga practice is uniting our limited consciousness with the unbounded infinite awareness that is the Self of all.

This yogic view of the Self is very different than usual views that emphasize the bodily self, the psychological self, or the religious soul as our true nature. Our ordinary view of the bodily self is of an entity that is born and dies along with the body and is as separate from the world as our flesh is from the ground. Our view of the psychological self is of an entity created by our personal history during this physical life. It has the unique characteristics of our upbringing and education along with the particular capacities that we develop through our own efforts, making us different than every other person. Our usual religious view of the soul is of an entity created by God, dependent upon the body and its resurrection, which can perhaps commune with God in some heavenly world but retains its separate identity and cannot become one with that supreme Reality.

In the yogic view, our true individuality is an inner consciousness that unites us with all — not a physical, mental or religious entity that keeps us apart. Our self is mirrored in all the selves in the universe. If we look deeply, we can see that everything in the universe has a personality or spirit within it, whether it is the Sun, the mountains, animals or human beings. Every form in nature from the rocks to the clouds is a face of Consciousness. All faces of all creatures, we could say, are masks of God.

This Cosmic Person exists in an embodied form as the soul within all creatures. We could say that plants and animals are evolutionary precursors of human beings or younger forms of ourselves, people in the making as it were. The Cosmic Person also exists in disembodied forms as the spirit behind the forces of nature. We could say that the Sun and Moon are cosmic, older or vaster forms of ourselves — spiritual powers and personalities. The whole universe is the cosmic human being taking many different appearances and assuming many different functions both individually and collectively as part of its manifold expression.

This view was known to the sages of the *Rig Veda*, in which the teaching of the Purusha first arose:

> *The Cosmic Person (Purusha) is all this, what has been and what will be.*
>
> *From his mind, the Moon was born, from his eye came the Sun. From his mouth arose the powers of fire and lightning. From the wind his breath was born.*
>
> *From his navel came the atmosphere, from his head Heaven, from his feet the Earth and from his ears, the directions of space. Thus all the worlds were formed.*[42]

The human being is a replica of the greater universe, which itself has an organic structure like the human body. We are an expression of the 'self-conscious universe' holding both spirit and nature within ourselves. This means that we exist in all things, not as a separate species but as part of the underlying fabric of awareness. Through the unity of consciousness, the human being is the universe and the universe is a human being. We could say that the material universe is the body of consciousness, while consciousness is the soul of the world.

This Cosmic Person is both man and woman, the Great God and the Great Goddess, both the cosmic masculine and cosmic feminine powers. It is not simply the essence of humanity but the prototype for plants, animals, stars and planets. The Cosmic Person is the universal form, the prime archetype behind all beings, the 'I behind the I' in all creatures.

This Purusha or consciousness principle of Yoga, however, is no mere philosophical concept, theological belief or abstract Absolute. It is the very fire within our hearts that is the light of the entire universe. The Purusha is Jyotirmaya or 'made of light'. To truly practice Yoga we must begin with an understanding of this being of light as our goal. However, few Yoga students today are aware of the Purusha, much less its connection to fire, though that has always been the key to the inner process and higher experience of Yoga. Most meditators aim at understanding the psychological self, not realizing that our true Self is the cosmic light expressing itself in all of nature, in which our personal psychology gets consumed as an offering in but an instant.

The Human Being as the Creator Awakening in his Cosmic Creation

The *Vedas* tell us that plants have feelings and animals have minds.[43] Other creatures are also aware. They want to live and experience happiness just as we do. But we humans do have an additional capacity of intelligence that affords us a better potential to know the Reality or Self behind the universe, should we choose to look for it.

Through the human being, the Creator can become consciousness in his own creation. God, the Creator is seeking to manifest through us, so that he can know his own creation from within, with the very creature realizing "I am all" and "I have become this entire universe."

The Self alone was there in the beginning. There was nothing else that winked. He thought, "I will create the worlds."

Having created the worlds, he thought. "How can this universe exist without me? How shall I enter into it?"

Having opened the top of the skull and through that means he entered it. He saw the Person (Purusha) as God (Brahman).

— UPANISHADS[44]

The human being is meant to serve as a vehicle for the entire universe to become self-aware. We are the instruments for God to perceive his creation through the eyes of his creatures. This is the great fulfillment that cosmic intelligence has planned through the long evolutionary struggle. The whole purpose of the evolution of the soul, which is also the evolution of life, is the soul's creation of a body through which it can realize God or the universal consciousness. This is achieved with the human body, through which we can practice meditation and find God within ourselves.

We are all sons and daughters of God. We are created in the image of God, which is as a power of light and consciousness! We are all meant to become God who is our origin and our home. That Divine Being dwells within us as our true Self, calling us to remember our greater nature as All.

The ancients referred to this Cosmic Person as the 'Person in the Sun'[45] as well as the 'Sun of suns' and the 'God of gods', meaning the consciousness principle inherent in light. The main dwelling for God in the external world is the Sun as the source of light and life. Similarly, God dwells within us as the soul, the source of life and feeling within our hearts, our inner Sun:

The Cosmic Person, the size of a thumb, dwells in the middle of the heart like a flame without smoke. He is the lord of what was and what will be. He is today and he is tomorrow. All this is That!

— UPANISHADS[46]

Our soul is this 'fire person' or being of light in the heart. This is what gives us individuality, character, vitality and creativity. The fire person within us reflects the Cosmic Person of pure light in the Sun and stars.

The human being, therefore, is a link creature between the animal and the god or cosmic being. It is the creature in whom the evolutionary fire is meant to come forth and connect itself with the universal light. Our inner imperative is to become one with the entire universe. We are not meant to rule over the world from the outside. Our task is to embrace the creation from within, according to the supreme power of love that is its true motivating force.

Yet we must remember that this special evolutionary position is not so much a privilege as a duty. To honor it, we must sacrifice our personal desires to the greater universal will. We must recognize the Cosmic Person as our real being and view all creatures as portions of our greater selves. This means to go beyond any mere bodily or mental definition of self.

The Great Equation Revisited

We can extend our original equation of light and consciousness:

Light = Perception = Consciousness = Human Being = Soul = Cosmic Person

The human being is meant to be a being of light. Our human head is like the Sun projecting the light of consciousness through its openings of the eyes, ears, nose and mouth. Our human heart is like an inner Sun projecting the light-blood of life throughout the veins and arteries of our bodies. Our true humanity is found not in the body, in our genes or in our social behavior but in the light of our soul that can feel oneness with all. Once we are liberated from a merely outward sense of self, our awareness will be as free and radiant as the Sun in the sky.

We are meant to be a walking, breathing, talking form of

the entire universe, each one of us with the vastness of a solar system or a galaxy! We haven't even suspected the great glory and beauty that we can project into the world. The universal being is meant to come to the front and awaken through us, seeing with our eyes, feeling with our hearts and thinking with our minds, remembering its journey from the stars to the Earth and through the entire domain of nature on this planet.

Our true humanity, therefore, does not reside in our mere humanity. Our humanness is a reflection of a Cosmic Person who pervades the entire world. Our true humanity resides in this Cosmic Human Being who cares for the entire universe as his own self. Our highest potential is not merely the scientific or social advancement of our species, but making our species the matrix for the universal being in its advent on Earth.

To realize this higher potential we must give up the arrogance of our species that has not only harmed our planet but also crippled our own inner creativity and awareness. We must honor that same conscious being in all nature from the stars to rocks, plants and animals. We must learn to see our Self in all beings and all beings in the Self as the *Upanishads* said so eloquently thousands of years ago:

> He who sees the Self in all beings and all beings in the Self henceforth has no fear.
> Where can there be any delusion or sorrow in whom all beings have become himself, for the knowing one who sees only unity?[47]

We must recognize the human face in the Sun, Moon, mountains and clouds. We must greet the Sun as our Father and the Earth as our Mother, with all the plants and animals as our brothers and sisters. We must recognize that whatever we look at also looks back at us with our own eyes, which are the eyes of our own soul and the eyes of God. Can you see your own face in every form of nature? It is only then that you will really see and all eyes will be yours.

CHAPTER FOUR

Transformations of the Cosmic Fire

Everything that can be found in the universe can be described as either fire or fuel for fire. All things are either burning or are combustible. Whatever fire can burn is also fire. Therefore, fire can be regarded as the underlying reality behind all existence.

Various forms of heat production are occurring throughout the entire universe from the cores of stars to our own bodily metabolism. The universe consists of interrelated transformations of fire and light from subatomic particles to the super galactic quasars. We live in a universe of fire, a universe on fire, a universe defined by fire in many forms. From the atom to a cell in the body, each unit of existence is a kind of oven, a fire vessel. As noted ecologist David Suzuki states in *The Sacred Balance*:

> *Living cells are like minute stoves, extracting energy from fuel so that they can do work such as maintenance, growth or reproduction.*[48]

All things in the universe are such fire cells in different shapes and sizes, including our bodies, minds and souls.

These various forms of the cosmic fire are the Divine children who build up the worlds from within, the children of fire. We ourselves are fire beings in this fire universe, the descendants of the cosmic fire that have traveled far. We create our life through various biological, psychological and spiritual fires that occur on conscious, subconscious and superconscious levels. As forms of fire, we are portions of the cosmic light. Hidden within the flame of our soul is the supreme Sun of the entire universe, the light of all the worlds.

The Original Cosmic Fire Ball

The entire universe was produced by a gigantic explosion of fire, the primordial Big Bang that scientists speculate occurred around fifteen billion years ago. Within less than a second this original flame, said to have at first been a singularity — a point smaller than an atom — erupted into a vast universe which has expanded rapidly ever since with its myriad galaxies, gas clouds and almost infinite space.

From this original 'Cosmic Fire Ball' all the galaxies and stars or smaller fireballs were created down to the atoms. These fireballs are not simply chemical reactions but are also eyes that see, hearts that feel and minds that know. We are all fireballs or 'spheres of light' in one form or another created by this explosive primal event, mirroring both its intelligence and its power. This original Cosmic Fire sustains the universe to this very day. We are part of its ongoing process and contain its essence within us. This original fire still burns in our own inner space at a metaphysical level as the power of awareness.

The *Upanishads* equate this primordial fire with the Divine Word:

> *This is the Supreme Truth: Just as from a well-burning fire, sparks of similar nature are produced a hundredfold, so from that imperishable Word, manifold beings are born and into it return.*[49]

The Cosmic Fire is not just a power of physics but the Divine Word or fire utterance.[50] It is the self-articulation of an infinite and eternal consciousness. The unfoldment of the Cosmic Fire is not just an expansion of energy that creates the material world, but an unfoldment of creative intelligence through which the soul takes birth within the worlds.

We usually approach the metaphysical through abstractions, logic or at best theology. In this cataclysmic universe, we can better understand both physical and metaphysical realities in terms of fire. Existence itself is like an inextinguishable flame. Consciousness is the undying awareness within the light. These metaphysical forms of fire underlie all physical manifestations of fire. To understand our reality we must grasp both the physics and the metaphysics of fire.

In Vedic thought, Agni, the Fire God — who is also the first or archetypal human soul — is born in the constellation of the Pleiades, the Seven Sisters and wives of the seven Rishis (who themselves are star beings).[51] This is not only an important truth of ancient Yoga and astrology; it reflects our inner connection to the stars. We are all forms of the Fire God, the Divine Child who descends to Earth from the stars, carrying the Divine light into the densest matter.

The Earth as a Fire Planet

The galaxies are clouds of fireballs thrown forth from the Big Bang or Cosmic Fire. The planets are smaller fire balls emitted from these greater fireballs of the stars. The Earth itself is a piece of fire that broke off from the Sun early in the development of the solar system. Yet it remains connected to the Sun by a stream of light, magnetism and an electrical connection between them.

The Earth is a fiery planet located in the hot interior of the solar system. It is only the third planet out from the Sun, within the inner fire zone of the solar system. At such a close distance to the Sun, only small and hot planets can exist. Yet the Earth is positioned at the outskirts of this ring of fire, where fire can be mediated by water and so allow for life. The Earth is warm enough at the surface to allow its water to exist in the liquid state necessary to sustain life, but not so hot as to make it evaporate entirely.[52]

As creatures of a fiery planet, we ourselves are fire creatures. We have evolved from the fire of the Sun to the fire at the Earth's core, into plant forms that catch the solar fire, into animals that carry their own internal fire of digestion, and finally into humans who can project the fire of intelligence. We are all transformations of the Cosmic Fire through the stars and planets. We are starlight and sunlight that continues to burn in ever new and miraculous ways. The story of fire is our story.

David Suzuki also notes:

> *Today we believe that life cannot arise spontaneously, that life can only come from life. But once, at the very beginning, that first organism from which we are all descended was sparked into being, full of a life-force that has so far persisted tenaciously for close to 4 billion years.*[53]

In the yogic view, that life-fire is the Cosmic Fire which gives light and warmth to everything. We are all part of the same cosmic evolution of light and life which pervades the entire universe.

Our Inner Journey as a Soul

I think all of us are aware that we are on some kind of a journey in life. We may define it in different ways. There is the journey of the aging process from birth to childhood, to maturity, old age and death. There is the journey of our career as we seek to make our mark on the world and build our fortune. There is our journey of family life as we bring children into the world and strive to raise them into good human beings. There is our intellectual journey to learn about life in many fields of knowledge or our artistic journey to express what we feel in many forms.

Above all, there is an inner spiritual journey to find meaning, truth or beauty beyond all the outer concerns of life. Our entire lives are a journey, a quest and a pilgrimage from the known to a greater unknown. We seek ever new horizons and ever new frontiers to cross. We also know that at death we will leave this world for yet another realm beyond and our journey will continue in another way, perhaps in another body or in another world.

I have always felt like a visitor in this world, though one who has been here many times before. At the same time, I have felt while looking at the stars that I could be equally at home in other worlds beyond. Probably most of us have had similar feelings. There is some part of us that reflects another type of being beyond our merely human personalities; a being that has its own history and strivings which are very different than our ego-based needs and desires. There is something of a cosmic wanderer in all of us, a sense that whatever happens to us in this world, it is not final but only part of a much longer process that we can at best only dimly intimate.

Yet if we are on a pilgrimage in this life, who are we? And where is our real home? Who is the real traveler that arrives at birth and leaves at death? *Try to remember your real journey in life as a traveler through all these worlds.* Clearly this inner journey reflects the greater mystery of your being that is more than your current human identity or bodily condition.

Our soul that has arisen from the stars takes its journey through the domain of matter on Earth. The evolution of life is really our own soul's pilgrimage through the world of nature as it participates in the cosmic creative process. This evolutionary movement, we could say, is a form of worship because it is a seeking of something higher and nobler, in which our consciousness comes to experience every aspect of life within itself as something meaningful or sacred.

All life is inherently a ritual, prayer and meditation — a seeking of ever greater light, life and consciousness, something we could call God, though it goes beyond all words and concepts. Once we recognize the soul or conscious being as our true Self, our lives will once more take on that dimension of the sacred and our journey in life will become a spiritual quest. We can once more return to the universal fire and light from which we have emanated.

Unfortunately, many of us are not aware of our souls and have forgotten that we are on an inner journey, much less its real purpose. We have forgotten how far we have already traveled and also lost sight of the ultimate goal that we seek. We have lost contact with the flame that is our true motivation and inspiration.

To discover the real meaning of our lives, we must remember the fire from which we have arisen, the flame that is still pushing us forward in our evolutionary journey from deep within. We contain the secret code of our cosmic journey, the inner map that we must travel and the tools of light that are necessary to lead us along the way.

Yet this journey of the soul or Agni is not merely poetry or spirituality, it also contains the essence of cosmology, geology and biology — of the entire evolutionary process. In it poetry, psychology, science and mysticism become one with the very power of consciousness, not in an abstract discourse but in an experiential vision of our true nature. This meta-language of the soul is the very expression of life.

II

The Journey of the Soul Through the Kingdoms of Nature

CHAPTER FIVE

Fire in the Rocks:
The Soul in the Mineral Kingdom

The Spirit dwells silently in the inanimate things of the mineral kingdom. In the stones the presence of immutable Being and its aura of eternity is not marred by the agitated activity of transient creatures such as ourselves. Being, we could say, is the very bedrock of existence out of which everything we see is made. It supports us like the ground on which we stand.

The Earth as a whole is alive. The very stones are conscious. They breathe, think, feel and know, though not in the same way we do. If we examine the process of how rocks grow, we see a tremendous intelligence, a wonderful beauty and marvelous order welded together. The crystalline structures of minerals, particularly gemstones, have an intricacy that vies with any human invention. Lava forms huge basaltic columns that resemble great citadels or castles equal to that of any grand poetic epic. Granite can be found in large blocks that look almost manmade — intimating the face of a hidden God wanting to be carved out.

Our soul begins its sacred journey on this planet, descending from its celestial home into the mineral kingdom. Its first level of earthly manifestation is the stone, from which it first learned to work on physical matter and create the substances necessary to build its bodies. Our soul fire enters like a spark into the rock and slowly begins to quicken it from within with the forces of life and consciousness. Along with all plants and animals, we humans have arisen from the Earth and are part of the land. We are creatures of the life that has evolved from the rock and carry its legacy within us.

The Magnetic Fire at the Earth's Core

The Earth has a metallic core composed mainly of iron and nickel at a very high temperature. The inner portion of this core is solid owing to the density of gravity, but the outer layer remains liquid. This means that the core of the Earth is a great 'metallic fire' that holds the planet together by its power.

The Earth's metallic core fire provides the foundation for evolution on the planet. It is the primal mother fire that sustains all the other fires on Earth. From it, the Earth's magnetic field arises along with the electrical currents that run through the interior of the planet to its surface, through its atmosphere and into the solar system beyond. It allows the Earth to receive magnetic forces from the greater universe, connecting us to the will and love that comes from the stars.

It provides the necessary force to hold the atmosphere together, assuring us our supply of life-giving oxygen. Without its gravitational and magnetic power, our bodies and the very air we breathe would disperse.

On top of this hot metallic core lies the Earth's mantle, which also exists at a very high temperature, though much less than that of the core. Its mainly mineral substance is the source of the minerals that cover the planet above it. Above the mantle is the crust of the Earth, from which magma or fiery liquid rock regularly intrudes to the surface of the planet.

The Volcanic Fire and the Origin of the Land

The connection between the Earth and Fire was well known to the ancient seers and yogis. They proclaimed that Fire (Agni) is the God or cosmic power at the level of the Earth (Prithivi). The Earth is the body while Fire is its soul, or more poetically stated, the Earth is the poem while Fire is its song.[54]

Placed in terms of human relationships, the Earth is the Mother and Fire or Agni is the child. The Earth itself is a cauldron or fire-altar for the Divine fire child of the soul as the *Vedas* state in this prayer:

> *As a mother carries a child in her belly, may the Earth carry the Divine fire as a child in her womb.*[55]

It is also a fact of science — the very cornerstone of geology — that all the rocks on Earth, whatever their form, originate directly or indirectly from only one source, from the fire of volcanic activity. This volcanic Fire in the Earth, or what could be called the 'mineral fire',[56] is the same rock form of Agni lauded by the Vedic sages.

All life on Earth, one could say, is a form of transformed lava. Lava or liquid fire is the very life-blood of the planet. The magma from deep within the Earth arises to the surface as lava and as it cools creates new land. This volcanic fire at the surface of the Earth is an evolution of the metallic fire at the planet's core, its outer blossoming and expansion.

The mineral fire has created both the continents and the ocean floors. It has raised up the mountains that are the backbones of the continents and the spine of the world. It releases gases that help sustain the atmosphere. It brings up chemical particles from deep within the Earth that carry the building blocks of life. The atoms that make up our own bodies have come to the surface of the Earth because of volcanic action. We are all, as it were, composed of the sacred ashes of this primordial volcanic fire.

The lava from volcanoes flows over the surface of the Earth building new land masses. Volcanoes encircle the continents where the continental plates collide with one another, as well as erupting at sensitive points (rift zones) within them. We can observe this land-building action in the Hawaiian volcanoes that are erupting today.

The mineral fire also builds up the great mountain ranges of the Earth from deep within. In this case, the magma may not reach the surface of the Earth in a molten form but pushes up slowly and breaks the surface in an already solid condition. This process results in a much harder and homogenous form of rock, mainly granite.[57] Such heavier rock forms the core of many mountain ranges.

The volcanic fire, as it were, is the first of the great Gods of nature, the very spirit of the Earth. It is the son of Mother Earth and carries her powerful evolutionary impulse. It represents the Earth's secret aspiration to ascend the heavens, inherent in all the creatures that arise out of her. We are all part of this striving of the Earthly fire to reach the Divine light. We are all manifestations of the volcanic fire as it erupts and explodes in magical and mighty ways.

The Many Forms of the Mineral Fire

The volcanic fire creates the beautiful texture of the planet, without which the Earth would have an even surface like a marble. Its molten rock solidifies and forms the face of our living world. Rock creates many forms on Earth as mountains, hills, valleys and plains. It has many shapes and sizes as clay, sand, gravel, stones and boulders. Each of these adds another facet of beauty to the contours of our world.

The mineral kingdom manifests various qualities of fire — like color, heat and light — within its earthly matrix. The Earth creates rainbow-like displays as light filters through mountains, cliffs and stone formations of every sort. In geological wonders like the Grand Canyon we can read a mineral record of half a billion years in currents of light and shadow along the variegated and magical strata of the rocks. Natural geology defines many sacred sites that all cultures in the world have recognized and frequented for inspiration, including America's national parks, which for many of us are our greatest cathedrals.

The mineral fire grows crystals deep within the Earth, which are perhaps the first forms of life and can reflect light — particularly quartz, which is one of the dominant minerals on the planet. Crystals possess great conductive powers for spiritual and healing forces. They are the basis of our computer chips that hold sophisticated information and transmit subtle radio waves. Our civilization may have advanced to computer chips and Silicon Valley, but we are still using the silica of stones to advance our species. The Earth itself, with its many minerals, could be compared to a gigantic crystal for bringing in cosmic energies from the greater universe. The planet itself is a cosmic computer creating the code of life and consciousness.

The light quality found in crystals also occurs in metallic ores, particularly gold, the mineral of the Sun, which the ancients called the presence of fire in the mineral realm. Gold remains our main measurement of wealth, as we depend on the solid beauties of the Earth for our enduring sense of value in life.

This light quality of the mineral kingdom is most obvious in gemstones that have the power to project light and glisten like stars.[58] In Vedic astrology, called *Jyotish* or 'the science of light', certain gemstones correspond to the planets, representing their presence and power on Earth. These are ruby for the Sun, pearl for the Moon, red coral for Mars, emerald for Mercury, yellow sapphire for Jupiter, diamond for Venus, blue sapphire for Saturn, hessonite garnet for Rahu and cat's eye for Ketu. Through wearing the appropriate planetary gem we can increase the positive energy of the planet and bring a higher light into our lives. Such gems prove that minerals are merely crystallized light and contain secret powers of knowledge and healing that connect us to the entire universe.

Civilization and Minerals

The mineral fire has created tremendous material resources that remain a great reservoir of wealth and utility for all our human ventures. We use many types of stone and rock for building purposes, relying upon the mineral kingdom to create the artificial structure of our urban world that shines brightly with metal and glass. Pottery, the ability to create utensils from the soil, was one of the most important discoveries behind all early cultures and continues today as an important art form.

We extract metals from their mineral matrix, using copper, iron, tin and other metals for diverse purposes. Our tools are mainly made of the metal that we have forged from the Earth, as are our weapons. Our entire chemical industry and all of its wonders has arisen largely because of our ability to harness the forces of the rock using various technologies of fire. Even our nuclear technology has been possible only because of uranium ores that exist on the planet.

Yet instead of making our mining of the Earth a form of worship, done with love and discretion, it has become a cruel exploitation, leaving waste and devastation in its wake, seeking maximum profit with minimal concern for the future of the planet or the renewability of its resources. We must remember the consciousness in the rocks in order to use their gifts in the right way. All forms of nature starting with the rocks are first of all tools of worship to help us grow in consciousness. Once we forget this we set in motion a process of desecration in which all meaning in our lives will eventually be lost as well.

Sacred Mountains:
The Houses of the Gods

The most visible form of the mineral fire is the mountain. Mountains are built up by volcanic activity deep within the Earth and arise like flames to touch the sky. They hold a great diversity of plants and animals in great forests and meadows, as well as many mineral treasures in their caves and crevices. They gather in clouds, produce rain, and release the waters over the Earth, giving birth to great rivers. Poetically speaking, a mountain is a fire and the clouds at its summit are its smoke that rises to heaven.

Mountains are houses of the Gods or cosmic powers. They allow the Gods to descend and perceive the Earth through the eyes of the mineral kingdom. The mountain, we could say, is the main mineral manifestation of the soul. Mountains are the human beings in the mineral kingdom. They stand upright and survey their domain. To be a great person is to be like a mountain, unperturbed by all the changes and disturbances of life.

All spiritual traditions have their holy men of the mountains, whether mountain monks, mystics or yogis. Like many prophets and sages, Moses talked to God on a mountain (Sinai). Ultimately, the mountains themselves are the sages, and many sages have left their spirits in the mountains in order to guide us. We can contact these mountain spirits ourselves if we recognize the consciousness within their summits. Our soul itself is such a mountain creature, with a vision beyond time and space.

Earthly mountains reflect the cosmic mountain, the great pyramid of existence, like Mount Meru in the Yoga tradition or Mount Olympus of the Greeks, the abode of the Gods. Yet the cosmic mountain also dwells within us. In Yoga it is identified with the human spine and its chakra system. The universe itself is a sacred mountain from its material foundation to its spiritual heights. Our entire evolutionary process consists of our soul's ascent up this great mountain of life. This sacred world mountain is perhaps ultimately a volcano, releasing the fire of truth from its lofty summit.

I have spent much time hiking in the high country of the Rocky Mountains, what could be called the Himalayas of America, and have also visited other mountain ranges throughout the world. There is a particular exhilaration that comes when one gets above tree line, an elevation where the cold and wind prevent even hardy trees from surviving. It is like going beyond the world, if not going beyond the mind. One is open to the sky from the roof of the world, with only diminutive plants, tiny alpine flowers in their short season of bloom, as if the very Earth itself and its creatures had gotten smaller. The cities fade into the distance, and we realize that most of the Earth still does not belong to man, nor do we figure important in it. We recognize that there is a spirit in the universe that dwells far above our human concerns, scarcely taking note of them. We remember our soul's identity as a traveler through the worlds, ascending from peak to peak.

Ancient rocks dominate this high ground in numerous outcroppings. They reveal some of the oldest mineral formations on the planet, taking us back to an earlier geological era before man or even most of life had evolved. At such altitudes the thin air holds the Prana or vital energy of the heavens. Strangely, fatigue disappears, and one becomes capable of long journeys above the clouds, stepping from summit to summit. One gets a sense of the journey that will occur when one must ultimately leave this mortal world for the sky beyond.

This is perhaps why high mountain regions like the Himalayas are so powerful for meditation. One's very being, moving and breathing in such rarefied atmospheres is a kind of natural meditation. It is like living in the Void before matter had come to dominate the world. The astral or heavenly light is much more accessible in high mountain regions. The rocks become alive and their Shiva energy, their power of pure being and pure consciousness, becomes palpable, drawing us up into the stars.

After reaching the summit of the mountains, you can leave your body behind and soar in your spirit above this world, ascending the cosmic mountain of space. You can climb the mountains of the clouds and rise into the sky, following the rays of the Sun back to the Sun itself. You can go beyond the Sun into the stars and galaxies beyond, mounting space and time and leaving the formed universe altogether for the formless Eternal and Infinite. Try meditating in the high mountains and you can easily experience this for yourself. Such yogic, mystical or shamanic journeys are a part of the natural meditation that occurs when we contact the spirit behind nature.

We can also find many sacred mountains in desert regions where the ground easily erodes away, revealing the many layers of rocks. Sedona, Arizona typifies such a landscape, with rising spires, cathedrals and pyramids of sandstone towering high above the desert floor. Much of the southwestern USA, sacred to the Hopi and Pueblo Indians, has a similar terrain.

The high desert in particular is a special region of light where the very rocks seem to merge into the clouds and the sky. The light of infinite space above touches the fire of the earthlight below in an ethereal glow. New Mexico, where I live, is an area that has always attracted artists because of the mystical light that falls on the mountains and rocks, as it illuminates the sunsets after summer thunderstorms. We should remember that this primal connection of stone and light opens one of the secret doorways to the soul.

The Soil: The Sacred Earth

Rocks are gradually weathered into sediments that get deposited in low lying regions, particularly along river beds. Such sediments are the most active and evolving aspect of rock. Once buried beneath the ground and subject to high pressures, they create a new form of sedimentary rock — the shale, sandstone and limestone that cover about two-thirds of the continents today.

The sensitive surface of sediment, mixed with moisture and organic matter, becomes the soil in which plant life can grow. We could say that the soils make up the skin of the Earth, allowing the Earth to touch and be touched. The soil has been evolving for millions of years along with its special bacteria, molds and the many plants which grow on it. It carries the nutritive essence of the planet that is the basis for all of life. It is perhaps the ultimate evolutionary product of the mineral kingdom. Just as mountains are the Gods of the mineral kingdom, the soil is like the mineral Goddess and the Mother of life, particularly in fertile valleys and great plains. We must learn to honor them as well if we want our species and our planet to flourish and to flower.

Sacred Rocks and Sacred Pillars

Different cultures throughout the world have their sacred rocks. Perhaps most notable are sacred pillars such as found in megalithic sites like Stonehenge or in the obelisks of Egypt. Pillared temples were common throughout the ancient world from Greece to India, forming special halls for discussion, learning and the performance of rituals, including offerings to the sacred fire. Such pillars, like mountains, are stone images of fire or the flame of the soul.

The sacred pillar represents the cosmic masculine force of Being and power, the Shiva force in yogic thought. Complementary to it are the ring stones, altars and basins in which the cosmic feminine force or Shakti is worshipped. In India such sacred pillars and pillar-like smaller stones are called Shiva lingas. Some are large pillar-shaped crystals. Others are oblong-shaped river stones.[59] They are generally set in rings or basins to honor the feminine or Shakti principle as well.

In high mountain valleys, particularly just below tree line, we often find mountain lakes, frequently in old glacial valleys, below towering peaks or cliffs of rock. Such formations are natural Shiva lingas, embodying the mountain 'male principle' and the lake 'female principle'. I have found a number of such formations in the Rocky Mountains, which are a geologically young mountain range holding many sharp formations. But they are common in high mountain regions everywhere.

My favorite such spot is Lake Katherine below Santa Fe Baldy, one of the higher mountains in the Sangre de Cristo range in northern New Mexico. On three sides are the slopes and cliffs of the mountain extending well above tree line, with a large jewel-like azure lake in the middle. The fourth side looks down over the Pecos Valley far below. To view the lake calms one's mind and directs it upwards through the vortex of the mountains into infinite space, creating a natural form of meditation that takes us out of our bodies to the spirit beyond. Such sites are like launching pads for the soul.

Yet even our modern civilization continues to construct stone buildings in a monumental style with pillars, columns and domes. A good example of this is the Washington monument in America's capital, which is shaped like a gigantic pillar or obelisk. We naturally return to stone to express meaning and duration in our lives. Even our death is honored by the stone that marks our grave, our last testimony and epitaph as creatures on the Earth. Such words in stone are not only our last word; they echo the first words of creation which God speaks through the rock. Our life moves from stone to stone, though few of us really honor the rocks that sustain us.

Sacred Images in Stone

Artists since prehistoric times have sculpted rocks into wonderful forms of beauty, expressing powerful human sentiments fixed in stone as a message for eternity. Many sculptors have preferred marble, which has a fleshy quality to it, making the very stone alive.

Most religions have their own special sacred images molded in stone. Such stone images have much more power and sanctity than any image created artificially. It expresses a stronger spiritual presence than a mere picture, ornamental window or piece of calligraphy, however beautiful these may be. Even the clay of the soil can be molded into sacred images, expressing the deity latent in the Earth.

Metal has also been used to make sacred and artistic images, like the great bronzes of European art or of Asian temples. Life cast in metal can similarly reveal the enduring secrets of the soul, carrying an almost magnetic force for the spirit.

Everything that we see is an image of God or the universal light. The entire creation is a reflection of the Divine down to the very rocks, which perhaps best represent its timeless presence. All such sacred images show us how Earth, rock and metal can hold a power of grace. This is the spiritual gift to us from the mineral soul. Such images are not mere idols but vital icons, sacred forms that remind us that God dwells in all things.

Alchemy and Sacred Geology

Geological time, the time of the rocks, proceeds slowly in periods of thousands, if not millions of years. Comparatively speaking, our own human life is but a hundred years at best, and we change perceptibly on a yearly basis. However, our soul as a universal principle lives in eternity. Its sense of time is more akin to geological time. It is more like a rock or a mountain than a person.

The mineral evolution takes much longer than that of plants and animals, which occurs within its field. We could say that evolution on Earth is mainly a mineral phenomenon. The rocks are our elders or gurus, reflecting the greater process of which we are but a recent and perhaps fleeting manifestation. To discover our true being we must honor their wisdom and respect their presence.

This is the work of a 'sacred geology', whose concern is not merely the utility of rocks but the consciousness or sacred being within them. Such a sacred geology honors the foundation of all life in the mineral kingdom. It studies how the geological structure of the Earth helps create the forces of life on the planet and also transmits the energies of cosmic intelligence from the greater universe beyond. It maps the force fields on the Earth that transmit such influences. There are many forms of this sacred Earth science, which is perhaps the first of all natural sciences. Such are the Chinese system of Feng Shui and the Vedic science of Vastu, which are now becoming popular aids for architecture and building today.[60]

In Vastu, certain directional forces are recognized and related to specific cosmic powers or deities. By properly orienting our buildings we can benefit from the cosmic energies that stream into our world from the different directions of space. In this regard, Agni or fire relates to the southeastern direction, where the main fire influence enters. This direction is the best place in the home for the kitchen and other activities centering on fire.

However, all the directional deities are ultimately forms of Agni as powers of heat and light connected to the Sun, which is the main force behind all directional and seasonal influences. The main direction for light is the east where the Sun rises. The northeast, where the first intimation of light occurs, is the direction of God or Brahman, through which Divine influences, specifically the Shiva force, enters into our spatial world. Meditation is best done facing east or northeast because of these influences.

For the ancients, mining minerals was a mystical process or sacred art. Imagine the wonder of primitive man finding a vein of gold or beautiful gem hidden in a cave. This led over time to the art and science of alchemy. Just as rock can be heated and a pure ore extracted from it, it was felt that metal could undergo transformation into yet purer metals. This became an analogy for the evolution of both the universe and of the human being, with the gross making way to the subtle through the application of heat and pressure. Ayurvedic medicine today still uses special alchemical metallic preparations, called *rasas* and *bhasmas*, for treating more severe diseases, including degenerative disorders. These are thought to be more powerful than herbs and to work at a deeper level of the brain and the nervous system.

The same metaphor was applied to human nature. The

base ore of our bodily ego can be transmuted into the pure gold of the enlightened soul through the inner fire of meditation. In the Vedic view this is transmuting the iron of the body and the Earth to the silver of Prana and the Atmosphere and finally to the gold of the higher mind and Heaven. All evolution consists of alchemical transformations of matter, bringing new forms of life and intelligence out of unconscious substance. This reflects the fact that all life is an evolution from the mineral kingdom, which itself is a secret power of cosmic consciousness waiting to unfold.

Your Internal Landscape

Just as the outer world has different landscapes of mountains, plains, rivers and seas, so we each have our own inner or soul landscape, what could be called our 'inner Earth'. This is composed of the outer landscapes that we have viewed along with the inner meaning we have extracted from them. It is also the 'landscape of our dreams'. When our inner eye is open, our dreams reflect wondrous landscapes, great mountains, forests and seas, the world or paradise of the soul.

Meditate upon the great landscapes of the Earth as various facets of your own greater being. You can hold all the landscapes of the Earth within you as part of the fabric of your own nature. Learn to create your own internal landscape as majestic as anything on the Earth. Discover the great mountain ranges and powerful rivers of the soul through which you can wander at leisure forever from one cosmic mystery and wonder to another.

It is into this inner landscape that we go at death. The soul is not buried in the outer ground but returns to its own sacred ground. The outer Earth is but a reflection of the inner Earth of our hearts. Make sure that you have created a rich inner Earth fruitful with your higher wishes and aspirations.

Reclaiming Your Soul in the Mineral Kingdom

The soul exists in a kind of deep sleep in rocks, in a latent and undifferentiated condition, not yet individualized. It rests in a state of peace, sustained by the forces of eternity. It resembles a dark night lit up by stars. In deep sleep, our soul returns to this mineral-like level, where it naturally gets renewed in the basic substance of its being. Remember this silent ground of your being, the serenity within as a source of inexhaustible strength without.

To reclaim your mineral soul, go out in nature and commune with the rocks as you would with an old friend or with an elder. Climb up a mountain or hill, ascending from one strata of rock to another as the different levels of your own being. Find a special summit that provides a vista in which you can survey the horizon. Look upon your own life and the whole of civilization from the ancient heights of the mineral kingdom, in which our mere human problems are little more than dust. Contemplate our creaturely insignificance in the older and much wiser geological world.

Make the land where you live sacred in one way or another. Recognize its contours, soils and textures as a temple open to the sky. Look into the caverns of your heart, your inner domain of stone, where your soul remains wakeful in deep meditation, at peace in your own inner Earth.

Reclaim your soul memories of its pilgrimage through the mineral kingdom. Remember the rocks, soils and mountains that your own soul's energy has helped to build up and whose nutrients still circulate inside you. Honor the Earth as your home, your matrix and support. Feel your body as a mountain holding you strong and straight, with the power of all the Earth. Remember the stone as your own more ancient flesh. Let the mineral fire burn within you with the light of the entire planet.

CHAPTER SIX

Fire in the Waters:
The Seed of Life

According to many ancient mythologies, space is a great ocean of light. The Sun, Moon and stars are like lotus flowers blooming on the cosmic sea.[61] This equation of water and light has a deep significance. Water and light have an inherently close relationship. Water reflects light, shining like a gem. We could say that water is the feminine form of light. Water can receive light and through it conceive life. This is the fact of our planet's evolution. Water is the matrix of life, the prima materia of the soul's manifestation.

Water is perhaps the ultimate mineral, holding in itself all the minerals necessary for life to occur. It stands apart from more earthy or solid minerals as a special domain in its own. Life itself can be described as a special form of heated or fiery water.

The Oceanic Fire

The surface of the Earth, most of which is covered by the ocean, is like a vessel that holds water. Where did this water come from? According to recent scientific theories, most likely it condensed from the steam produced by primordial volcanic eruptions. The ocean is a child of the volcanic or mineral fire, whose gases also produced the atmosphere as its other offspring. The volcanic fire built up not only the ground but also the waters on the ground, and the air and clouds that circulate the waters above. It is the original source of both the sea and the rains.

There is a special volcanic fire connected to water that exists deep beneath the sea, building up the ocean floors. An 'oceanic or submarine fire' burns in the mid-ocean ridges spreading the ocean floor with its lava flow. Fully eighty percent of the Earth's volcanic activity occurs beneath the sea as part of this life of the waters. We could say, therefore, that the submarine or watery fire is the main fire on Earth, supporting the waters which themselves are the very support of life.

The oceanic fire heats and energizes the waters, adding important minerals and gases to them. Strange new forms of life have recently been discovered living on the hot sulfur-based minerals arising from these deep mid-ocean vents. We ultimately derive from this volcanic womb of life hidden beneath the sea. As David Suzuki notes in his book, *The Sacred Balance*:

> *Where did the energy come from to create life over hundreds of millions of years in those primeval oceans? The guess is that the first complex molecules were formed with energy contributed by lightning and by liberation of heat from molten magma, streaming down from volcanoes and up from sea vents.*[62]

The oceanic fire creates undersea mountains, some which rise above the surface and become islands of fire. A good example of this is the Hawaiian Islands where perhaps the purest form of fire creation on the planet is occurring today as the Hawaiian volcanoes continue to erupt and create new land. We could perhaps say that the continents themselves are only greater islands of fire floating on this watery planet.

The Cloud Fire and Thunder Gods

Water is not only a mineral but also a gas. It has a special amorphous nature that easily accepts transformation. Liquid water easily evaporates into the atmosphere, rising up into the sky and forming clouds. When the moisture content of the air reaches a high enough concentration, the water particles precipitate and fall in the form of rain. This atmospheric water is driven by the air or 'cloud-fire', which works on it through the forces of thunder and lightning. Water links the surface of the Earth with the sky. It traverses from Earth to air and back again. Falling from Heaven, it brings atmospheric energies and heavenly blessings to the ground.

Just as the mountain volcano can be called the image of the God in the mineral realm, the thundercloud is the main image of God in the atmosphere. Whether Biblical Jehovah, Greek Zeus, the Vedic God Indra or the Native American Thunder God, we find the same image of the deity riding the clouds and speaking through the thunder. This Thunder God is often the king of the Gods and the Great Father of the world.[63]

In the ancient Vedic view, Wind (Vayu or Indra), the power of thunder and lightning or the air fire, is the deity of the atmosphere. Yet the atmosphere, the second or mid-world between Heaven and Earth, was often regarded as the central world. Heaven and Earth were its upper and lower limits or the two firmaments. Because of its special importance linking Heaven and Earth, the deity of the middle realm, Indra or Shiva, became the supreme deity, carrying both Heaven and Earth as the two sides of himself.

Yet beyond the earthly atmosphere is the heavenly atmosphere between the stars, which carries its own special electrical forces that flows through the wormholes of space. This higher or cosmic lightning energy is what starts or brings the light on all of levels of its manifestation. Lightning in one form or another is the fire-starter for all forms of light. There is a cosmic lightning, the lightning of God that causes the stars to shine — the electrical current in clouds of interstellar gas that turns them into shining stars.

The thundercloud, we could also say, is the mountain of the sky, holding the bounty of the air, with the Earth at its base and Heaven at its summit. The thundercloud carries the lightning that impregnates the Earth, releasing the rains that make the Earth fertile. Through lightning, fire descends to the Earth, not only as forest fires but as electrical and life currents of all types — the Earth dragons of ancient mythology. The lightning seed is the catalyst of life on the surface of the Earth.

Lightning or atmospheric electricity is magnetically connected to the ground where it strikes and stimulates the flow of life energy. The rain itself is a kind of electrified water that refreshes and revitalizes the ground. Water itself is a good conductor of electricity. This is the basis of building dams and creating steam in order to generate electricity. Water generates its own life-force or bioelectricity, the light seed that stimulates life to evolve. Through this water cycle, the biological and electrical fields of the Earth are intertwined. Life itself arises from the waters, with the ocean as the origin of both plant and animal life. Life is a kind of 'electrified water' or 'fire water'.

Fire and Water: The Sacred Male and Female

Water and fire are sacred companions like the female and the male, yin and yang, night and day, cold and heat. Water is also the fuel or food for fire which burns on a liquid or oily matrix. Even solid matter like wood only burns because of the oily or liquid resins within it. Fire in turn liquefies solid objects, like the metals that it burns. Similarly, water remains liquid only to the extent that it holds heat or fire.

Water and fire are not simply opposites; they complement and support each another in many ways. We could call water the 'feminine side of fire' as the Moon complements the Sun. Water keeps fire in balance as well as serving as its vessel. We could say that water is a slow burning or cool fire. Its smoke is its evaporation.

Fire, particularly the life or soul fire, is called the 'child of the waters', expressing this connection between the two elements.[64] The life-fire in the body depends upon the vital fluids to hold it. The soul fire dwells in the ocean of the heart, giving heat to the waters of the blood. While inanimate fire is put out by water, the animate or soul fire flows through water, just as water conducts electricity.

The Sacred Waters

All cultures have their sacred or holy waters. These take diverse forms as sacred rivers, lakes, pools, springs and fountains. Sacred waters are usually related to the Goddess or Divine Mother because the female represents the watery aspect of creation. All rivers are forms of the Goddess flowing her grace, beauty and bounty over the Earth. The Hindus have their many sacred river Goddesses like the Ganges and Sarasvati. Ancient Europeans also had their many river Goddesses. Their ancient water Goddess and World Mother Danu has left her name on many rivers of Europe like the Danube and the Don.[65] Our civilizations have grown up along great rivers and their agricultural wealth, reflecting this grace and bounty of the waters.

Waterfalls are particularly important forms of Shakti or Goddess energy, the spiritual power that cascades downward from the mountains of meditation. The water from mountain streams has strong healing properties. Mineral springs, mainly found in mountains, are a special form of fiery water that contains powerful healing and rejuvenating forces, carrying the very vitality from deep within the Earth.

Sacred waters are placed in special rock basins or in metallic vessels like copper or gold. Water can hold not only the power of life but also the power of thought and the feeling of love. It can be energized with prayer or mantra for healing or religious purposes. We can use water to magnify and empower all our aspirations in life, to anoint all that we do with consciousness.

Each house should have its own sacred waters. No temple or church can be holy without it. Bathing is one of our oldest religious rituals. Water cleanses the body of impurities and renews our vital energy. Cool water refreshes our eyes and allows us to see more clearly. Metaphorically speaking, the water of truth cleanses the soul. Baptism is a sacred water ritual that symbolizes a new birth, the awakening of the soul.

Make sure to have your own sacred waters, whether a small fountain in your home or a small pool in your garden. Energize these waters with your thoughts, prayers and wishes. Keep your sacred fire balanced with sacred waters around it. *Remember not only the fire of the soul, but also its waters that are deep and pure enough to reflect the infinite light.*

Discovering Your Soul in the Waters

We all sense a great beauty, peace and joy in bodies of water, watching the ebb and flow of waves by the sea or a wide meandering river. Water gives us joy because our soul is connected to the waters. The meditative mind resembles a calm pool. The inner waters of light stream forth from the higher realms of consciousness. Like a lightning flash, the insights of the soul release the rain of bliss and the floods of inspiration.

For the soul, the universe is a series of oceans. The heart itself is our doorway to the cosmic sea. Meditate upon the ocean of your heart, the ocean of immortality. From this, the heart's ocean of universal life, the life in the earthy ocean arose. Your sacred flame dwells in that inner ocean like a ship, carried and nurtured by the waters.

In the realm of the soul, fire and water are one. The unity between fire and water is the unity of the soul with all opposites and with all the dualities of creation. It is the unity of the seer (fire) and the seen (water or the mirror). Unite fire and water in yourself as consciousness and its creative power. In this regard there is a beautiful Upanishadic verse:

> The solitary swan (hamsa) in the middle of the world, he is the sacred fire that has entered into the waters. Knowing him, one goes beyond death.[66]

CHAPTER SEVEN

Absorbing the Light:
The Soul in the Plant Kingdom

With plants the light brilliantly enters into the world, spreading its rays in a rainbow display of shapes and colors. The Sun touches the Earth and unites with the soil, creating glowing currents of energy and life. While the soul dwells behind the mineral kingdom, it finds a real home and beautiful flowering in plants.

Adding water, the sap of life, to the earthy matter of the rock, the living plant becomes fertile, creative and abundant in a variety of growing forms. The soul seed is quickened in the plant, entering into the Earth below and reaching out to the sky above. From the twilight of the rocks, the soul awakens in the dawn of the plants. The soul that was asleep in the rock slowly stirs in the plants, feeling life within itself for the first time.

The plant kingdom arises as the soul's second level of manifestation after its initial birth through the mineral or volcanic fire. Plants mark the second stage or dimension of our pilgrimage through nature. While minerals have a secret life and consciousness that we can only vaguely intimate, the life of plants is evident to all. From mere bacteria hidden in the ground and air, which provide an important link between the mineral and the plant, plants evolve into a great diversity of grasses, herbs, flowers, vines and trees that clothe our world in splendor and delight.[67]

Carriers of life prior to the often violent struggle for existence that we find in animals and humans, there is something spiritual or etheric about plants. Like rocks they have the aura of eternity and help elevate our minds beyond our often transient personal and social conflicts and concerns.

The Digestive Fire in Plants

The plant has a unique and new type of fire to sustain it — the fire of photosynthesis, the first digestive fire in nature. Plants are able to digest sunlight and convert it into life-energy. This 'solar fire' of photosynthesis is the basis of the plant soul and its main contribution to the evolutionary process. Plants are 'solar cells' on Earth, responsible for the free production of life-energy for the planet. Their solar power sustains all life on the planet, upholding the very atmosphere with the oxygen that they release.

This sunlight-transforming digestive fire of plants is one of the great creations of the evolutionary process and a qualitative advance over the mineral kingdom, which is inert in its processes. As David Suzuki notes in *The Sacred Balance*:

> *Eventually life learned to eat sunlight through photosynthesis to stay alive — it was a giant step for evolution, a new level of metabolic innovation and biological adaptation.*[68]

The plant can absorb sunlight and conduct it through its own water or juice. It can transform light into life and circulate it within itself. The plant fire is the basis of all life on Earth, which depends upon photosynthesis for the creation of all nutrients. The plant is a slow burning fire, turning the fire of sunlight into the fire of life.

The plant fire ushered in manifest life on Earth and

brought about a series of revolutionary changes in physical matter of which we humans are the final product. We are descendants of the plants that have learned to uproot themselves and move on their own. But we cannot happily go far from our plant home as our gardens, parks and houseplants so clearly reveal. In Vedic thought the human being is the essence of the plants:

> *Of all beings, the Earth is the essence. Of the Earth, water is the essence. Of the waters, the plant is the essence. Of the plants, the human being is the essence.*[69]

In fact, all creatures and all worlds are essentially plants — organisms that contain fire and convert sunlight into energy and consciousness. The planet itself is a plant, an organism that converts cosmic light into life and intelligence.

Sunlight in the Waters

The plant is not only connected to the Sun but also to the Moon. The sap of plants rises and falls, ebbs and flows, like the tides, according to the phases of the Moon. Plants, like the Moon, one could say, represent reflected sunlight.

Plants are sunlight reflected into the waters. Their watery sap holds the sunlight and extracts the life inherent in it. Plants use sunlight to convert mere water into the liquid life, the sap or milk of existence. The essence of plants is this sap or vital juice, which carries a fiery energy or heat, what we could call the 'plant-fire'. The sap of plants is a kind of bio-electrically charged water containing select nutrient minerals in a special solution.

In this regard, the plant fire is more of a 'water-fire', while the mineral fire is more an 'earth-fire'. This fire in the waters is the life-force called Prana in Sanskrit or Chi in Chinese medicine, the vital energy that runs through our internal waters, our plasma and blood.

Plants as vessels for living water depend upon rain and groundwater to fill them up. Plant life first developed in the ocean because of the ability of water to hold the life-force. Water creates the chemical soup in which life-energy can emerge in the form of island creatures. The soul enters into the womb of the sea, the bosom of the waters, in order to be born as life.

This bioelectric fire conducted through the waters endows plants with their vitality. From it plants gain a tremendous power and will to live with a tree, for example, being able to split open a rock with its roots. Though plants are soft, if not weak, compared to minerals, their vital energy makes them the lords of the mineral kingdom, which in turn becomes their soil, their field and their home.

Plants, Food and Medicine

All life on Earth is rooted in food, which is the mother of all creatures. Plants provide the foundation for all food. Plant matter, whether leaves, flowers or fruit, becomes the main food for animals from which they derive their heat or fire. We humans derive most of our food from plants — from grains, vegetables, fruit and nuts — converting the food energy from plants into our own bodily heat, nerve impulses and light for our mind and senses. Sugars, starches, oils, carbohydrates and proteins extracted from the plants are the main fuel for our digestive fire.

Feeding off plants, humans and animals are metabolic transformations of the plant kingdom. We ourselves are specialized plants, children of our plant mother who nourished us with her juice. Our human culture arises from agriculture, the cultivation of the plant. Agriculture, the culture of the plant, the tending of the plant fire, is the basis of human civilization.

Our medicine also arose from the use of herbs, from the healing power of plants. Even today the majority of people in the world use mainly plant-based medicines.[70] Most important advances in modern medicine are owing to the special chemicals found in plants.

The Many Displays of Fire in the Plant Kingdom

The plant kingdom has many domains of its own as trees, shrubs, vines, herbs, grasses, lichens, algae and mosses. Each of these has its own display of form, color and beauty. There are varieties of plants for all the climates on Earth from the sub-arctic regions to the hot tropics, from the high mountains to the deep valleys, from the dry deserts to the wet rainforests.

Plant materials of all types contain fire. Plants, when dry, easily burn as is the case of wood, dry grass or peat. Plant remains buried in the Earth create fossil fuels like coal and oil that are our main energy sources today. While rocks are produced by fire (volcanic activity), all plant material is ultimately combustible and can itself produce fire. Plants themselves are creators of fire. We could say that all plants are 'fire-plants' because they contain heat and exhibit color.

Plants burn largely owing to their high carbon content, which itself is the chemical record of life and photosynthesis. This fire-bearing carbon of the plant kingdom is the fuel for the oxygen fire of the animal kingdom. Such combustible plant matter represents the sunlight that plants were able to digest during their lives.

Plants manifest fire in a more colorful way than rocks, particularly as flowers, but also as colored fruit, bark and leaves. The new leaves of trees assume a bright green color in the spring sunlight. Autumn leaves put on a brilliant display as they take fire as it were and consume themselves before they fall. Many varieties of flowers grow in diverse colors and different climates and seasons. Plants give vibrant color to the Earth, adding rich highlights to the more subdued earth tones of the rocks and the ground.

The Sacred Plant

The plant is a presence of light, beauty and fertility. Not

surprisingly, all cultures have their sacred or special plants. Plants hold a special psychic energy through which we can feel something ethereal beyond this Earth. Both traditional peoples and poets regard plants as dwelling places for Gods and Goddesses, which combine human and plant characteristics in their forms.

The Gods or cosmic masculine powers are reflected in large forest trees, like tall solitary conifers on high mountain ridges. The towering coastal redwood is such a tree of the Gods. The Goddesses or cosmic feminine powers are particularly fond of plants, preferring colorful flowers, herbs, vines and delicate deciduous or fruit-producing trees, particularly as growing in valleys or along waterways. The aspen that develops many trunks from a common set of roots and turns gold in autumn is a typical Goddess tree of the mountains. The recognition of these plant spirits is not mere superstition but an appreciation of the powers of consciousness working through such forms of nature.

The religion, mythology and legends of all lands have stories of sacred plants. Among the most important are ambrosial plants that yield the nectar of immortality. Perhaps the most famous is Soma, the legendary drink of the Gods. Ayurvedic medicine, the medicine of Yoga, retains a knowledge of special Soma-yielding plants like the famous amla fruit that can be used to rejuvenate both body and mind.[71]

Yet the sacred plant is also an inner symbol. According to the Yoga tradition, Soma is a special secretion of the brain and nervous system, creating a feeling of bliss and contentment in the mind. The sacred plant is symbolic of the inner nectar of peace that deep meditation releases within us. The immortality that it grants is of our inner consciousness, our soul. This yogic 'plant alchemy' consists of distilling the essence of our experience, like the honey taken from flowers, to realize the bliss behind all creation and at the very root of our own life-energy.

Poets all over the world from China to France have their 'wine' of poetry. Even Christianity has its sacred wine that represents the redeeming blood of Jesus. Such symbolism indicates an inherent recognition of the power of plants both outwardly and inwardly.

The Sacred Tree

The most developed of all plant forms is the tree, which is the highest plant manifestation of the soul. Trees, it has been said, are the human beings of the plant kingdom. They stand upright and open their branches as arms to the heavens. As the human beings among plants, trees are our ancestors and our gurus. They led the way and set the trail for our evolution. Resins from special trees like frankincense and myrrh or special fragrant wood like sandalwood can be used as incense to purify the mind and heart and send our prayers and aspirations heavenward along with their smoke.

On a spiritual level, trees mirror the process of the One Being becoming the manifold universe. Just as one tree has many roots, leaves, branches, flowers and fruit, which all remain part of itself, so the One Being of the universe has many diverse worlds, creatures and forces that can never be separated from it. This image of the Cosmic Tree is one of the great teaching symbols in all spiritual traditions. The *Upanishads* speak of the entire universe in the form of a banyan tree:

> This is the eternal banyan tree with its roots above and its branches below. That is the luminous. That is Brahman. That they say is the immortal. In it all these worlds are placed. Nothing goes beyond it.[72]

Sacred trees are common objects of worship throughout the world. Great mystics have always frequented the forests, where the plant force and its energy of peace acts as a powerful catalyst for meditation. Great yogis traditionally retired into the forests and imparted their instructions to disciples while sitting beneath the trees. Perhaps the highest form of Lord Shiva, the God of the yogis, is the youth

Dakshinamurti who enlightens his disciples through the power of his silence alone, teaching them while seated in front of a banyan tree. The Buddha also achieved his enlightenment while meditating under a banyan tree. In this regard he appears like an incarnation of the sacred fire, the flame of mindfulness that is enkindled out of the tree of our own life-experience.

The ancient Druids gathered in sacred oak groves, which were open air temples of nature. Even our modern western culture carries a sacred tree culture from ancient Europe in the Christmas tree, an old Germanic practice. Such sacred trees like sacred images magnify the spiritual power of those who gather around them. They are living images of the deity that is the entire universe.

The fire naturally produced through rubbing the wood of trees is regarded as especially powerful. It is the very life fire in manifestation. Such a natural fire is very different from any fire produced artificially. It is aware and can convey the powers of consciousness. Through such natural fires, Divine forces can descend into our environment and bless us. Ancient fire rituals were based upon such naturally produced fires. In India special 'fire sticks' made with sacred wood were rubbed together for this purpose.[73] By kindling fire we enter into the universal process of growing the light; we link ourselves with the development of the light of consciousness in the greater universe.

Learning to gather wood, build a fire, and keep it going is a skill that connects us to the deepest memories and aspirations of our species. It can be a great spiritual adventure for anyone who wants to look upon it with an inner eye. Go out in nature and make your own sacred fire to the universe under the canopy of the sky. Use the wood that you yourself have gathered with reverence. This is one of the greatest forms of worship you can offer.

Fire is the God (cosmic power) that rules over the forests, which themselves carry the fire absorbed from the Sun. Fire regulates the forest and its growth. At times it must burn down the forest in order to eliminate old wood and create new growth. The ashes created by forest fires purify the land, renew the soil and stimulate new seeds to grow.

During the last century, our national policy in America has been to try to eliminate forest fires mainly because they threaten the houses that we often carelessly build in the wilderness. This has led to a build up of dead wood in the forest that is causing extremely destructive forest fires, which represent the plant fire gone wild.

This attempt to suppress fire reflects the many ways in which we have tried to eliminate the powers of nature that we cannot control or which may be harmful to our human interests. The forest fire, like all others in nature, must be given its place. If we suppress it, it will only arise with a greater fury later. The Earth is produced by fire and ruled by it. Fire descends through the lightning to keep the Earth renewed. We humans are only here because of the fire that has evolved within us. We must strive to become custodians of that fire and not usurp its place on the planet. Often the best way for us to administer nature is to leave it alone. The action of non-interference is often the highest and most compassionate action.

The Soul as a Flower

Thou, O Fire, the sage Atharvan enkindled from the lotus, from the head of every seer.

— RIG VEDA[74]

The soul is a fire whose flames form a flower. The soul naturally reveals itself in flowers, which reflect its inherent love and beauty. Flowers represent the unfoldment of the heart of nature as it reaches out lovingly to the greater universe. Wonderful flowers of all colors can be found throughout the world blooming from bulbs, herbs, bushes or trees, whether in the wild or in special gardens. Consider the light and energy necessary to make these displays possible. Their natural fireworks are there for all to enjoy.

Flowers contain not only the beauty of color but that of fragrance as well. The sweet aroma of flowers reflects the pure fragrance of the soul. This natural form of incense calms the mind and gladdens the heart. Aromatic oils derived from flowers are an important tool for healing body and mind. The honey gathered from their pollen is also an excellent medicine and rejuvenative food for our long-term well-being.

Flowering plants are a relatively new species in evolution, dating only from the period of the mammals, after the age of the dinosaurs. They have grown up with mammals and added to their evolutionary development. We human beings have ourselves cultivated and bred many new flowers, showing how we can exert a constructive role in creation. Flowers have evolved to help the soul come forth and to serve as companions in our evolution of consciousness.

Flowers reflect the creative forces of cosmic intelligence in the material world. That is why they are ideal offerings for rituals to honor the Divine, particularly the Goddess or Mother of the universe. There are many forms of the flower Goddesses, like Our Lady of the Flowers in Christianity or the yogic Goddess Tripura Sundari, the Beauty of the Three Worlds, in Tantric Hinduism.[75] Part of real culture is recognizing such divine forms of beauty in nature and the spirits behind them. It takes us from art to Yoga, from mere aesthetic appreciation to a deeper meditative perception of the Divine.

Many religions have flower rituals as well as fire rituals. Most notable perhaps is the *puja* ritual that goes on in Hindu temples even today.[76] Generally, flowers are offered to statues of deities. The stone image represents the enduring presence of God in nature. The flower represents the delicate and spontaneous opening of our heart to it.

The sacred flower also exists within us as the various chakras strung like lotuses along the spine, which the practice of Yoga seeks to open. It is important to cultivate these inner flowers and help them bloom, offering them to the deity within our hearts. Remember that your soul is a flower offering, a flower of light for the greater universe of light.

The Sacred Grass

Grass, the ancients have said, is the milk for the animal kingdom, the very milk of the earth that all grazing animals depend upon for life. Grass is an extraordinary plant form that can grow in nearly all climates and ecosystems. The Earth has many great prairies, steppes and grasslands, like those of the central United States, which have become the bread baskets of the world, with fields of grain replacing native grasses. We could say that just as fire aspires upward or vertically in the form of trees, it spreads outward or horizontally and shares its bounty in the form of grasses.

Just as fire administers the forests, it is a part of grassland ecosystems as well. Many native people burn their grasses. Fire renews the grassland, removing old grass, making way for new grass to grow and eliminating competing plant species like trees and bushes. Ancient fire religions like those of India and Iran included spreading special sacred grass around the fire altar, reflecting this connection between fire and grass.[77] We still spread special grass as lawns and gardens around our houses to make ourselves feel more at home and at peace. As the *Rig Veda* II.4.4 notes: "We spread wide the sacred grass that encompasses the Divine."

Sugar is another product of the grasses, with the sugarcane itself being a special type of reed grass. Sugar derives from the sun as a kind of concentrated sunlight extracted by the plants. The honey produced by flower pollen is another example of the sweetness of light. In Ayurvedic medicine both raw (unheated) honey and fresh sugarcane juice (pure and unrefined sugar) are regarded as powerful foods and rejuvenative medicines. Honey is an ancient form of Soma as well. It is often mixed with ghee (clarified butter) for this purpose.[78]

The plant fire creates the sugars, the very sweetness that is the essence of food, from the sunlight. This means that light has an inherent sweetness or bliss, one manifestation of which is food. The delight that we experience while seeing beautiful colors is another form of this sweet essence of light that nourishes the soul in many ways. Plants convey the delight and sweetness inherent in light.

The Fire Seed

Plant seeds are like a spark or small flame that can produce a larger fire. The whole design and development of the plant is already present in the seed. When the right forces of heat, light and water come together, the seed sprouts and gradually unfolds the entire plant concealed within it. The plant seed is a form of the fire seed that creates the entire universe.

Seeds are sacred because they carry the soul force of life from one generation to another. They mirror the soul that is the Divine seed that contains the blueprint of all life. *Remember the power of the soul whenever you plant any seed.* That is the real force behind its growth. All our actions are casting seeds that carry the power of our soul for good or for ill.

The Soul and the Sacred Ground

Directly connected to the mineral soul that sustains it, the plant soul dwells primarily in the roots of plants, particularly trees, perennial herbs and bulbs. That is why the roots of herbs are the strongest medicinally, such as powerful tonic and rejuvenative herbs like ginseng, astragalus or ashwagandha. These 'man-roots' or 'spirit-roots' carry the power of the soul that is hidden in the ground. A good herbalist knows how to communicate with these sacred roots and uses their powers to strengthen the roots of our vitality.

Yet the plant soul also pervades the soil. For some annual species, like certain grasses, their soul pervades the region, valley or hillside where they grow. Some souls or nature spirits inhabit mountains or streams, sustaining the many plant species around them. These are not simply creatures of poetic imagination but the living consciousness behind these ecosystems, each of which has its own unique personality. That an ecosystem has its own consciousness may sound strange, but once we recognize consciousness as the wholeness principle in nature we must accept its action in all organic systems, which are all living beings of one kind or another.

One can sense the plant soul in the ground as one walks through the forests and hillsides. It is part of the atmosphere of peace that one feels in the land. I have often felt the presence of the living soul from the Earth, beckoning from the roots of plants like an ancient ancestor or guide. One can sense it particularly hiking on rainy days when one can smell the pungent ground. It is more evident in deep forests that have rich soils and thick coverings of leaves and other organic matter. Yet even in the winter one can sense the plant soul sleeping dormant beneath the snow, conserving its energy for a new flowering in the spring.

This plant soul will teach us the secrets of the Earth and give us the healing powers of nature if we but listen to its call. This is how native peoples learned about their healing herbs in the first place. Their own greater soul residing in the plants taught them. The soul in the ground can teach us more about life than we can learn from any school or institution. This voice of the Earth is more important than any media broadcast, as it carries the wisdom of the entire evolutionary process.

Cultivating Our Sacred Ground

The very ground on which we walk is always sacred as many native tribes like the Navaho have long proclaimed. When we walk, we step upon the soul and the remains of our ancestors of all species. Our cultures have grown up along the ground they have sanctified, which mirrors their relationship with the Earth.

Our current commercial culture honors neither the Earth nor the soil. This is one of the greatest environmental tragedies today. We are not only eliminating many plant and animal species, we are blindly damaging the very substance out of which they grow. We have forgotten our own sacred ground. This means that we no longer have any place where we can truly abide and there is no sacred place for us to rest.

To make the ground sacred is essential for spiritualizing our lives and for imparting meaning to anything that we do. This requires honoring the soul in the soil. Without nourishing the soil on which we build our lives, we cannot expect anything enduring to come forth from our endeavors. It is like planting seeds in barren ground. *When you dig into the ground, remember the soul that dwells there.* If you have never touched the ground with a recognition of the soul beneath it, you have missed one of life's greatest miracles. You have yet to know the Earth on which you live.

Working with trees and herbs in different climates from California to New Mexico, I have grown a large variety of species, both ornamental and agricultural. I make sure to plant a garden every year to keep in touch with the Earth. I try to know the plants in the different ecosystems around me, not as a mere curiosity but as a form of worship and meditation. I believe that writing is a lot like cultivating a garden. You don't create a book by committee or force it along according to a preconceived plan or system. You work the ground well, cast good seeds, allow for time, honor what sprouts and help it grow in its own way. The words grow organically, creating a structure as natural and inevitable as any plant.

Healing is also a lot like cultivating a garden, with your own body as the sacred ground. The Ayurvedic approach emphasizes your own daily life-style, the ground of your activity, as the main factor of health and disease. Take the proper nutritious foods and healing herbs for your unique constitution, do the right exercises, making sure not to trouble your mind about getting better, and let time bear the fruit of wellness.

Meditation is another form of cultivation; a term commonly used by the Chinese Taoists who were very close to the Earth and its yin spirit. *Perform your Yoga and meditation practices gently, slowly and consistently on a daily basis, letting the process be its own reward, cultivating the ground of your being, and the cosmic spirit will come to you as naturally as your breath.*

Such cultivation, like tending a big fruit tree, works through the seasons, undergoing cycles of dormancy during which nothing seems to occur. It creates the space that allows things to grow, trusting their natural potential, which we often do not know, to come forth in its own way. It is very different from assembly lines and mass production that force preconceived results and cannot produce anything of lasting value. Inner cultivation cannot be rushed or postponed according to the demands of the market. Yet it creates an abundance far beyond our expectations that continues to grow of its own accord. We could say that everything in life is only cultivating the ground, creating a cover crop to enrich the soil of Being into which all things must eventually return.

Connecting to Your Plant Soul

Plants are conscious beings with feelings and an awareness of their environment. They have senses, though these function in a more general way than ours.[79] They see the sunshine with their leaves and taste the Earth with their sap. They respond to music, to touch and to love. They are strong psychic conductors, picking up vibrations at an intuitive level and magnifying them to the world around them.

Plants are our companions, our mothers and friends who can reflect and refine our moods. They can augment our aspirations, connecting us to the universal life and the worlds of light beyond. *Place your prayers and wishes into the plants, the trees and flowers around you and discover this for yourself.* Plants can absorb and transform not only sunlight but also the light of the soul into a greater beauty and delight.

Our very nervous system follows the blueprint of a great plant or wonderful tree, with its roots in the brain above and its leaves and branches extending throughout the body below. Looking within ourselves we find the template of the plant existing at our very core. If we nourish nature's plants, the soul plant in us will also be well cared for.

We thoughtlessly and carelessly use so many things on Earth. The result is that our lives have lost their meaning. Just think of the abundance that nature has given us through the plant kingdom. What would our life be without trees, flowers, fruit or grass? Have you ever offered your appreciation to these silent partners of the earth and the soil? When you die your body will return to the Earth. The flowers may be your last companions and the last gift of life to you. They will carry your spirit forward into the next world with nature's love and wisdom if you honor them while you are alive.

Recognize that plants are akin to you as another manifestation of the Cosmic Person, that the beauty of the flower or the green grass is part of your own inner light. Feel yourself to be like a tall tree on a high mountain slope quietly surveying all the land around it. Feel yourself as a flowering meadow in the springtime, full of life and beauty for all. Embrace the life-sap of the plants as your own blood.

Learn to cultivate the garden of your soul. Care for your soul and its aspirations with the same patience and consistency as you would a delicate orchid. *Choose a special plant as your own sacred plant,* whether in your house, your garden or out in the wild.[80] Honor the sacred plant within you and around you. Then the plant kingdom will support you with all the light of the Earth.

CHAPTER EIGHT

Fire Roaming the Earth:
The Soul in the Animal Kingdom

The soul in plants continues to evolve, seeking yet greater powers of movement and expression. After great struggles, it breaks free from the dense and fibrous net of plant tissue and develops a more fluid and elastic body. It leaves the womb of the ground and sets off on its own. The plant picks up its roots, becomes an animal, and begins to explore the planet on which it was born. Plant sap gives way to blood as the fluid of life. In place of branches and leaves, eyes and ears emerge along with hands and feet in a new display of life, energy and curiosity.

The soul that stirred in plants but could not move of its own accord, now ventures forth in a wide array of forms — with animals moving in the sea, roaming over the earth, digging into the ground and flying on the wind, spreading wherever plants have prepared the way for them. The animal fire burns at a higher degree than the plant fire. This makes it a stronger and more dynamic fire, but also more dangerous and wilder. Life takes on a new drama and dance in the animal kingdom, with the struggle for survival[81] and for mating.

The animal kingdom is the third level of manifestation for the soul after its earlier births in the mineral and plant kingdoms. While plants contain life internally, animals express it externally, imparting life and motion to the world around them. In animals the soul first becomes a creature in its own right, moving freely on the Earth, no longer tied down to it.

The Digestive Fire in Animals

The animal realm brings in several powerful new biological fires that we humans, as a type of animals, also share. First and most important is the animal's digestive fire, the 'fire in the belly',[82] which is the driving force behind animal existence. The digestive fire in animals is able to convert food, whether of plant or animal origin, into heat, energy and the tissues that make up the animal body.

Each animal contains a core fire within itself, at the center of the digestive system, the main canal around which its body is formed. This 'material' fire, like a wick flame burning on oil, burns the food that the animal has eaten and reduced to a semi-liquid state. It coverts this food into animal flesh, which is a much more plastic and malleable substance than plant tissue. In turn, the animal excretes the waste matter from its digestion of food, which becomes food for the plants and then nourishes the soil.

This moveable fire of animals is a great evolutionary advance over the stationary plant fire. While plants gather nutrients as they are rooted in the ground, animals must move to find food. This makes animals into wandering creatures. Animals roam over large areas of land in search of food, creating territories much larger than what plants can reach with their roots. Their activity has a transformative effect on the plant and mineral realms as well, shaping the Earth into animal homes, colonies and dominions on land, sea and air.

The Fire of the Breath

In addition to the digestive fire, animals have a second biological fire — the fire of the breath. The breath fire propels their circulation and energizes their limbs for movement. Animals are creatures of these two fires — the earthy food-based fire and the solar air-based fire — which are the two levels of their energy. The food or material fire in the belly, which is connected to the Earth, builds up the animal body. The breath or gaseous fire located in the chest or forward part of the animal, which is connected to the Sun and the wind, builds up the animal mind and senses.

While plants can only move if stimulated externally by the wind, animals have their own internal wind or breath to propel them. Their digestive fire draws in the wind to feed it and convey its heat throughout the body. This internal wind gives rise to the animal nervous system, which generates nerve impulses like various electrical currents, lighting up the animal mind and senses.

While plants must rely passively on vital energy from the sunlight, animals actively create their own vitality through the breath. This provides animals a much quicker means of response to their environment and its greater challenges. While the mind and senses in the plant function in a generalized manner, these become differentiated organ systems in the animal, which can be individually employed and directed. The animal life is driven by these powerful currents of sensory activity.

The Fire of the Blood

Just as the plant soul dwells in its sap, the animal soul dwells in its blood, with its focus in the heart through which the blood circulates. Blood holds the animal heat, light and fire. It conveys the life-force from the breath and circulates the nutrients from food. The red blood of animals carries their vitality, instincts, passions and aggression. We humans, as red-blooded animals, share these animal impulses and energies,[83] which often overwhelm our conscious mind.

The main mineral found in the blood is iron, the same mineral that predominates at the core of the Earth. This means that our blood is magnetized to the Earth's core and reflects the central Earth fire and its energy.

Sense Organs, Motor Organs and Mind: The Tools of the Life Fire

The animal fire builds up the appropriate organs to acquire food, along with the mental functions necessary to direct the process of food-seeking. Animals develop limbs mainly to catch or to hold food, or to escape predators so that they themselves do not get eaten. This results in various arms, legs, wings, claws, fins and tentacles in a vast array of sizes, shapes and forms.

Animals develop eyes, ears, noses, mouths, tongues, skin and antennae of various numbers and types in order to gather information about their world. Their sense of smell is particularly important because it provides special knowledge of the ground, the Earth and the creatures that have moved upon it.

Animals also proclaim their presence, communicating in various ways both to their own and to other species. While plants are mute, animals develop every sort of song, cry, chirp, bellow and roar. They bring a new music into the world, a cacophony of calls and utterances. In animals the voice of the soul first begins to speak.

The animal mind coordinates the senses and the motor organs to facilitate its food-seeking activity. The mental cunning of animals arises primarily from the needs of hunting or searching for food. Animals, one could say, are the 'intelligence of food'. Food is their God, the sacred form that they worship, to which they offer their enrapt attention, such as we observe with our pets when we feed them. Animals are the emerging consciousness of the food chain. As animals ourselves, we are a refinement of this intelligence of food and our every meal is a participation in the sacred order of life.

The animal fire, centered on food, is connected to other vital impulses like sex and survival. The animal sexual fire creates a variety of mating habits, some quite aggressive. The territorial instinct builds up animal communities that compete and overlap in different ways. The animal fires build up the realm of instinct, the main power of the animal domain.

Animals as a Living Fire over the Earth

While minerals manifest the 'earth-fire' and plants manifest the 'water-fire', animals have a more 'fiery-fire', as it were. The animal fire is impetuous and hard to tame or control. Animals are like a wild fire wandering on the earth, driven by strong hunger and desire. The animal is a living fire in motion. Animals must work to stay warm, to preserve their internal heat and bodily fire and to maintain its proper fuel.

The animal kingdom itself has many domains, manifesting as fish, amphibians, insects, reptiles, birds and mammals, each with its characteristic digestive and respiratory systems, each with its own sphere in nature, its communities and its struggle for existence. Each of these has its own sacred fire and soul energy.

Animals demonstrate many aspects of fire in their colors, bodily heat and passions. Their fur, feathers, markings and sense organs reflect various forms of fire and light. Animal matter is not as combustible as plant matter, but oils and fats derived from animals are flammable.

Mammals, perhaps the most evolved branch of animals, are especially fiery creatures. Their digestive fire is strong enough to allow them to live in cold climates (as opposed to reptiles that are cold-blooded and limited to warmer regions). Such a powerful digestive fire produces a rich warm red blood that can energize a sharp mind and senses and afford great powers of movement and adaptation. We humans are the products of this mammal fire.

Companion Animals: Our Friends around the Fire

Animals have been our long-term companions on our evolutionary journey, particularly those we have domesticated. Few of us have a house without a dog, a cat or a bird; without them near, we feel incomplete. The dog has been our main companion around our fires and has shared our food since the Stone Age. Our companion animals have been present at our fires, both ordinary and sacred, and have added their energy to them as well.

Such companion animals help us spread our consciousness into the world of nature. They help us reclaim our animal soul and our links to the pre-human world. Look into the eyes of your pets to see this reflection of yourself and your direct connection to the rest of nature.

Sacred Animals and Mythic Images

Most cultures have sacred or at least special animals that represent their key energies and values, whether it is the sacred bull of ancient Egypt or the bald eagle of the modern United States. While we may dismiss such practices as superstitious, there is an ecological as well as spiritual basis to them. The idea of sacred animals represents a human recognition of the spirit in animals and an honoring of their place in the cosmic order.

Our inner consciousness reflects a language of symbols and archetypes, among the most primal and powerful of which are animal images. This symbolic language of the soul is evident to children, whose less conditioned minds are naturally drawn to animal images both for entertainment and for learning, whether those of common animals like dogs, ancient creatures like dinosaurs or mythical animals like dragons. Children naturally gravitate toward animal images, finding the magic and joy of existence in them. We should not simply dismiss this language of children but see how it reflects the soul or Divine child within us.

Animal images are part of mystical and poetic languages worldwide and appear in many of the greatest stories of humanity. They reflect the language of the soul, which is one of life-images not abstract concepts. Many religions portray God as the lord of the animals, with our human soul symbolically regarded as an animal itself. Christ was seen as the good shepard, Krishna as the benevolent cowherder and Shiva as the lord of the wild animals.

Perhaps the greatest story of Asia, and the most commonly performed from India to Indonesia, is the *Ramayana,*[84] the epic poem of the great Sun king Rama, the incarnation of dharma, who was aided by an army of monkeys and bears in his struggles with the powers of darkness. Such animal images represent our own soul that is a servant and child of God. They communicate to us at a level that is both preverbal and trans-verbal, connecting us to our core vitality, not simply to our intellects. They also serve as powerful artistic images, like how a beautiful landscape painting of plants and animals awakens us to the sacred presence in life.

The ancient sages, it is said, learned more from nature than from humans. They saw each animal as a prototype for certain universal processes. For example, the great yogis first learned the knowledge of yoga postures through observing the movements of different animals. The signature movement for each animal became the basis for the particular yoga posture in which the human body simulates the animal and its energies, gaining its powers. The *Vedas* say that God speaks to us in the form of animals. "The Gods generated the Word Goddess. Animals of all form express her power."[85]

Animals embody the Divine Word in various ways, each manifesting an important aspect of universal life. Each animal is a poetic, spiritual and Divine image made in the flesh. Each species is a unique form of the sacred fire. The

cow symbolizes the nurturing force of nature, the Earth
Goddess who suckles and carries our soul through its many
incarnations. The bull reflects the creative power of
Heaven whose rains fertilize the Earth. The horse reflects
the cosmic life-energy rushing forward in its march, gaining
velocity as it seeks to reach the stars.

Birds, particularly eagles, falcons and hawks, reflect our
aspiration to transcend the body and symbolize the rising
up of the soul through the power of the breath. Snakes and
serpents reflect powerful electrical energies of life and consciousness arising from deep within the Earth. The union
of the bird and the snake, the feathered-serpent as in the
Mayan tradition, indicates the forces of wisdom and energy, sun and lightning harmonized.

Animals as Vehicles for the Gods

In the Yoga tradition, sacred animals function as the vehicles (vahanas) of the Gods. They are part of Hindu mythology as taught in the numerous ancient sacred texts,
the *Puranas*.[86] The eagle is the vehicle of Lord Vishnu, who
represents the indwelling cosmic intelligence that maintains harmony and peace in the universe. It indicates his
power of insight and speed of action. The bull is the vehicle of Lord Shiva, who represents the cosmic masculine
energy and power of will and insight. It indicates his spirit,
vitality and endurance.

The lion is the vehicle of the Goddess Durga who represents the ruling and protective aspect of feminine energy or
Shakti, the Queen of the world. It indicates her courage,
valor and power of victory.[87] The peacock is the vehicle of
the Goddess Sarasvati who represents knowledge, art, music and literature. Its colorful wings indicate her creativity,
beauty, charm and wisdom.

Some deities have the heads of animals on a human
body. Ganesha with an elephant head, for example, represents the Divine will and intelligence that can overcome
all obstacles and remove all doubts. The elephant's head

symbolizes the power of memory and the full development of the capacities of the brain.

Sometimes animals become our spiritual teachers or gurus. In a famous Upanishadic story,[88] the student Satyakama was sent out into the wild along with a herd of cattle. After bedding down the animals at night, he was taught in turn by a bull, a swan, a crane and the sacred fire itself, which came and related to him different aspects of existence. When he later returned to the hermitage, his guru noted that he appeared radiant with the knowledge of Brahman (the Godhead) and asked who taught him. Satyakama replied that it was other than humans.

In many Yoga teachings, God is worshipped with the help of animal forms. This is not mere superstition but a recognition that all creatures are part of God, each expressing an important aspect of Divinity. Why can't we feel the same love for God through an animal form, just as through human figures like Jesus or the Buddha? Even in Christian religious imagery Jesus is called "the lamb of God who takes away the sins of the world." Perhaps the animal form of God can save us (impart wholeness to us) even more effectively than the human form because it restores our unity with life.

Experiences of Hanuman, the Monkey God

For me the figure of Hanuman, the monkey companion of Lord Rama, is the most interesting of such animal forms. Hanuman can fly through the air and become as large or as small as he wants. He has the very body of yoga that can be as light as a feather and perform even the most difficult yoga postures with ease. As the son of the Wind god, he symbolizes the life-force or Prana that can accomplish miracles in service of the Divine. Hanuman is the head of the Divine army of nature, composed of animals, monkeys and bears. All the healing powers of nature, including the rejuvenative herbs of the mountains, are at his disposal.

There are many prayers to Hanuman in Sanskrit literature:

> *Who has the speed of thought, with a velocity equal to the wind,*
> *Who is the master of the senses and the foremost among the wise,*
> *Who is born of the Wind God, the leader of the monkey army,*
> *I take refuge in Hanuman, the messenger of Lord Rama.*[89]

Hanuman represents the forces of nature that protect the Dharma represented by Rama, the Dharma king. Hanuman alone could find Sita (the symbol of devotion), Rama's wife who was kidnapped by the demon king Ravana.

While visiting the Hawaiian island of Kauai and its great Shiva temple a few years ago[90], I had a visionary dream of Hanuman coming down from the lush mountains along with his monkey band. His message was that as a protector of the Earth, he was growing impatient with how we humans are mistreating the planet. The forces of nature are replete with such guiding spirits. We humans are not the only guardians of the Earth and should we fail in our duty, these spirits will hold us accountable as well. We must remember the soul and intelligence of the Divine animals that oversee our world.

Honoring the Soul in Animals

If we look at other human beings, we can often see the face of an animal within them. We can see the movement of an animal in how they move or in the gestures that they make. This fact has entered into our language in many ways. We speak of a person being like a lion, a serpent or a swan. Each animal typifies various attitudes and energies that are mirrored within us.[91]

Each animal teaches us something about the universe and about ourselves. We only become a complete human being when we integrate all the animal selves within us.

Learn to discover the many animals inside you. One of them may better represent the face of your soul than any human form.

Remember your many lives in the animal kingdom. You have been a bird, an amphibian, a reptile, a fish and every sort of mammal. You have experienced birth and death in every sort of animal body. Each has helped your soul develop in its own way.

Look into your soul as if it were a wild animal, never cornered, caged or controlled but still firm in its primal will and independence. Look into the eyes of wild animals to see the reflection of God and the unknown, God who is perhaps first of all the lord of the animals.

Animals carry the sacred fire in many ways. *Revere at them as amazing formations of cosmic vitality that can give you the strength and energy for your soul's great labor in life.* Their spirits can take you into the realm beyond the human if you embrace their consciousness as your own. To discover your true Self you must discover the inner animal of your spirit.

III

Human Evolution and the Fire of Yoga

CHAPTER NINE

The Fire of Intelligence:
The Soul in the Human Realm

After its long pilgrimage through the mineral, plant and animal kingdoms, building up its bodies, building up its worlds, the soul or cosmic fire emerges in an extraordinary new form, finally taking birth as the human being. It stands upright, has the power of thought, and works consciously to shape its environment. We humans are a new emergence of the sacred fire, which continues to grow in us and develop new forms of light, expression and action. We are that fire as it walks and speaks on the planet it has forged.

We humans are the fourth birth of the sacred fire after the rock, plant and animal. We are the fire that has come forth from the animal kingdom as a result of its striving for the light. We humans can be defined as animals that consciously create fire, harnessing its energy to improve their lives. The kindling of fire is the primal act that defines the human species and allows it to stand apart from other animals. In starting their first fires, early humans gave birth to their humanity, displaying the new intelligence latent within them.

All that we do is a product of the forces set in motion from this first fire. We are the descendants of the first fire people who have wandered far, carrying their fire over the Earth — traveling so far that we have forgotten where we came from and the original purpose of our long journey. In Vedic thought, Manu, the first man and prototype for the enlightened human being,[92] established the religion of fire and the practice of Yoga as the cultivation of our inner fire:

> In the manner of Manu, we place you down. In the manner of Manu, we enkindle you.
> Sacred fire and primal seer, in the manner of Manu, bring the Gods to the person who seeks them.[93]

All ancient and indigenous traditions recount similar tales as to the sacred origin of our species in the cosmic light:

The Fire of Intelligence

The human species evolves a new type of fire, the fire of intelligence. This mental fire manifests in various ways through our special manual and vocal skills and, above all, through our extraordinarily intricate brains and nervous systems. Around these new fires of the human body, a new fire kingdom emerges — human society — creating new spheres of activity and expression made possible by our new powers of hand, speech and mind.

What makes us unique in the animal kingdom is our special intelligence — our ability to think, reason and perceive. Through it we seek to grow in knowledge and not merely accept our evolutionary programming. We are not simply content to live; we want to grasp the meaning of life. We are not content merely to exist; we want to know the meaning of existence. We are not satisfied merely to have a place in the world; we want to understand what the universe is and who we really are. This is because the fire of intelligence burns deep within us. While this intelligence is not absent in earlier life forms, we have a special brain and nervous system through which it can more easily come to the front of the other life powers.

We humans have not only an instinctual mind that looks for food; we have a higher intelligence that searches for truth beyond all bodily concerns. We can look beyond the outer forms of nature presented by the senses to the inner spirit and indwelling deity that transcends all forms. We have a conscience, an ethical sense that can determine right from wrong and truth from falsehood, allowing us to erect an enduring set of values apart from the shifting phenomenon of the outer world.

We can develop kingdoms of the mind and heart as philosophy, art, religion and spirituality. We can have an inner life along with or even apart from our bodily striving. Even in our current materialistic culture, most of us are not satisfied with outer affluence but desire something intangible, priceless and sacred. This fire of intelligence is called Buddhi or 'awakened perception' in Sanskrit. When it is fully developed one becomes a Buddha or enlightened one.

Our Unique Digestive Fire

Our unique human body also provides new biological forms of fire that go along with our intelligence and aid in its workings. These new fires can be found in all aspects of our organism, starting with the digestive fire that is the root of our physical existence.[94]

We do not have the teeth or digestive tract of carnivorous animals necessary to digest raw flesh. Nor do we have the extra stomachs of grazing animals that allow them to digest grass and leaves. We can easily eat and digest many fruits, nuts and vegetables. But we have to cook most of our food to suit our different and subtler digestive system. For this purpose we have learned to cook not only meat but also grains, root vegetables and other foods that we could not digest in the uncooked state. Cooking our food on a daily basis is a natural fire ritual that we depend upon for our survival.

Our Breath Fire and Pranayama

Our species also has a special breathing ability. We can control our breath at will, breathing slow or fast, shallow or deep, or holding the breath altogether. We can develop the energy of the breath for greater vitality, creativity and spirituality. By increasing the fire of the breath, we can also increase our mental energy, our acuity of perception and the strength of our will power. We can transform inhalation into inspiration and exhalation into effort.

The fire of intelligence arises out of the fire of the breath. It is an etheric fire, produced by the purified essence of the breath fire that is gaseous in nature. To develop our higher intelligence, we should remember the power of the breath that can stimulate it. This is one of the great secrets of Yoga.

While minerals represent the 'earth-fire', plants the 'water-fire', and animals with their moving energy the 'fire-fire', we humans manifest the 'air-fire', the lightning or electrical force. We have developed many technologies of speed through which we can move faster, leaving the surface of the Earth for the atmosphere, outer space and worlds beyond. Similarly, through the 'inner fire of air', the human soul can transcend the bodily realm and enter into the cosmic spirit, becoming a flame that can freely wander through the universe. We can release the bird of the soul from its bodily cage. Yoga has many special breathing practices or forms of pranayama that help us develop this capacity.[95]

The Human Voice as the Soul Fire in Expression

Our lives consist of what goes into our mouths — namely food — and what comes out of our mouths — namely speech. Food feeds our digestive fire, which in turn provides the energy for our activities, the foremost of which is speaking. Speech is the main expression of our biological fires. That is why in Vedic thought the cosmic fire (Agni) as it enters the body becomes speech, which is the primary form of fire at a physical level.[96] Speech is a kind of fire or heat coming forth from the mouth.

Our human voice is the product of our special digestive system starting with the mouth. The tongue itself is a kind of flame, revealed by its triangular shape. It has a dual capacity as a sense organ to taste food and a motor organ to articulate sounds. It is our only sense organ that is also simultaneously a motor organ. It is both the eater and the speaker. In Vedic thought the tongue is the primal form of the Fire Goddess and the consort of the Fire God who himself is the power of speech.[97] This implies that the language of Fire, the language of Agni, is the basis of all our human languages.[98]

Our voice and digestive system have evolved together to allow our intelligence both to nourish and to express itself. Our speech has created our entire social order based upon word, name and idea. It has allowed us to unlock the secrets of nature through science and technology. It has given us great powers of expression through poetry and literature. Most importantly, it has connected us to the Divine Word, the cosmic fire, through prayer, mantra and chanting.

Our special voice allows us to sing, through which we add a dimension of beauty and emotion to our communication. Our fiery joy of song reverberates in many forms. It is part of the rising flame of our souls and sets the rhythm of our lives. *When you speak or sing, remember the fire of your soul propelling your voice from deep within.*

Our Fire Body

Our human body itself is a kind of 'fire body'. Our species originated in tropical lands of heat. As special two-legged creatures, we stand upright like a flame. Like a flame, we flare upward and seek the heavens. Our skin, particularly our face, has a glow or luster of light, especially when the soul is awakened within us. Our head, round and luminous like the Sun, looks down upon and surveys our world. Our upright posture makes us look beyond the limitations from which we have arisen and connects us to a higher will and purpose.

Our hands are the tools of fire. Building fire was the basis of most of our other manual skills. It was the first industry that eventually gave rise to everything from cooking to chemistry. Our hands are the hands of fire and convey the fire of touch, which can be one of love, a warm soothing sensation, or one of hate, a sharp strike or blow. Our hands can be fire weapons or fire healers. They can be important tools of communication as well, with gestures that imitate flames.

Our unique and sensitive skin is incomparable in the animal kingdom. We are special naked creatures. We require protection from the external elements that can easily damage our skin. This sensitive skin makes us develop clothing for both protective and ornamental purposes, which helps us see our body as a cloth or vesture for the soul. Our sensitive skin allows us to absorb sunlight, which adds vitality to the body, senses and mind. Notice how sunbathing energizes you, clears your mind and makes you feel more alive. Like a plant you are taking in sunlight to feed the fire within you.[99]

Our human skin affords us a powerful sense of touch, through which we can transmit love and healing energy. The fire of the skin transmitted through the hands conveys our inner fires of caring and feeling. We have a unique ability to touch our world and to touch each other. Our face is our most sensitive region, with special powers of expression, particularly our ability to smile, which is the expression of the soul's light of happiness within us.

The Fire of our Sexual Vitality

Sex is the vital fire from which all creatures take birth. The fire of sex conceives us, gestates us and brings us forth into the world. As human beings we have a stronger sexual fire than other animals. While other animals only mate season-ally, we can be sexually active all year round. Our sexuality is part of our strong life-fire that drives us to be passionate and creative. It can be a source of vitality, creativity and spirituality that can enrich our lives; or it can drive us to lust, emotional agitation and violence that imbalances us, depending upon how we use it.

As sexual beings, we are much more defined by our sexuality than are other creatures. Sex is not merely a tem-porary mating urge but a lifelong drive that helps maintain our social order and the family system necessary for our offspring's long period of education. Sexuality is our main drive not only for reproduction but also for upholding our social order defined by male and female roles.

The sexual distinction of male and female is also more defined in human beings than in other species. It is a deeper and more lasting feature, pervading our entire lives, with profound psychological and spiritual ramifications. The sexual fire burns differently in men and women. We could say that the male has his own fire and the female has hers. The male fire is an assertive force that is posi-tively a drive for achievement but negatively a destructive aggression. The female fire is a power of attraction that can be positively a force of love and beauty but negatively a power of attachment and seduction.

Our sexual fire is a powerful force that we cannot ignore without consequences.[100] It is part of an urge not merely to perpetuate the body but to express the soul. Its power can be used to bring about a second or spiritual birth within us, if we link its power to our soul's higher evolu-tionary potential. This requires offering our sexual vitality into the fire of the soul.[101]

The Fire of the Home

As fiery beings we are intolerant of cold. The sensitivity of our skin requires that we live in houses heated by fire. Our need to cook our food also necessitates a dwelling built around fire. Our first dwellings in the caves were made into homes by the presence of fire. Our earliest houses were built around a central or primary fire.

Fire was the first lord of our house and our life long guest and companion in the home.[102] The kitchen or dining table remains for us today the center of the house and the main site of family gatherings. The fireplace is still a center around which we gather for association, relaxation and intimacy. We still look to home as our place of rest and peace at the end of the day. The home fire remains the basis of our social life and the foundation of all our relationships.

It is important today that we restore the sacred fire of the home that is the basis of all our other social fires. We should install a sacred fire in our homes in one way or another, whether it is a candle or a light or a fireplace. We must remember that our kitchen fire is always a sacred fire and that our home is always a place of worship. A family meal of home-cooked and home-grown food remains perhaps the greatest sacrament that we can offer.

The Development of Civilization: Our Collective Fires

The human kingdom is not just that of a single species but constitutes its own domain of nature, almost as diverse as the animal kingdom. We humans are distinctly social creatures living in groups, communities and cities. We have specialized roles like cells or organs of a greater body. We organize ourselves into various professions, classes or subcultures, each with its own type of fire or particular energetic activity of the body and mind.[103] There are many different breeds of people, as it were, expressed through various races, ethnicities, cultures and languages. The different shapes and colors of humanity are the different colors and rays of our single sacred fire.

Our fire of intelligence affords us a unique ability to shape our world. We are no longer merely part of nature but have an almost separate realm of existence. We have developed a society and civilization that looks to harness and transcend nature for its own purposes, good or ill.

The fire of intelligence allows us to probe into the world around us and discover its laws and powers. We don't simply accept things as they appear but look into what is behind them, what makes them tick. Our intelligence works to extend the range of our bodily capacities developing tools, machines, vehicles and instruments of different types. It has enabled us to produce technology in all of its forms from stone tools up to modern computers.

We have extended the range of our eyes through telescopes and microscopes. We have extended the range of our ears with every sort of sound system and hearing device. We have extended the range of our feet with every sort of vehicle from the simple bullock cart to the modern rocket that can take us into outer space. We have extended the power of our hands with tools and machines from the spinning wheel to rapid assembly line equipment. We have extended the range of our speech with every sort of written and spoken media, filling vast libraries and data banks with detailed information on every sort of subject.

We can delve into nature with our tools and extract her essences. We have learned to mine metals and facet gems from the rocks. We have learned to extract fibers, dyes, oils and medicines from plants. We have hunted and domesticated animals, using them for food, clothing and transportation. We have unlocked the very power of the atom.

We have become creators in our own right, developing our own plant varieties and breeds of animals. We have fashioned our own landscapes, reshaping the surface of our world with great cities and roads, using the substances we have extracted from nature like metal, glass, stone and wood. We have created our own race of machines through cars, televisions and computers and now look to create automatons or even clones of ourselves.

Yet even with all this growth of civilization, our higher intelligence has yet to really express itself. Its true function is not merely to exploit our outer resources, but to take us to a higher state of consciousness in which our human intelligence unites with the cosmic intelligence that is its true origin and support. We have yet to create a real civilization of the sacred fire whose home is in the entire universe and honors all life. This means that the work of our species and its special fire is just beginning.

Agriculture and Fire

Agriculture was the basis of the first human communities or villages. We could say that fire was the first farmer. Our role in clearing the fields and the forests was often a fire role. Early agriculture began with burning down the forests or the grasslands, which not only cleared the land but also added to its fertility. Slash and burn agriculture was an early farming stage throughout the world. The plow itself can be viewed symbolically as a flame, bringing light out of the ground. Crops ripen owing to the fire of the Sun.

Not surprisingly, the ashes from sacred fires have long been used to purify and fertilize the soils. They increase the power of the soul in the soil. Vedic agriculture uses ashes (bhasma) from the Vedic sacred fire in order to counter the effects of the pollution of the soil. It is an important method to help restore our depleted soils, uniting once more the ground with the light. Soil is, metaphorically speaking, the ashes of the Earth's plant and mineral fires. By adding the ashes of our human sacred fires back to the soil, we can enrich it with a spiritual light.

In our age of factory farming in which we work the ground like an assembly line, we should remember the sacred root of farming. Agriculture is our first culture and perhaps the basis of all our other arts and sciences. For our civilization to flower, we need to turn it once more into a form of worship.

The Fire of Education

We humans have a long period of childhood that requires an extensive education so that we can mature and function independently in the world. This fire of schooling is the key of how we develop in life. We move from the family fire to the school fire in our growth and development. Schools are meant to light the lamp of learning in the student and pass on the flame of truth from one generation to another.

Yet in our current commercial age, education transmits more an artificial light of information than any real flame of learning. Training is aimed at providing high paying jobs, not at any deep understanding of life. Our schools are not so much temples of learning as factories to produce drones for our latest job specifications. Even the humanities departments that still might exist in universities today are more caught up in politics than in any study of the soul of man or our spiritual heritage as a species. Art, literature and philosophy mainly continue as the ghosts of previous ages, with religion as a fossil that has been fashioned into a weapon of war. We must remember learning has its own value as the real unfoldment of our inner flame. We must once more cultivate its priceless light or whatever jobs we create will only lead to exploitation, not the freedom of the spirit.

The Fire of Justice

The aggressive aspect of fire that developed in the hunting skills of animals led over time to the martial skills of human beings. Warriors had their own special fires that were the center of their gatherings, which were used for taking oaths or even for forging weapons. Each king had his royal fire, which represented his ancestry, lineage and power. Before battle, special war fires were lit, not simply as a necessity of the encampment but as a ritual to prepare the soldiers to fight. The War God in all cultures is usually a fire god, like Mars among the Romans, Ares among the Greeks and Skanda among the Hindus.

Fire was the basis for the first laws or dharmas, which were generally formulated around a council fire or fire of the elders. Fire was the first judge who determined right and wrong by recourse to the laws enshrined in the sacred fire of the community. All legal authorities take such a fire role in their work. This 'fire of justice' upholds the moral authority of a culture.

Each country today still has its military fires and the armies and weapons that go along with them. It also has its legal fires and the punishments they decree. Yet seldom in the world today is the real sacred fire of justice honored. We have forgotten the sacred and universal basis of the law. We have covered it over with the smoke of vested interests — politically, socially and economically. We must remember that true justice rests upon the fire of the soul and its connection to universal truth and ethics. Otherwise such aggressive and punitive fires will only result in more conflict and inequality and will never bring peace.

The Religion of Fire

Our fire of intelligence directs us to religion and spirituality as the crest of its flame, to the awakening of the soul or eternal element within us. Religion deals with the outward tending of the sacred fire through ritual, prayer and ethics. Spirituality is concerned with the inner fire of meditation for realizing the Divine light within us. Spirituality is the inner fire of religion, which is often no more than its ashes.

The religious guide is first of all a fire priest who maintains the fires of our faith and directs our aspiration to the light. This fire priest became the prototype for all our spiritual guides appearing as shamans, prophets, saints and yogis.[104] The ancient teachers transmitted the Divine message to us that they had received directly from the cosmic fire. Through it they established the first *dharmas* or spiritual laws behind civilization.

Our natural religion is the religion of fire and light. The fire built on a stone altar is perhaps our original sacred image of God. When we kneel to pray, we naturally assume a fire-like position, we place our body and our hands in the gesture of a flame, looking upwards to the light.

Our places of worship are houses of light, fire temples or

resemble flames. Many great churches, particularly the Gothic cathedrals of Europe with their spires, look like flames rising up to heaven. The great pyramids of the world from Egypt to Mexico have the triangular shape of a flame. Domes such as adorn many temples, churches and mosques reflect a similar fire-like image.

Most religious rituals center on offerings of fire and light, from the lighting of candles in Christian and Jewish rituals, or the burning of special fires in Vedic and Iranian rites. All ceremonial functions in Hindu and Buddhist cultures, whether religious, cultural or educational, begin with the ceremonial lighting of the lamps. While such fires may appear to be only a formality or a spectacle, their recognition of the Divine light is easy to discern.

There are also many religious festivals of light like Christmas, the Jewish Hanukkah, the Celtic Beltane festival of August where great fires are lit, or Hindu Diwali, which features massive fireworks. These are among our greatest collective celebrations and form our fondest memories as children. Every native culture has its own great festivals of color, fire and light, which are often associated with the change of seasons and the renewal of life. Even our political holidays like the Fourth of July reflect such special community displays of fire and light.

Yet this religion of fire, we must carefully note, is not simply a worship of fire as a material element or unconscious force of nature.[105] It reflects a direct experience of the Divine, which is the light of lights, the consciousness that illumines light itself. We should remember our soul, our inner fire as the indwelling deity in the temple of our body and enshrine it in the temples of our society. It is that flame that makes things holy, not the pronouncements of any religious authority or tradition.

Learn to see the inner flame of the soul behind the forms of whatever religion you may choose to follow. That inner fire can teach us the universal language of light, through which we can go beyond all division and conflict, taking us to the unity of truth behind all spiritual striving.

Carriers of the Flame in Humanity

There have always been those among our species who are awake to the soul and its eternal striving. These are the spiritual guides who have led humanity from the very beginning of time. I have met several such masters still alive in India, including Sivananda Murty, a great teacher in the south of the country, who has a beautiful hermitage and retreat center by the gentle hills along the coast of Andhra Pradesh on the Bay of Bengal.

Murtyji, as he is called, knows the very cosmology of the universe and recognizes all the planes of existence, as residing in his own consciousness. The universe for him is not an external reality but an inner vision. While living on Earth he can access all realms of existence. One can ask him questions about almost any yoga practice, any mantra or even any aspect of human culture and he can reply with an experiential knowledge of its essence. Yet he responds to all questions with humility and respect and never tries to impose his views on anyone. He does not try to broadcast, much less preach what he knows. People visit him and he replies according to their needs, talking to everyone from common villagers to the wealthy and the talented. His guidance is succinct and to the point without any effort to embellish even the most extraordinary subjects.

Specifically Sivananda Murty taught me about the soul and the subtle body in the heart, and how to enter into it through various Yoga practices. The subtle body or interior person, the Upanishadic Purusha that is the size of a thumb,[105] holds our bodily image and all of our experience in its awareness in the heart. The subtle body mirrors all the movements of the gross or physical body. When the outer body or person moves, it is because the inner body or person is moving. Through visualizing changes in the subtle body or real person in the heart, we can change the physical body as well. Entering into its sphere of light we can change ourselves and alter our karma from within.[107]

Visualize your physical body and personality existing in a small form of about an inch inside a flame in the center of your heart. Consider whatever changes or improvements you would like to make in yourself in order to better express the Divine will within you and become a better human being. Whatever you hold to and meditate on through this inner soul body of the heart must eventually occur in your outer life as well.

The wisdom of such spiritual masters has come down to us in many forms, not simply as religion but also as poetry, art, music, science, philosophy and medicine. However, its main form is secret or esoteric teachings, transmitted directly from teacher to student as the light of wakeful awareness directly transmitted from one soul to another. Though such teachers still reside among us, they are very hard to find. They often live in retirement like a fire hidden in darkness, working in the background, emphasizing the essence and avoiding any outer displays. We must be receptive to the teachings of these great sages again, wherever they may be and whatever forms they may adopt, as they maintain the soul's transmission of the light that is the crowning labor of our species.

Humanity as Nature's Flame

Our species has come forth from the Earth and carries its planetary heritage. Our face and form is in all of nature, which has eyes and ears everywhere, only a few of which take shape in the bodies of creatures. We represent the intelligence that has worked its way up from the stone, releasing the hidden potentials of life and mind held in the primordial rock.

All planetary evolution is hidden within us. Just as rocks contain the fossils of previous life-forms, so too the rock of our mind, our deeper subconscious nature, contains the imprint of all previous life on Earth. We have a reptilian and instinctual part of the brain as well as our self-conscious and human side. The mineral, plant and animal still work within us and allow us to function. Only in our case they work in the background and we miss the importance of their contribution. But we could no more function without them than our head could function without its feet or arms.

Much of what we call ourselves is the continuation of forces set in motion earlier in the evolutionary process. Our hungers and urges are powerful biological forces etched deeply within our cells. They are like great Gods or titans that rule over us, making us want or feel things that otherwise we would not consider at a conscious level. Most of what we think is unique to ourselves is just the perpetuation of deep-seated compulsions that arose long before our species.

Even the better part of humanity — the spiritual and creative urges of the soul — existed before our species arose and already produced much beauty in nature from the mountains to the flowers before we appeared. Similarly, the worst part of our nature — our violence and intolerance — represents an animal aggression that we have distorted and exaggerated. We must recognize these evolutionary powers for both their constructive and destructive potentials. We must honor all the fires that have gone into creating our species and afford them their appropriate places. We must continue with the evolutionary march of fire from a mere material force that is hostile to life to a spiritual force that brings joy to all existence.

Remembering Your Soul in all Humanity

Look deep behind your mind and your personal memories, beyond the veils of sleep and death. Recognize your many human births that linger as a vague intimation of times before your body was born. You have been a man, a woman, a boy and a girl. You have been a father and mother, brother and sister, husband and wife. You have been rich and poor, happy and sad, fortunate and unfortunate, dying as a mere child and living for over a century. You have been an artist, farmer, priest, warrior and sage. You have been a member of many different villages, cities and countries, in both the highest and lowest strata of humanity. You have followed every type of religion, assumed every nationality, and been of every race and ethnic group. You have traveled all over the Earth and yet spent many years alone in your own house.

You are humanity in its many forms. All people are your different faces, your various masks. Look at those around you, your family and friends who mirror your current life and recognize that you dwell within them also. Consider all people in the world today. You are as much akin to them as you are to your present family. In this regard there is a beautiful Upanishadic statement:

> *You are the woman and you are the man.*
> *You are the young boy and you are the girl.*
> *You are the old man who totters on his staff.*
> *You are born with your face to every side.*[108]

CHAPTER TEN

The Fire of Yoga and Higher Human Evolution

Most of us have encountered the practice of Yoga in one form or another. Many of us have taken it up as part of our own life-styles. We usually view Yoga as a special physical discipline with spiritual overtones that provides greater flexibility to the body and relieves stress and tension from the mind, restoring our natural sense of well-being. Yet most of us are not aware of Yoga's profound connection with the world of nature or its great diversity of practices for all aspects of our being.

Yoga in essence is not a mere human invention; it arises from nature itself, from the very intelligence of life. The entire philosophy of Yoga is based upon an understanding of nature called Prakriti and its evolution from matter to life and mind.[109] It sees nature as the manifestation of cosmic intelligence, not simply as a material force.[110] Most importantly, Yoga recognizes an inner or higher nature, our true Self and being, the Atman or Purusha, as the real power and presence behind the outer forms of nature. Yoga regards the outer world of nature, life on Earth, as a vehicle for unfolding the inner world of nature, the life of the

Spirit, which takes us beyond time and space to pure exist-ence, consciousness and bliss.[111]

Yoga is the very movement of nature toward greater life and awareness. It is the integrative approach of evolution itself, seeking ever greater forms of wholeness and univer-sality, not simply as abstractions but as new states and conditions of body, mind and awareness. Yoga is the es-sence of our evolutionary journey and an important tool to carry it to the next level.

Yoga, one could say, is a natural approach to spirituality, working with our life-given powers of body, breath and mind according to the secret evolutionary intelligence be-hind them. Yoga is not simply an exercise system or even a meditation approach but the way of action of the soul or wholeness aspect of our being on all levels. The soul al-ways seeks unity, but in a natural way, embracing multi-plicity in a greater totality, like the ocean absorbing all the rivers without losing itself. Yoga harmonizes the different aspects of body and mind into a higher flame to take us beyond their limitations.

Yoga and the Spirituality of Fire

I taught this imperishable science of Yoga to the Sun God (Vivasvan) who taught it to Manu.

— BHAGAVAD GITA[112]

According to the *Bhagavad Gita* — perhaps India's greatest scripture and the most important work on Yoga philosophy — Yoga was first taught by God in the form of Lord Krishna, who related this teaching at a cosmic level to the Sun God. The Sun God in turn revealed it to Manu, the progenitor of all humanity and himself a great Yogi, from whom it spread to all peoples.[113]

This story may not be only a Hindu account. The an-cient Germans also traced their origins to a primal man called Manu, as did other Indo-European peoples. Accord-ing to the Roman writer Tacitus in his *Annals and Histories*, the Germans claimed to be descendants of Mannus, the son of the Sky God Tuisto. Tuisto or Sanskrit Tvashta is another name for the progenitor Sun God called Vivasvan.[114] We are all creations of solar energy, which inwardly is the light of intelligence. Its mode of operation is Yoga or harmonious development and integration of all evolutionary potentials for consciousness.

According to classical Yoga, the original teacher of Yoga is the Sun God called Hiranyagarbha, the golden embryo or Sun seed, which is another synonym with Vivasvan.[115] This Vedic Sun God, similar to other solar deities of the ancient world like the Greek Apollo or Egyptian Amun-Ra, is symbolic of the light of truth within us. Its embryo state is the seed of truth or inner fire latent within our own souls.[116]

Patanjali, to whom is attributed the *Yoga Sutras*, the chief classical text on Yoga, was a mere compiler of Yoga teachings at a later stage of history, with the Yoga tradition already very old when he put it into a few succinct verses. Patanjali never claimed to invent Yoga but only to be carrying on a much older and broader tradition. In a statement of the great epic *Mahabharata*, in which the *Gita* occurs, Hiranyagarbha gave his teaching to Vasishta, the foremost of the Vedic rishis,[117] showing the connection of Yoga with the older Vedic science of light. Patanjali received it from this line of the Rishis and was himself considered to be a great Rishi. This means that the Yoga tradition and the Rishi tradition are essentially the same.

The ancient Rishis were the original great Yogis as well. Even the Yoga postures that modern Yoga so emphasizes were originally designed by the Rishis to bring the energy of Yoga into the physical body. Several asanas are named after Rishis like Bharadvaja-asana, after the great rishi Bharadvaja, or Vasishta-asana, after the great rishi Vasishta. Asana traditions are related to Vedic martial arts[118] and Vedic dance traditions.[119] Many Yoga postures can be found in Indian art and temple sculpture.

Hiranyagarbha or the solar flame represents the seed of

enlightenment that unfolds the transformative process of Yoga from the fire of our own souls. *Yoga, therefore, is the living essence of the ancient solar and fire religions that are our oldest spiritual heritage and as such it belongs to everyone. Yoga is the very purpose of our existence on the planet.* This yogic fire religion is an experiential form of spirituality that transcends all dogmas, definitions and ideologies. It proceeds through cultivating our internal fires in order to reach the supreme light of reality.

This ancient Fire Yoga, what is called *Agni Yoga* in Sanskrit, is arguably the origin of all yogic paths. The fire of Yoga leads us forward in our evolutionary march towards greater wisdom and devotion. It is our chief priest and guru of the internal rite of self-transformation, working through many names, forms and teachers according to the needs of time, place, person and culture:

> *First yogically controlling the mind, developing the power of intelligence, discerning its inner light, the Solar Creator brought the sacred fire up out of the Earth.*
>
> — UPANISHADS[120]

The fire brought up out of the Earth by the power of Yoga is that of our own soul. Yoga's main concern is a higher human evolution — the development of an unconditioned consciousness within us. *The fire of Yoga helps prepare our fifth birth beyond the mineral, plant, animal and human to the Divine.* It takes us from a limited body consciousness to a universal awareness in which we can see our Self in all beings. Through the process of Yoga, the individual soul can expand into the universal soul, which is the real goal of our pilgrimage through all the kingdoms of Nature. The soul originally enters into this world in order to become all creation. This movement of the soul is inherently a process of Yoga or integration.

To really embark on this yogic quest, therefore, we must practice Yoga from the level of the soul, which is the level of the spiritual heart. We must remember our spiritual journey — that we are seeking immortality through many bodies and births, many faces, forms and inspirations. We must recall our Divine mission of Self-realization, which is the liberation of consciousness, not just for our individual benefit but for the benefit of the entire universe.

Yoga and Self-realization

The individual soul is symbolized by fire. The body and mind are the two fire sticks that when rubbed together (brought into a state of balance) bring this fire forth. This Divine fire is born within all creatures as the sense of Self — the 'I am that I am' behind all our thoughts and feelings. Through Yoga, the little I am of the bodily self expands into the universal I am of 'I am all', the Self that is Being itself. In this process, the Self reclaims the universe and the world regains its soul.

Our own soul as the sacred fire unfolds all the powers of the conscious universe — the great Gods and Goddesses — which it secretly contains within itself. It takes us through all the realms of consciousness from the Earth to the highest formless heavens at the origin of creation — to the very world before the world. Through it we can know not only the creatures that manifest in this world but also the Divine powers that guide them from above and within.[121]

Whatever we see on Earth in the rocks and plants is a form of fire as light and color. All animals and humans are forms of fire as life, perception, love and intelligence. The Sun, Moon and stars in the sky above are forms of fire, the eyes of God that ever watch over us. The highest form of fire is the Fire of Pure Being, the fire of Brahman or the Absolute. This supreme fire is also the great God Shiva, the eternal lord of Yoga who unfolds the cosmic dance of fire that creates, preserves, and transforms the entire universe.[122] Shiva is anointed with the ashes (bhasma) of the sacred fire that consumes all things. We are all part of Shiva's fire dance. We are all Shiva himself. We are the light of the all-consuming fire and the Self of all creatures that have been or are to be.

The evolutionary fire of Yoga works to turn our crude

human nature, our frail human desires, fears and ambitions, into something genuinely spiritual, sublime and vast. It transmutes our egoic mindset and circumscribed personal concerns into an immutable awareness beyond any disturbance, desire or distraction. It unfolds a higher human potential in which we go beyond our mere humanity to the Cosmic Person of pure light.

Our soul carries the Divine will within it to return to the Godhead that is the very source of our body, life and mind. We must bring forth that spiritual fire out of the Earth of the body. We must purify ourselves through the fire of Yoga in order to go beyond death and suffering. This is our true resurrection, that of our spiritual Self, the Divine light or secret Sun hidden within us. We need to create a new body of consciousness beyond the limitations of the physical body as the *Upanishads* say:

> *Those who have gained the fire-made body of Yoga suffer no disease, old age or death.*[123]

The Eight Yogic Fires

Yoga is the spiritual science of fire that works with our own natural energy and intelligence. It provides many tools and methods for the process of growing the light, working with all the main forms of fire within us. It has special postures for the body, special breathing methods for the vital force, visualization practices for the senses, concentration and meditation methods for the mind, and devotion for the heart. At the same time, Yoga reminds us that the process of Self-realization is natural and all tools are just expedient aids to eventually be cast into the fire themselves.

Yoga is classically defined in the *Yoga Sutras* as the 'control of the modifications of the mind' (chitta), which results in the realization of the higher Self or Purusha.[124] In Sanskrit, the term Chit refers not only to consciousness but also indicates a layer of the fire altar (Agni-Chit).[125] Control of the mind means creating the proper fire altar or state of consciousness to support our inner flame. The Self so realized is Agni or the sacred fire of the soul both within us and enshrined throughout the entire universe.

The disturbances of the mind that we must control are the smoke that comes forth from an improperly burning flame of awareness. Once we cultivate our inner flame properly, it will burn clearly, revealing the nature of reality. All Yoga practices can be understood in terms of such fire practices and fire offerings.

Classical Yoga consists of eight branches (Ashtanga),[126] each of which develops a certain portion of our soul's fire in order to transform a corresponding aspect of our nature from the gross physical to the highest levels of the mind. These eight branches (loosely translated) are:

1. Right attitude (Yama)
2. Right life-style (Niyama)
3. Right posture (Asana)
4. Control of the breath (Pranayama)
5. Control of the senses (Pratyahara)
6. Concentration (Dharana)
7. Meditation (Dhyana)
8. Absorption or bliss (Samadhi)

For any yoga practices to really work, we must first live according to the principles of natural law or the principle of dharma, respecting all beings and honoring the sacred flame throughout the universe. This means that to really begin the practice of Yoga, we must first awaken at the level of the soul. Our inner fire must be enkindled. The purpose of our practice must be to increase the Divine light both within and around us. This is the concern of the first two steps of Yoga (Yama and Niyama) that involve creating dharmic values and dharmic action as the basis of our life and thought.[127]

1. The Fire of Right Attitude

The yogic fire process begins with right attitudes in life. In order to handle this spiritual fire energy we must have the fundamental values that can support it. Otherwise this fire can consume us as well. These yogic values are defined mainly in terms of self-control. Only those who have some degree of self-mastery can reach a deeper level of self-transformation.

The first step in Yoga consists of five factors of self-control (Yamas); non-violence, truthfulness, responsible use of sexuality, non-stealing and non-coveting.[128] These fires of character help us restrain our outward going tendencies and gain mastery over our internal urges. They help build our character so that we can become an appropriate vessel for higher forces to descend.

- The fire of non-violence destroys our main destructive tendencies in life, which involve violence, aggression and domination.
- The fire of truthfulness purifies the mind, which is obscured by the darkness of falsehood and deception.
- The fire of sexual restraint allows us to use our sexual energy as a healing and spiritual force.
- The fire of non-stealing allows us to burn up the unhappiness and resentment that we have created by taking things from others.
- The fire of non-coveting allows us to keep our minds free of any excesses or attachments and from accumulating too many things either within or around us.[129]

The first and foremost ethical principle of the yogic life style is non-violence or non-harming (ahimsa). We should have an attitude of not wishing harm to any creature or any aspect of our world. We should act in such a way that we not only avoid violence, which is a passive approach, but also strive to reduce the amount of harm occurring in the world, which is an active approach. This effort to reduce the amount of harm in the world is particularly important today when so much destruction is going on all over the planet.

The fire of non-violence has a special power to purify

the heart. Casting all enmity into the fire of non-violence, we gain a tremendous power of truth and conviction. Even if we must confront or challenge hostile forces in the world and work to counter their wrong actions — as often must be the case — we must remember to wish their souls well. We must remember not to direct any thoughts of harm against others, even when we must oppose what they may do or represent outwardly.[130]

2. The Fire of Right Life-Style

The second foundation for the yogic approach is right life-style (Niyama). This is defined according to five factors of self-discipline, self-study, surrender to the Divine, purity and contentment.[131] These fires, which all involve different forms of self-discipline, provide us with the way of life necessary to reach a higher level of awareness.

- The fire of self-discipline, emphasizing control of body, speech and mind, allows us to transform the fire of blind desire into the fire of conscious will power.[132]
- The fire of self-study allows us to penetrate through the ego and conditioned self to our true identity in consciousness.
- The fire of surrender to the Divine allows us to access cosmic forces of energy and aspiration beyond our personal limitations and work with the creative forces of the entire universe.
- The fire of purity and cleanliness helps us reduce impurities and toxins of body and mind through such practices as right diet, right exercise and emotional integrity.
- The fire of contentment keeps all our inner fires in balance through an evenness of mind, emotion and attitude.

3. Yoga Asanas and the Bodily Fire

Yoga postures (asanas) purify, balance and energize the digestive fire that propels the physical body. They bring calm, flexibility and equipoise to our entire organism, countering agitation, stiffness and fatigue. In the balanced state created by asanas, our circulation flows unhindered, our metabolism is optimal, and there is a minimum amount of resistance and friction in our movements. Yet asana does not simply have physical benefits; it calms the body, opening up a space for the inner fires of prana and mind.[133]

When we gently but firmly stretch ourselves in Yoga postures, a special heat is created that frees the muscles, releasing any emotional stress or nervous tension held within them. This 'fire of stretching' changes our bodies from a heavy weight upon our soul into a fluid or plastic tool of its expression. It unlocks our joints, allowing the life-force to flow freely within us.

The natural form fire takes when it burns is an upward-facing triangle. In sitting postures like the lotus pose we put the body in such a triangular position. We place it in a 'fire position' in order to let its inner fire come forth. Sitting cross-legged is an imitation of fire and allows the mind's fire to develop within the body. That is why sitting postures are emphasized in Yoga. They are fire postures that prepare the way for inner transformation. Recognizing the sacred nature of the body, Yoga asanas enable us to turn it into a tool for meditation.

4. Yogic Breathing and the Fire of the Breath

Yogic breathing (pranayama) works to purify, balance and energize the pranic or breath fire, the source of vitality within us. When inhalation and exhalation are balanced, the fire of Prana bursts forth at a deeper level and opens the subtle channels of the mind and senses, providing a new energy and motivation for change and growth.

Through yogic breathing we gain the 'breath of fire' and can ride the waves of the wind throughout the universe of the mind. We contact a perpetual source of internal inspiration that stimulates our inner creativity and daring. We discover an almost unlimited internal energy source to provide added strength and ease in action. We can literally breathe our problems away and breathe new life into the world. We connect our soul with the spirit that pervades all nature.

Actually Prana is the real Yogi, not any human person. Even asanas are expressions of Prana and best done by Prana, not by the ego of the practitioner. Many great Yogis learned their asanas from Prana alone, not from books. For them, the asana was an extension of the breath and even complex asanas came naturally along with deep rhythmic breathing and even suspension of the breath.[134]

5. Internalizing the Fire of the Mind

Yoga as the realization of the inner Self requires an interiorization or introversion of the outgoing mind and senses. To discover the inner reality of both ourselves and the universe, we must first redirect our attention within. We must create a revolution in our consciousness, through which we move from our fixed bodily view of reality to an inner view of the world as light and consciousness. This stage is marked by yogic internalization practices (Pratyahara). Once our life-fires are turned within, they can gather strength, gestate and bring about a new birth or manifestation of the soul.

Turning our senses within, they become instruments of insight and contemplation.

- Turning the eyes within through the practice of inner seeing, we can develop the inner or third eye and learn to perceive the light within and behind all beings.
- Turning the power of speech within through the practice of silence, we can create a fire of silence that purifies the mind.
- Turning the mind within, we can discover the nature of consciousness beyond all thought and imagination.
- Turning our self within, we can discover our universal Self beyond all sorrow.

6. Concentration and the Flame of the Mind

The mind is like a flame with the power of attention as its

point of focus. The more intent the focus, the more the mind can see and the greater its power of knowing. Focusing the mind in concentration, we bring forth the light of one-pointed awareness that can reveal the secrets of any object we choose to examine. In concentration, we gather the mind's light to illumine reality, collecting its rays to expand our perceptual capacities far beyond their ordinary boundaries.

Whenever our minds are one-pointed, our lives gain meaning and power. Recollect the times in your own life when you were really intent, whether in a creative project, some new research or just getting out into nature. At such times you felt the most alive and energetic. These are also the times that we most remember. To be truly successful in life, we must act in a whole-hearted manner, concentrating the light of our heart's purpose towards its highest goal.

There are several methods of concentration using fire itself. Gaze on a candle flame or the fire in your fireplace for fifteen minutes or so in the evening. The flame will make it easy for you to concentrate and bring your mind into a state of meditation. It will help you to rediscover the flame within you. Or visualize a golden flame of truth within your heart and concentrate on it as the source of all your being. *Hold an image of light within yourself as a reminder of your deeper Self.*

Another method is to concentrate on a particular mantra or sacred sound like OM or HREEM, repeating it on a regular basis until it becomes the dominant background thought or sound in the mind. Owing to the connection between fire and speech, Mantra Yoga is one of the best ways of developing and concentrating the flame of the mind.

7. The Fire of Meditation

Meditation is the balanced state of awareness, the tranquil mind and heart that is the essence of true Yoga. Calmly holding the mind in meditation, we enter into a state of peace and contentment in which the soul's natural fire of wisdom spontaneously rises up and blesses all things. Our mind itself mirrors the depths of existence and embraces the very origins of time and space.

The easiest way to begin your practice of meditation is to observe nature. Go outdoors and open up to the presence of Being from horizon to horizon, offering your thoughts and attention to the greater universe beyond yourself.

- Look up into the day sky and contemplate the shifting clouds. All things in existence are like passing clouds in the infinite space of consciousness.

- Contemplate the night sky and its endless stars. We are all but points of light in the unlimited glittering canopy of existence.

- Contemplate the endless expanse of the ocean and its innumerable waves. We are but waves of bliss on the cosmic sea.

These are but a few typical approaches. Examine any aspect of nature that inspires you for its contemplative value, from the streams and rocks to the plants and animals. Be aware of your natural environment and you will discover that your awareness is everywhere in nature. *Each ecosystem in nature can function as a doorway to the infinite if we approach it with a meditative mind.* That is its real value for the soul. Learn how to use the mountains, plains, deserts and jungles as doorways to enter into the Divine. See how all facets of nature contribute to the soul's return to the Godhead.

Once you can restfully hold your attention on various forms in nature, you can discover the deeper nature inside yourself as well. Enter into the greater world within your own mind. Look deeply into the ocean of your heart in which all the worlds are but waves. Travel through the infinite sky of your mind that extends as much inwardly as space does outwardly.

Ultimately your mind must become the entire universe. When you close your eyes you will see all nature as the very field or garden of your soul. Develop a mind that is vast enough to encompass the entire world without losing its own peace or equipoise. *Such a 'mind of nature' can become any ecosystem.* It is its own inner ecosystem holding minerals, plants and animals, planets, stars and galaxies in a harmonious awareness of the sacred.

Meditation naturally occurs when we return to ourselves, when we rest content in our inner being without distractions or desires. Though many methods can aid in the process, these are only tools to bring us to the meditative state in which all action naturally subsides into Being Itself. We should follow whatever techniques accomplish this for us, disregarding their forms and differences.

Cultivating the fire of meditation is the main practice of Yoga. All other practices are preparatory. It is the main way to enlightenment and Self-realization. The fire of spiritual knowledge created by meditation destroys all our negative karmas, purifying the soul for its realization of the Divine Self:

> *Just as a blazing fire reduces its fuel to ashes, the Fire of Self-knowledge reduces all our karmas to ashes.*
>
> — BHAGAVAD GITA[135]

8. The Fire of Bliss

We are not meant merely to survive or to struggle for happiness. We are meant to live in joy, love and inspiration. We are meant to melt in the flame of bliss and transcend time, space and limitation.

Merging into our hearts in meditation, we discover the fire of bliss and Divine love (Samadhi), in which we are inherently one with all beings and can embrace all nature from within. We merge into the boundless sea of light, with our soul fire but a wave of light pulsating across the boundless shore, where world and no world become one in the ineffable. The fire of meditation naturally culminates in the fire of bliss, which is the ultimate state of pure unity that real meditation brings us to. True bliss is the oneness of meditation, not merely an emotional state or achievement of desire. It is the happiness of the natural Self that is one with all. It occurs when we become one with the light.

Following our bliss in life does not mean running after pleasure in the external world. It means returning to the joy of the spiritual heart which arises from the state of peace and surrender to life. Such bliss is the inner motivating flame that has been guiding us throughout our evolutionary journey.

Discovering the Yogic Fire God

Most of us consider that great spiritual masters of antiquity like Krishna, Buddha or Christ cannot be found in modern times. Actually there have been several comparable great yogis and sages over the past century alone. Ramana Maharshi (1878 – 1950), probably the most famous enlightened sage of modern India, is such a figure. He was the very personification of Self-realization, which he achieved as a mere lad of sixteen through a short twenty-minute inquiry into the deathless Self.[136] After that experience he lived in the highest enlightened state without fluctuation for the rest of his life of over seventy years. No other practices were necessary for him. It was though he was born in the highest spiritual state and merely waited until his body was mature enough to manifest it. His life, teachings and character easily compare with the great teachers of old.

Ramana meditated in silence at the base of the sacred hill of Arunachala, the reputed fire center of South India, the fire form of Lord Shiva himself, with which he himself was identified. Though he never sought to gain any disciples, people spontaneously gathered around him as his influence naturally spread. Up to the time of his death, he expressed no need to travel much less to seek the attention of anyone. He was completely merged in both the Divine Self and in the mountain, which he saw as one. He himself was the sacred mountain of fire. One of his own verses states:

> In you, O Mountain of the Dawn (Arunachala), all this
> manifold universe takes birth, in you it abides and in you

*it dissolves. As the "I" in the heart, by the power of the
Self you dance. O Lord, they call you the heart of all beings.*

— FIVE VERSES IN PRAISE OF ARUNACHALA[137]

Arunachala is one of the most sacred sites in all of India. It
is a reddish granite mountain among the oldest exposed
rock formations on Earth. Like the much higher Himalayas
to the north, this fire hill of the south was a place of refuge
for the great Rishis at the time of the great flood many
thousands of years ago.[138] Its connection with Ramana,
perhaps modern India's greatest sage, can hardly be coinci-
dental.

Ramana's teaching has a great appeal to the rational
mind seeking to transcend name, form and culture in order
to reach a pure deathless awareness. This began with Paul
Brunton, who through stories of his meetings with the
sage in the nineteen thirties first brought world attention
to Ramana.[139]

The very picture of Ramana's face conveys the deepest
insight, love and compassion. For many it is enough to take
them directly into deep meditation. His ashram remains a
powerful pilgrimage center for meditation visited by many
people East and West. Though Ramana passed away decades ago (1950), his large picture in the meditation hall
appears alive and pouring out his grace, particularly if one
visits before dawn when few people are there.

Yet, what I discovered during my first visit to his ashram
many years ago was something very different from what I
was expecting. I came to pay homage to Ramana for his
teachings of Self-inquiry, his simple and direct method of
the Yoga of Knowledge leading to the state of pure awareness. What I actually discovered was the God Skanda, the
child of fire, who demanded purification, death and spiritual rebirth. I stumbled on the yogic Fire God, not as a devotional or cultural image but as a primordial and awesome
power both within my own psyche and within the sur-
rounding world of nature.

In Hindu mythology, the Fire God called Skanda is the

son of Lord Shiva, the deity of meditation, and his wife Uma, the personification of selfless devotion. Skanda is the fire child who takes birth from the union of Shiva and Shakti (Uma) in order to destroy the powers of death and ignorance that oppress the universe. He defeats all these deep-seated negative forces, the demons of duality, as a mere child six days old. In this regard, Skanda personifies the childlike or innocent mind, the mind of the Divine Child that has the power to overcome all negativity and duality.

When I came into the town (Tiruvannamalai) on the outskirts of which Ramana's ashram is located, I felt the presence of a tremendous spiritual fire, which also had, in its more benefic moments, the face of a young boy. The image of a small boy carrying a spear, rising out of a fire, kept arising in my mind. This brought about an intense practice of Self-inquiry, a questioning of 'Who am I?' I began to realize that all that I called myself was just an illusion, a confusion of a deeper consciousness with the changing body and its shifting sensory images. This brought about a deathlike experience, an immersion in the fire of the spirit, though it was the ego's death, not that of the underlying Self.

I felt my body gradually lose consciousness as my awareness became focused in the flame of the heart. I could see my whole body and entire life becoming consumed in that flame. My awareness gradually became concentrated into a point of pure light inside the flame. That point opened inward as a mysterious door to a world of pure light beyond this shadow realm of name and form. It took me into a new dimension of consciousness in which my Self was the universe, not just the world that we know but all potentials of existence and the supreme space that never enters into form.

Going through that fire was perhaps the most intense spiritual experience of my life. I had to pray at times that it would not become too strong! It is not easy to face the inner fire. I found that when real spiritual experiences oc-

cur it is we who go, it is not we who witness it. Our ordinary self is effaced. Only the core essence, the most
stripped bare portion of our heart, remains. Yet afterward
this experience, I felt refreshed and cleansed, with a purity
of perception that was extraordinary, though the 'I 'that
remained was never the same again. It remained more as a
flame than a person — an awareness from the core of my
being, not a mere bodily identity or self-image.

Up to that time, with my western background, I had a
limited understanding of the role of deities in spiritual practice, which we easily dismiss as primitive or inessential. I
had little knowledge of Lord Skanda, though he is a popular
deity in South India, particularly in his Tamil name of
Murugan. I was aware of Agni or fire as a spiritual and natu-
ralistic power from my earlier Vedic studies but had never
experienced him so vividly through a human form. I was
surprised to come into a direct contact with such an entity,
not as a mere fantasy but as a concrete and vivid inner experience. That the process of Self-inquiry, a formless meditation practice, could be aligned to such a primeval power,
was something that went beyond my conceptions.

I eventually came to understand Ramana himself as
Lord Skanda, the embodiment of the flame of spiritual
knowledge. This was how his chief disciple, perhaps modern India's greatest Sanskrit poet, Ganapati Muni, lauded
him in the following poem:

Your spotless form blazes with lightning.
Your vast vision shines with radiance.
My mind, O Lord, has been swallowed by your heart.[140]

Over time I learned more about Skanda, the yogic Fire God.
He is the inner Being born of the process of Self-inquiry,
which itself is like a fire. He is the inner child born of the
death of the ego on the cremation pyre of meditation. This
fire child represents the direct insight of the innocent mind,
free of ulterior motives. He can destroy all illusions, our
negative conditionings, with his spear of discrimination.

I felt Lord Skanda most keenly at the great temple of

Arunachaleshwara in the nearby town of Tiruvannamalai. The thousand-year-old temple still holds the vibration of Ramana, where he stayed and did ascetic practices for many years when he was young and unknown. It has also nourished many great sages and yogis throughout the centuries. The temple is said to hold the fire linga of Lord Shiva, his fire form among the five elements. This fire form of Shiva is like Ramana's spiritual father. The Devi (Goddess) at the temple functions as the mother of Ramana and Skanda and of all true seekers.

One day at the temple I decided to purchase a statue to take back home for my altar in America. I found a small statue of Lord Skanda for sale that I bought and put into my nap sack. One of the Brahmin priests in the temple noted my acquisition and asked for the statue, which I gave to him. He took my hand and led me through the temple, using the statue for performing puja (devotional worship) to all the main temple deities. He started with the Devi (Goddess) temple and then to the Shiva linga and finally to the Skanda temple. My statue was placed on all the main temple icons and was consecrated as part of their worship. It was as if I myself was reborn as Skanda during these rites. The deities in the temple came alive for me as the parents of Lord Skanda, who was not only Ramana, but also my own inner child of immortality. I felt the strongest energy in the shrine of the Goddess, who represents the power of self-discipline and self-surrender.

The story of the birth of the Goddess Uma (Shiva's consort), her tapas (ascetic practices) in the Himalayas, her marriage with Lord Shiva, and the birth of Lord Skanda began to unfold in my meditations as a symbol of the process of Self-realization.[141] The myth became real, while our human lives became mere shadows. The realms of these deities (Devalokas) emerged as states of higher awareness in which we can participate in their energy. My pilgrimage to the inner Himalayas began.

That initiation into the Fire God led to many more experiences and many encounters with different sages both outwardly and on a meditational level. It took my previous work with the Vedic fire to a much higher level. It led me from a mental appreciation of the yogic path of Self-realization to a deep understanding of its extraordinary fire that puts our entire human world to rest and can consume the entire universe. When one experientially knows that fire, the reality of this material world fades in comparison, becoming little more than its sparks or its ashes!

My experience of Skanda brought me contact with the teachings of Ganapati Muni, whose unpublished writings I later received from his oldest living disciple, K. Natesan of the Ramanashram. Natesan, a disciple of both Ramana and Ganapati since he was a child, had carefully gathered all of Ganapati's works, most of which were only written by hand, and carefully transcribed them in his own handwriting. He guided me through Ganapati's works that cover all aspects of Yoga, Tantra, Ayurveda and Vedic astrology, the specific fields of my own studies. Natesan also related his own direct experience of both Ramana and the sacred hill of Arunachala that opened many inner vistas for me. Ganapati's Sanskrit works taught me many secrets of Yoga, of the worship of the Goddess, Lord Shiva, the Vedic Gods and the sacred fire, including the inner yogic experience of the creation of the entire universe.[142]

Ganapati's own disciple, Brahmarshi Daivarata,[143] later became one of the main inspirations for Maharishi Mahesh Yogi and his Transcendental Meditation (TM) movement, which also looks back to the *Vedas* and has proposed its own new model of Vedic science. Maharishi referred to Daivarata as the greatest living Rishi. It was claimed that Brahmarshi Daivarata created his own new Vedic verses today much like the Rishis of old. He explains the sacred fire in the following verses:

> *This Fire is the Universal Person and pervades everywhere.*
> *He has entered into all souls and becomes the fire in the belly that digests our food.*
> *He is worshipped as the Self of all.*[144]

CHAPTER ELEVEN

Ayurveda, Yogic Fire Medicine

A good general indication of harmony with our soul is physical and psychological health and well-being. Similarly, disharmony with the soul causes disease and unhappiness. The proliferation of chronic diseases and emotional distress in our present society mirrors the lack of harmony with the soul and a neglect of its sacred fires.

In spite of the sophistication of modern medicine we have failed to utilize the great healing powers of nature. We are not even able to recognize the great medicine that native peoples and traditional healers can so easily sense in the plants, the waters and the wind. Instead, we have gone to great time, labor and expense to create an elaborate system of inorganic, drug and machine-based medicines, to which we are becoming ever more addicted, if not enslaved.

Our diagnosis of disease depends upon high tech equipment and detailed medical testing, though even this often proves inconclusive. We no longer examine the whole living patient but emphasize extracted bodily by-products analyzed in a laboratory, showing that we don't know how to read the energy of the person as a whole or even regard it as important. We must go beyond this reductionist chemical view of the body and look to the more observable reality of our life fire and how it is shining through our bodies and minds.

We have forgotten to create a sacred ground to support the healing process. Instead we remove the sick from nature, leaving them in sterile hospitals that are often devoid of real vitality. Yet as organic beings, our kinship is with the forces of nature. Unless we return to our natural healing sources, we cannot expect to be healthy as a species, even if we can make ourselves live longer artificially.

The key to health and well-being is to carefully cultivate the fires of body and mind, each of which has its own place in the sacred order of life. As we learn more about our biological fires, we can develop them consciously to improve the quality of our energy on all levels. Our soul fire in the heart is the central fire, what I like to call the 'pilot light' that enkindles and supports all the other fires within us. Keeping it burning with the proper nutrition, energy, love and clarity holds all our physical and psychological fires in balance, attuned to their source in the Divine light.

Ayurveda, Yogic Fire Medicine

The role of fire is well known in traditional systems of medicine, which use the great elements of nature for healing purposes. However, one system in particular is built around a profound understanding of our biological fires. This is 'Ayurveda', the traditional natural healing system of India, the healing branch of Yoga and Vedic science dating back thousands of years to ancient Vedic Rishis like Bharadvaja.[145] Ayurveda means the wisdom (Veda) of life and longevity (Ayur).

Ayurveda is a complete system of natural healing using food, herbs, bodywork, yoga and meditation for both physical and psychological healing. Recognizing consciousness as the primary force in the universe, Ayurveda is a mind-body medicine that considers all of what we do as promoting health or disease, wholeness or fragmentation.[146]

Ayurveda is not simply a physical or even a human-based medicine. It views human health as intimately connected with the well-being of the environment and with the forces of nature, which it recognizes as powers of a greater universal life and consciousness. It recognizes that epidemic diseases — which can destroy entire civilizations — must arise whenever there is significant damage to the land, water, air or seasons, with the damage to the land being the worst of these factors. [147]

In this regard, Ayurveda regards our current civilization out of harmony with nature as a diseased society that must cause health problems on individual, collective and planetary levels. We have created an environmental and ecological propensity to global disease that must manifest unless we change our societal life-styles. Unless there is both an ecological and a spiritual awareness brought into our medical system, it will be unable to deal with the increasing health and environmental threats that are now manifesting all around us.

Ayurveda and Agni, the Sacred Fire of Healing

In the *Rig Veda*, the most ancient Vedic text, life or Ayur is defined as Agni or fire, which is our soul or life-essence.[148] Ayurveda, therefore, is not only a 'fire medicine' but a 'medicine of the soul'. Its definition of well-being is harmony with our inner soul and the soul of the universe, not just absence of physical disease.

If we remember that our lives are a sacred fire, this recognition itself creates a power of awareness that keeps us in harmony with the entire universe. As the soul is the consciousness principle within us, Ayurveda is also a 'medicine of consciousness' stating that only what we do with awareness really heals us. All true healing works through the giving of care, love and consciousness. This means that consciousness is the ultimate healing force, the real healing fire.

Ayurveda recognizes fire or Agni on a physical level as the key to all bodily processes from cellular metabolism to perception in the brain, which all involve the burning of energy and the generation of light. It regards the digestive fire or 'fire in the belly', called Jatharagni, as the basis of physical health. If the digestive fire is kept burning in a consistent and clean manner, then health is guaranteed; our food is digested properly, our tissues and waste-materials form normally, and there is the necessary internal energy to ward off any pathogens that may attack us from the outside.

Along with the digestive fire, Ayurveda recognizes the 'life-fire' or fire of Prana (Pranagni) as the key to healing on an energetic level. If our breath is deep and full, calm and consistent, then our vital force will maintain harmony and balance between all our bodily systems and mental faculties. Our life-fire is a force of nature that can bring us all the healing energies of the universe. It holds the natural intelligence of healing that is responsible for the wonderful intricacy and marvelous order of our organism and its amazing ability to repair itself from injury and disease. Unless we learn to harness our own fire of healing, how can anything else really help us?

In my own work as an Ayurvedic healer, I always emphasize the role of Agni as the most important factor in health. Putting patients in touch with their different Agnis, showing them how to understand and regulate their internal fires of digestion, breath and mind makes Ayurveda and natural healing very simple and easy to apply. I call this 'Agni-Ayurveda', fire Ayurveda or 'fire-medicine', which was probably the original Vedic form of Ayurveda.[149]

We can easily assess the state of our digestive fire through the conditions of our appetite, digestion and elimination. We can diagnose our life-fire by how we breathe, by our level of strength, energy and endurance. We can determine the state of the mental fire through noting our acuity of perception, power of reasoning and ability to deal with emotional challenges. You can check your own signs in this regard:

• If your appetite is regular but not excessive, your digestion smooth and elimination regular and, above all, if you have a pleasant breath and no tongue coating, then your digestive fire is functioning at an optimal level.

- If your breath is full and deep, without coughing or gasping, if you have good circulation, good strength in your extremities and good resistance to disease, then your life-fire is functioning at an optimal level.
- If your senses have good acuity, your reasoning powers are sharp and you are content and at peace with yourself, then your mental fire is functioning at an optimal level.

Noting the condition of these three main biological fires, we can regulate them through diet, herbs, exercise and meditation so that we can manifest the full potential of our lives.

Ayurveda as it is usually applied works to balance the three doshas or biological humors of *Vata* (that which blows), *Pitta* (that which cooks) and *Kapha* (that which sticks). These represent the vital energies of the three elements of air (Vata), fire (Pitta) and water (Kapha) as they both create the physical body and put their distinctive mark on our individual constitution, creating Vata (airy), Pitta (fiery) and Kapha (watery) types of people. Patients follow recommendations of diet and life-style or more specific disease treatments to counter any excess or toxic conditions of the doshas within them.

However, Agni is the main factor behind all three doshas.

- VATA or the biological air-humor is the pranic or bioelectrical force that comes forth from Agni.
- PITTA or the biological fire-humor is the vital substance, the flammable oil that holds Agni in the body.
- KAPHA or the biological water-humor makes up the bulk of our bodily tissues and serves as a container and support for this internal fire.

The three doshas are rooted in Agni and can be treated through it. Vata people need to cultivate a more consistent internal fire to keep Vata, whose energy tends to be erratic, in balance. Pitta people need to keep their fire from getting too high, as it naturally tends to be excessive. Kapha people require a higher internal fire to burn up the excess weight and water that they tend to accumulate.

As we are fire beings possessing a fire body, the regulation of our internal fires is the determinative factor for our happiness and well-being. By learning how to balance our internal fires or Agnis on physical, pranic and psychological levels, we can connect to the deepest level of Agni, the soul in the heart, the flame that sustains all of our biological fires. This not only facilitates health but also opens the wellsprings of creativity and aids in rejuvenation.

Fire and Disease

As fire creatures, most of our diseases are born out of cold that prevents our inner fires from burning fully. Cold reduces our digestive power, weakens our vitality, inhibits our movement, impairs our circulation and causes pain. An increase of cold can be caused by exposure to the elements, by wrong diet, by overwork, by the aging process and by other factors that wear down our fire.

However, diseases can arise from excess fire as well, such as conditions of heat, inflammation and bleeding in which we have overly elevated or improperly burning internal fires. There are also unhealthy fires born of poorly digested food or the accumulation of toxins which produce the 'smoke' or 'ash' of disease. In such conditions our fires need to be purified, regulated and restored to their proper function.

The negative 'fire of disease' fights with the positive 'fire of health' in the body. We must learn to increase the fire of health and decrease the toxic fire that is seeking to replace it. It is easy to see the difference between these two fires. The fire of health gives clarity to the mind, luster to the skin, good circulation and good digestion; the fire of disease results in emotional agitation, poor complexion, poor circulation and poor digestion.

To counter imbalance, whether due to cold or to toxic fire, we must promote the fire of healing. Our inner fires have a healing potential, a 'fire of healing' that can overcome all diseases. This arises through the natural effort of our internal fires to protect our organism and restore its internal balance.

Fire both within and around us provides many tools for healing. In various forms as heat, light, energy and color, it is the main force for healing both the body and mind. *Fire, we could say, is our main natural healer.* It is not our therapies or our medicines that really bring about healing. These are at best vehicles for the healing fire. The therapist is also not the source of healing, but functions mainly as a form of fire or a fire priest, providing warmth, guidance and comfort.

A true doctor should be able to access the wisdom of fire to help balance our bodily fires. He must both know the laws of fire as well as how to work with the healing tools of fire. Above all, he must be able to take the role of the sacred fire in treating others. The true healer must become Agni as both an organic and spiritual force.

Cultivating Your Digestive Fire

Eating is the most basic ritual that sustains life. In the eating process, food is the sacred offering, our digestive fire is the sacred fire, and nutrition is the Divine gift, through which the body is sustained. The fire of eating maintains our physical life. Food (Anna) is the first name for God in the *Upanishads*.[150] Food was probably the first name of God for all of early humanity and remains the center of our lives, which depend upon it. When we eat it is important to remember the sacred fire of digestion within us as a gift of God.

The digestive fire is the central force of the body, providing the heat and energy to operate all the other bodily systems. It is a material fire that burns the fuel of the food and beverages that we take in through the mouth. Our entire metabolism or metabolic fire depends upon it. The digestive fire works through the digestive fluids; hydrochloric acid, enzymes and bile salts that with their heat are able to digest our food.

If our digestive fire burns too low (as is common in Ayurvedic Kapha types) then we accumulate weight and water and our functional level gets reduced. We get lethargic, tired and congested. If it burns too high (as in Ayurvedic Pitta types) then we burn ourselves up as it were, overheating the brain, heart and liver. We suffer from fever, inflammation, bleeding or hypertension. If it burns irregularly (as in Ayurvedic Vata types) then we have an agitated or disturbed energy in life. We experience nervousness, anxiety, insomnia or tremors. Keeping our digestive fire balanced is the key to health for all body types.

Food contains fire in a latent form, which our digestive fire converts into energy. Taking our food cooked (but not overcooked) aids the digestive fire in its functioning. Different foods hold energy to various degrees, releasing it quickly or slowly. Grains are the basis of our natural diet because they represent the concentrated energy of sunlight gathered by the grasses. Legumes (various types of beans) are very helpful as well, carrying a similar concentrated energy but with more protein and less carbohydrates. Fruit and nuts also represent the light gathered from the sun by trees and carry much solar power that can be extracted directly and require no cooking.

Different types of vegetables provide us different forms of heat as well. Green, leafy vegetables and cabbage family plants generally hold the energy of the sun from the spring season, helping to purify our inner fires. Squash, gourds and root vegetables like potatoes contain a concentrated energy that can sustain us through the cold of winter.

Our digestive fire requires the right oil for it to burn steadily and clearly. Nutritive oils feed our internal fires, particularly the fire of the nervous system that has an oily nature to its tissue. For this reason it is best to take our food cooked with an appropriate amount of oil. Natural oils from seeds and nuts are the best, like sesame, olive, safflower and sunflower.

The yogis of India regard dairy products an ideal food because of the energy of sunlight that comes through the cow's digestion of grasses. Good dairy products, however, require treating cows with love, which is hard to find today in the modern age of factory farming. So if we want to benefit from dairy products, it is necessary to get the most organic and natural forms that we can find.

Milk and yogurt are particularly good for keeping our biological fires energized but not overheated. Ghee or clarified butter is an especially nourishing food for Agni in Ayurvedic medicine.[151] As the essence of milk, it represents sunlight refined from the grasses to the cows into a nutritive oil to sustain our inner fires. Ghee is used to treat many diseases and also serves as an ideal food for the brain and nervous system. It is one of the best cooking oils, feeding our nerve tissue without overheating our system.[152]

The most direct form of fire in food comes from spices, which is why they taste hot. Spices can either feed the digestive fire or function to aid in digestion in its absence. Using the appropriate spices to improve the digestive fire is an important herbal therapy for both health maintenance and for the treatment of all kinds of diseases. Hot spices like cayenne, ginger, black pepper and garlic are the strongest. They help burn up toxins, improve circulation and stimulate vitality at a deep level. But all spices have this effect, including common culinary herbs from basil and bay leaves to parsley, rosemary and sage. Such milder spices are often better for maintaining a balanced digestion.

Yet the strongest way to increase the digestive fire is through fasting. Fasting is the prime means for detoxifying and cleansing the digestive tract and purifies the entire body. When we fast, our digestive fire, deprived of external food, turns within and burns up unneeded waste material and residual pathogens instead.

When our physical fire is turned within, the fire of our mind also gets elevated and opens up to higher levels of consciousness. That is why so many mystics and yogis have taken to fasting as a spiritual practice. Through fasting we can reconnect to the soul fires within. Moderate seasonal fasting (particularly in the spring) is an important tool for improving health and increasing longevity for everyone.

The Fire of Exercise

Exercise is the dynamic expression of our bodily fire. Strong exercise increases our bodily fire and creates its own power of purification through sweating. It draws the digestive fire from the center to the periphery of the body, cleansing our blood, muscle and bones. It raises our bodily temperature and improves circulation, helping to eliminate toxins from the tissues and organs. While we have all experienced such results as we exercise, we usually don't consciously recognize the power of fire behind it.

Without sufficient daily exercise our metabolic fire remains low. This results in the accumulation of excess tissues and toxins that clog both body and mind. However, exercise is best done only to the extent necessary to tone our bodily fires, not so much as to overheat or to exhaust them. Yoga asanas are a special form of balanced exercise designed to strengthen our internal fires without agitating the body or disturbing the emotions. They can be done safely by everyone as a part of a good daily health regimen.

The Fire of Herbs

Herbs bring the plant fire, which is the life-fire, into our body to strengthen our own biological fires. Herbs are part of the healing gift of fire given to humanity by Mother Nature. They contain special fire agents that can promote processes either of growth or of elimination. Different herbs stimulate digestion, circulation, elimination or detoxification. Others are special powerful foods for the deeper tissues and internal organs. To bring out the healing effects of herbs, fire is often required in the form of heating, boiling or other chemical processes of herbal preparation.[153]

Traditional systems of medicine like Chinese Medicine or Ayurveda classify herbs according to their heating energy, their 'fire capacity', as the main factor for determining their therapeutic effects.[154] Spicy hot herbs like cayenne, ginger and black pepper are the strongest fire herbs. We can easily experience the fire-power of these herbs for ourselves noting how, for example, a cup of ginger tea will raise our temperature, improve our circulation and stimulate our appetite, feeding our biological fires. Most spices fall in this category of warming herbs, including the commonly used cinnamon, cardamom, turmeric, mustard, bay leaves, basil and sage.

Herbs that are cooling in their energy, on the other hand, can help regulate our fire by preventing it from getting too hot. Bitter herbs like golden seal, echinacea, barberry and aloe reduce excess or evil fire, such as occurs from infections in the body and toxic heat in the blood. We can easily note how a little aloe vera juice will counter acidity and cool us down. These fire-reducing herbs are good aids in the healing process and can serve as natural antibiotics. We should not overlook the role of herbs in carrying the fire of healing. Our life-fire has its root in the plant-fire which, therefore, has a special regulatory effect upon it.

Fire Therapies, Fire as Our Response to Disease

An increase in bodily temperature is our main physiological response to disease, starting with the common cold. The body manifests its 'fire function' in the form of the fever, a rise in bodily temperature to burn up the viruses attacking the body. In this way, fire is our own natural defense force. The fires of our immune system naturally arise when our body is threatened by pathogens.

Fever causes sweating to drive pathogens out of the body and restore proper circulation and flow of energy. Sweating is an important 'fire therapy' for dispelling colds and flu, for countering arthritis and allergies and for overall stimulation of our vital functions. Sweating promotes our bodily fire peripherally to drive out toxins from the plasma and blood. Many herbs of a spicy and aromatic quality like ginger, cinnamon, sage or mint promote the fire of sweating.

Many healing traditions use sweating therapies through the use of saunas, sweat lodges and steam heat. Sweating therapy is called *swedana* in Ayurveda and used for a large variety of ailments as well as for health maintenance.[155] It can be combined with exercise as another means of increasing sweating. A seasonal usage of sweating therapies in the fall and winter helps guard us from cold and debility in the darker and colder part of the year.

Native Americans use sweat lodges for spiritual as well as physical healing. In cleansing the blood (the soul's fluid in the body), sweating can purify the senses, emotions and mind and open us up to the powers of the spirit. Sweating helps liberate the soul from its bodily limitations, taking our life-force beyond the boundaries of the skin.

Massage and Our Body Fire

The body as a whole is like a contained fire whose presence is conveyed through the warmth of the skin. Through massage and bodywork, particularly with use of heavy massage oils, we can nourish the fire of the skin and through it the fire of the body as a whole. Warm oils like sesame, almond or apricot increase fire at the level of the skin, improving its luster and warmth. Cool oils like coconut, sunflower or ghee counter excess heat and inflammation of the skin. Just as oil feeds a flame, oil applied to the skin allows the bodily fire to increase.

The Fire of the Breath

The breath is our internal life-fire, whose power of circulation regulates all other physical fires. The breath is the fire of respiration. It is a gaseous fire fed by the air that we take in through the mouth and sinuses. Of these two, the air filtered by the sinuses has a more immediate effect upon the brain and goes deeper into the lungs. For this reason, to be truly healthy and clear-headed we need to both breathe adequately and through the nose. Breath taken in through the mouth can increase toxins and build up mucus that clogs the body and suppresses the digestive fire.[156]

Deep breathing fans the fire of the breath, just as bringing in air through a vent helps a fire to burn better. The fire of the breath aids the digestive fire in its function by providing it more air as well. Rapid deep breathing through the nostrils quickly improves the fire of the breath, increasing energy, promoting circulation, clearing the mind and the senses, and helping eliminate toxins in the sinuses, lungs, skin and digestive system.[157]

Another important technique to bring balance to the life-force is *alternate nostril breathing*, breathing in through one nostril and out through the other.[158] In this regard, *Yoga teaches us that the right nostril breath has a solar, fiery and heating nature, while the left nostril breath has a lunar, watery and cooling nature.* Breathing in through the right nostril increases the fire of the breath, while breathing in through the left nostril provides more fuel for it. By breathing in and out alternatively through each nostril we can balance the fire of the breath and ensure ourselves maximum vitality.

While we increase the breath fire we can also direct its healing power to the various organs, limbs and systems of the body that require attention. This healing power of Prana can be enhanced with therapeutic touch outwardly, placing our hands or fingers on the areas of the body to be treated; or it can be enhanced inwardly using visualization, mantra and meditation along with the breath.

Sleep and Returning to the Source of Life

We usually experience sleep as a kind of darkness and forgetfulness. Yet deep sleep is the state in which our bodily
fires get naturally renewed. Without this state of rest, our
organism will be unable to maintain its balance or its
strength. In the state of deep sleep our awareness returns
to the primary inner or soul fire that lies behind the mind.
Our biological fires re-attune themselves to the central life
fire of the soul. We rest in the all-nourishing flame of the
heart through which our entire being is revitalized for another day.

Proper rest, relaxation and deep sleep are necessary for
all healing, which may require retreat or retirement from
our ordinary life-style. We must also allow our bodily fires
their period of rest. We cannot expect them to burn per-
petually. Only the inner soul fire never sleeps. The other
fires must wax and wane through the cycle of time.

The Fire of Rejuvenation

The body contains a special power that can inhibit the aging process and renew our vitality. There is a secret
rejuvenative fire hidden deep within us. It also rests upon
our connection with the fire of the soul. The soul fire pos-
sesses all creative and transformative powers as the very
power of life.

After we have balanced our biological fires of body,
breath and mind, we are prepared to access this fire of rejuvenation. It is specifically linked to the breath. That is why
pranayama is important for all rejuvenation practices. It
also requires 'conscious' deep sleep, putting the body to
rest without losing awareness, which is rejuvenating meditation, internalizing our mental energies for self-transformation.[159] For such processes to occur, we must go beyond
our own limited vital energy and access the cosmic life-
force that is unlimited. We must connect with the Divine
fire in nature in the rocks, plants, atmosphere and sky.

Special minerals, waters and herbs contain a rejuvenative power of fire.[160] Hot springs, mountain streams and wild mountain herbs are among these, including special tonic herbs like ginseng, ashwagandha, shilajit or amalaki,[161] or special tonics for the mind like shankha pushpi, brahmi or manduka parni.[162] Sacred places in nature, like high mountains or tropical beaches, which are free of stagnant air, are homes to such healing powers. Ashes (bhasma) from special sacred fires, like those from the ashrams of great gurus, have this power as well.

Ayurveda uses ashes (bhasma) from special alchemical or rasayana preparations to aid in this process, including those of minerals like sulfur, mercury, mica and gold or gems like diamonds and rubies. These bhasmas — specially prepared by repeated heating in powerful fires — have their unique rejuvenative powers for different aspects of the body and mind.

However, to really use these we must first purify ourselves and regulate the natural fires that we already have. This requires activating the fire of purification through internal cleansing practices like the Pancha Karma system of Ayurveda[163] or special purifying forms of pranayama. When we are internally in a state of balance, the soul fire will take us to the next level of our development, the nature of which only it can decide. True rejuvenation is not just a question of living longer but living in our highest flame and inspiration.

CHAPTER TWELVE

Yoga Psychology and the Fire of the Mind

It is not only our physical medicine that requires a new casting in the sacred fire; our psychological medicine is even more in need of such a spiritual renewal. Without being aware of the sacred fire in our hearts, emotional balance, happiness and contentment is not possible, whatever else we may do. For this we need a new 'psychology of fire' that shows us how to properly cultivate the fires of our minds and hearts. This is the basis of Yoga psychology which emphasizes aligning our emotions with our higher Self.

Psychology must take us back to wisdom of the soul for emotional healing. It is not enough merely to analyze, remember or relive psychological traumas, thinking that this might heal us from them. We must create a fire that has the power to burn them up and free us from their imprint, eradicating their scars deep within the mind. This means that we must elevate our minds and hearts to the level of the soul and its transforming light.

Emotion itself is a very powerful fire that can fill us with loving radiance or cast us into a dire conflagration of agitation, depending upon its nature. Positive emotions like love nurture the flame of the heart and allow it to burn with clarity and light. Negative emotions like anger create a harmful fire that chokes or stifles the heart.

Just as at a physical level, as fire beings we also suffer emotionally mainly from cold. This arises from a lack of emotional warmth and connection, from loneliness, from what is essentially not having the fire of love. Such emotional coldness leads to unhappiness, depression, fear and anxiety in which our heart flame flickers or even goes out. To counter this, we need to increase our fires of love and compassion, reaching out and helping others rather than contracting into our own darkness.

Conversely, we must learn to reduce excess fiery emotions like anger, jealousy and hatred. These cause our emotional fire to burn with a toxic smoke that harms others and ourselves. When this occurs we must learn to counter harmful emotional fires with those that are helpful, turning anger into forgiveness and hatred into love.

The Mind as the Fire of Space

To arrive at psychological healing we need to understand that the mind is an etheric fire — a fire which arises from space. Adequate space is necessary for the mind to function properly. *Without the proper space for our mind and senses to expand, we become narrow and disturbed, mentally and emotionally.* On the other hand, whenever we create a space to grow in our lives, our minds are able to flower, new learning spontaneously occurs and new creativity blossoms within us.

To heal the mind, we must create the right space inside ourselves, which is not a space of external separation but an internal field of freedom and growth. We need a sacred space within our hearts that is not invaded by our personal or social cares, worries or ambitions. When we have such space we have the room to accommodate life and to deal with all of its problems without losing peace of mind.

The best way to create this internal space is through the

practice of meditation, particularly meditation emphasizing space, emptiness and silence. To aid in this, you can visualize an unbounded space within your own heart that can contain the entire universe. Remember that wherever you place your attention you can create space and silence if you hold to the root of your awareness in the heart.

Similarly, we need sufficient space around us externally. The mind gets narrow if we do not afford it the space of perception, by keeping ourselves indoors or behind computer or television screens for too long a period of time. A good way to do this is to regularly go out into nature where our minds can expand to the distant horizon and renew themselves with the unlimited space of nature. Otherwise the mind, like a caged bird, will never be happy and will develop various neurotic tendencies to compensate for its confinement. Stillness, space and inaction can be the most powerful forces for psychological healing, more than any overt efforts we may make to change ourselves. One of the best ways to deal with our emotional problems is to leave them alone and let them go, trusting the space and the silence to absorb and transform them.

I find that after a busy day either working with people or writing at the computer my mind often feels constricted, if not agitated, burdened by the weight of its own activity. When this occurs I make sure to go outdoors and let my mind go to the clouds, the sky or the trees, which are its natural home, forgetting the affairs of the day and our human concerns. If my mind is too tense, it may be necessary to take a walk, go for a hike or dig in the garden — using bodily activity to help the mind release itself into nature.

Before sleep I also let my mind sink into the space within itself, releasing the burden of the day for the renewing force that dwells in what has no form. Often the answers to life's problems come from such moments of emptiness in which there is room for a new and higher energy to come into the mind, not through our own overt efforts to solve them.

Food for the Mind

The mind has three levels of nutrition through which it takes in the energies that sustain it. The first two are the indirect results of the digestive and breath fires that support the mind from a physical level. The third is direct as the nutrition that comes to the mind through its sensory openings.

The first fuel for the mind's fire comes from the essence of the food that we eat, as a product of the digestive fire. This means that it is necessary not only for physical but also for mental health that we have pure, natural food cooked with love and kindness. The second level of mental nutrition comes from the essence of the air that we breathe, as a product of the breath fire. To keep the mind and the senses sharp we must breathe deeply a clean natural air energized by the plants and the breezes.

The third and most important level of nutrition for the mind comes from the senses themselves, which are like mouths for the mind. Our ears, skin, eyes, tongue and nose ingest sensory impressions that are the main food for the mind. According to yogic thought, sensory impressions are forms of the subtle elements (their etheric counterparts).

- The ear brings us sound, which is the subtle ether element.
- The skin brings us touch, which is the subtle air element.
- The eyes bring us sight, which is the subtle fire element.
- The tongue brings us taste, which is the subtle water element.
- The nose brings us fragrance, which is the subtle earth element.

Just as solid and liquid food (the gross elements) builds up the tissues of the body, these subtle elements (sensory impressions) build up the mind. Just as the body requires its appropriate natural food, so the mind has its appropriate natural nutrition as well. Just as we must watch our physical diet in order to maintain physical health, so we must watch our mental diet of impressions in order to maintain psychological health.[164]

The eyes are our specific fire-sense that takes in light from the external world. The light they absorb nourishes our internal faculties of perception and imagination, giving color and light to the mind. It is particularly important for a healthy mind that our visual impressions are filled with natural light and beauty.

Our proper sensory diet consists of impressions rich in Prana or the life-force. Such are natural vistas, gardens, buildings decorated with wood or other natural substances, inspiring music and pleasant fragrances. On the other hand, junk impressions like those of violence that abound in the media dull the mind, just as junk food dulls the body. A mind filled with the noise of the streets or computer images also tends to become confused, frenetic and agitated.

Most of us are unaware of sensory perception as a kind of nutrition. We fail to notice the deleterious effect of disturbed sensations, even when we experience mental unrest and emotional turbulence after being exposed to them. We should take at least as much care with our diet of impressions as we do with the food that we eat. It becomes the very substance out of which our thinking occurs and our judgments are made.

Nature is our natural form of entertainment. Watching natural scenery, like sitting on the banks of a river and enjoying its flow, is our natural pastime that quickens the soul and stimulates its higher intuitive powers. Natural impressions are food for the soul. We were meant to look at the sunrise and the sunset, the clouds, trees, mountains and streams, not at entertainment boxes flashing violence, news emergencies and political turbulence. That is why we feel so at peace in nature and seldom find real contentment in our social pleasures, which are usually mere addictions, not a source of real joy.

Nature is meant to be our launching pad into the world

of the spirit. We were meant to follow our natural inspiration upward from the Earth to the Heavens. Unfortunately, today we are closing these spiritual doors of nature as we eliminate our natural surroundings, reducing them merely to forms of business and entertainment.

Mental and Emotional Digestion

Most of our psychological problems result from faulty mental and emotional digestion. Repressed feelings ferment in the subconscious mind, breeding fear, anger or attachment, causing depression or agitation, just as undigested food sitting in the stomach disturbs our entire body. We must maintain a strong mental fire to digest the complex, if not contradictory food of experience that our present world offers in such excess. This requires that we keep our minds clear, observant and aware, and also afford them rest from our artificial human world in the open spaces of nature.

Just as our bodies get clogged by improperly digested food, so our minds get clogged by undigested experiences, mental attachments and emotional clinging. To counter this condition, we can benefit from the practice of 'mental fasting', sitting quietly with our eyes and ears closed and looking within. When we turn our attention to the inside, closing the gates of the senses, our mental fire is able to burn up residual impressions, just as our digestive fire burns up residual toxins when we fast from food. We discover an inner space in which the mind's etheric fire finds purity and freedom and can shine with radiance. Make sure to give your mind its quiet time also. Try to give at least half an hour a day for your mind to renew itself.

However, it can be hard to keep the mind in an empty or quiet condition. If this is the case, visualize expansive impressions like the blue sky, the ocean or a field of flowers. Let these soothing influences draw the mind gradually into its natural state of peace. Such a 'diet of pure impressions' purifies the mind like a diet of pure food purifies the body.

Along with mental fasting, the practice of non-speaking or silence is very helpful.[165] We can turn the fire of speech within to purify our expression and control our outgoing urges and emotions. Then when we do speak our words will carry weight and have power, reflecting the soul within us. Try fasting from speech one day a week or one day a month and you will see its healing effects upon the mind.[166] Through such practices you can discover how the power of non-doing can transform your being and reveal its inner light.

The Fire of Desire

Most of our psychological unhappiness arises from not getting what we want in life, from not having our desires fulfilled. It is our human condition that we are born and live full of many desires, often unrealistic, and that our society encourages their endless multiplication. Our unhappiness may start when our natural desires for food, shelter and relationship are not adequately fulfilled. But this is only the beginning of an almost endless net of desires that we spin trying to find fulfillment in the external world that is really only the shadow of our soul.

On top of our natural desires, we have added an entire set of unnatural, artificial and socially conditioned urges for wealth, power, possessions and position. As these longings are not based upon any natural necessity, they can never be fulfilled and their apparent fulfillment affords no lasting inner happiness. The fire of desire only burns more brightly when it is fed with the fuel getting what we want. It cannot be satisfied but only abandoned. Only the soul's fire of love is truly fulfilling, needing no fuel other than its own joy.

All desire is really a seeking for love. Love is the soul's fire that exalts all other life-giving fires. Love itself is the most powerful fire that can burn up all conflict and confusion. Only the fire of love can put out all the negative fires of want, fear and hatred. This requires offering our desires into the fire of the heart, letting it fulfill those it wishes and consume those that are not appropriate. Love is the only emotion that we can truly digest because it is food for the soul. Through it all our psychological problems can be easily solved. But for that to occur, we must become a source of love for all and cease expecting love from the outside.

The fire of unfulfilled desire leaves us in a state of want and inner poverty. It is the main force that keeps the soul caught in the cycle of rebirth because we must continue taking additional births until all our desires are either fulfilled or given up. Desire is the fire that keeps us bound to the outer world of time and death. If we cultivate the fire of desire, we end up ourselves getting consumed in the flames. If we cultivate the fire of love, on the other hand, we will give light and radiance to all. True love is a fullness of light whose joy is to shine. In it the pain of desire, which is a state of want and deprivation, has no place to grow.

The Fire of Self-Remembrance

Memory is the continuity of our inner fire of awareness. We need to remember our true Self and the light from which we come. This is not simply to recall the events of our outer lives but to revive the aspiration and the striving of our souls. It is to awaken our species memory, our planetary memory and, ultimately, our memory of the universe itself. We are all linked in a planetary memory that is the very web of life connected to the stars. We can remember the entire universe inside ourselves. We can ultimately remember God. This type of self-remembrance is a special yogic practice.[167]

In crucial life moments, like approaching death, we naturally contact our deeper soul memories, examining our lives, seeking forgiveness and responding to others with compassion. We should learn to cultivate such a 'soul reckoning' on a daily basis. Before you go to sleep at night, make sure to remember your eternal mission and thank the wonderful and unfathomable universe in which you have taken birth for all it has given you. This is a great tool for psychological and emotional cleansing. That we exist at all is a great wonder and joy because Being is eternal. Whatever pain we may suffer is only a temporary alienation from our true nature of bliss.

The Fire of Death

All the fires of life naturally reach their culmination in the fire of death, which is the ultimate life-fire, revealing the light of our entire lives. At the moment of our death, our vital energies along with the mind merge in the fire of the soul. From its station in the heart this soul fire leaves the body and ascends upward, returning to its own nature as the bodiless light of awareness. The soul retains the seeds of karma and uses them to create a new birth after it has finished its period of rest in the after death state that is much like the state of deep sleep.

We need not fear death. Death is not the end of life, which comes from the soul, but only of a particular body that is no longer useful. The soul leaves the body but itself never passes away. Yet death is a fire of purification that we all fear because it ends our attachments to our particular lives. Only if we cultivate our spiritual fires in life can the fire of death not harm us. Once the evolution of our soul is fulfilled we merge back into the Divine Light from which it came and find our true and everlasting home.

We journey from light to light in our cosmic journey. We are actually never away from the light, even for a second. Even our ignorance and suffering is only the shadow of the light at the front of our being. *If we would but remember this inner light, all our psychological problems would disappear forever.* Whatever we offer into the fire, even our deepest suffering, must be transformed into joy. There is a famous Upanishadic prayer for merging into the Divine at death:

May my spirit enter the immortal spirit as the body ends in ashes.

OM! O Will remember, remember your labor. O Will remember, remember your labor.

O Fire, God who knows all the ways of wisdom, lead us by the perfect path to reality. The most complete utterance of surrender may we offer unto you.

The Being in the Sun, He am I. OM! Space, Brahman.[168]

IV

A Call for
a New
Sacred Fire

CHAPTER THIRTEEN

Our Current Evolutionary Crisis

Our present humanity is caught in the midst of an enormous crisis. We cannot fail to see this in the growing destruction of our natural environment, the increasing stress of our daily lives, the continuing conflicts between communities and countries, and the unhappiness so many of us feel even if we have achieved affluence and success. The current wave of terrorism shaking the world is but a manifestation of the greater problem of a species out of balance with its world and with itself.

Our civilization may have made great advances in terms of technology and the spread of information but our planet as a whole along with its natural resources of air, water and food appears to be in an unprecedented decline. Our species has spread far beyond its natural frontiers and overpopulated itself to the detriment of all other life forms. We have arrogated so much of the planet's resources to ourselves that the Earth itself is suffering and numerous other species have lost their homes, if not become extinct.

This crisis is many sided, multileveled and wrought with many dangers. We have disrupted every ecosystem on the planet from the viruses and bacteria to the atmosphere itself. We appear as a species poised on the brink of its own destruction, carelessly harming its environment but thinking that the damage will not affect it. We are like a person burning down his own house, but oblivious to the danger because the fire has yet to reach the room where he is staying.

This current crisis is not merely one of the many that our species has faced in almost every generation. It is not simply an economic or political problem that can be solved through reorganizing our outer resources, by government action or by a better distribution of the wealth (though such factors can be helpful). *We are in the midst of an unprecedented evolutionary crisis in which the fate of our species hangs in the balance.* We are failing to adapt to our world. Instead we are trying to compel the world to accommodate us, as if we were the only real species on the planet. We are trying to evolve not with nature but against it — forcing nature to serve an artificial human development inimical to the rest of the planet.

This evolutionary crisis is not simply a failure in outer adaptation; it is a *crisis in consciousness*, which is the real force behind all evolution. The consciousness that we have developed as a civilization is insufficient to meet the needs of our species or to fulfill our planetary role. It is inadequate to handle the complex technologies that we have produced or to enable us to apply them in harmony with the greater life around us.

We have failed to understand natural law and the organic interdependence of all creatures. Our dominant mindset is not rooted in the sacred nor is it aware of the spirit. We are following a path not of compassion but of consumption, which means devouring our world with the fire of greed, increasing our desires each step along the way, so that we must ever take and use more and more. Our species seeks an unlimited expansion for itself in a world of limited resources that are shared by other species as well. We don't see that the ultimate result of this equation is destruction.

If this current evolutionary crisis can lead us to an inner spiritual awakening, it could help usher in a higher level of human development, harmonizing technology with the world of nature by the light and wisdom of the soul. But without such a higher awakening, it must eventually produce a global catastrophe that will also devastate our own species as we undermine the very natural factors upon which life depends. What will occur depends upon how we act and, above all, on the awareness that we bring into our action.

The question arises: Will we go forward as a species in the evolution of consciousness or will we halt or reverse the evolutionary process, not only for ourselves but for the planet as a whole? This is the real problem facing us today, but we seldom look at the big picture. Our concern is the next quarter's profit, the next election, or our national interests which blind us to the greater array of forces at work in the world. We are setting forces in motion like the starting of a forest fire. We may be able to control the beginning of this process but the resulting conflagration can go far beyond what we can regulate or even expect. We may be stirring primeval forces of nature that will carry us in a very different direction than what we have intended. The great fires of nature have their own indomitable will and tremendous power, which can bring us great suffering if we go against them.

We cannot escape universal law, what the Hindu and Buddhists sages call *dharma*.[169] Dharma refers to the ethical foundation of all life, the interdependence of all beings in the conscious universe. The real goal of human life is to further dharma, to uphold the laws of the universe that allow for the happiness of all creatures. Not honoring dharma we fall into negative karmas, actions that go against the universe and the greater evolution of consciousness, causing conflict and division that will make us suffer as well.

Examining our world history of but a few thousand years, we should recognize that the march of civilization, like the evolution of life, is not always forward. Entire civilizations, like poorly adapted creatures, can bring about their own demise or extinction. Many great civilizations like ancient Rome or ancient Egypt have declined and disappeared, sometimes quickly. Our own civilization could do so as well if we don't restore our balance with the Earth.

To put this in the root language of the Earth, which is the language of fire — where the sacred fire is not honored and kept burning with the appropriate offerings, other more destructive forms of fire must manifest. This is the current state of our planet wracked by the fires of greed, hatred and intolerance. Even nature must erupt with an uncontrollable fire if we do not honor the sacred fire within her.

Our Inner Battle: The Clash of the Two Fires

David Suzuki in his *The Sacred Balance*, while arguing for ecological responsibility in our species, notes about the reality of fire:

> *All the gods of our stories know that fire is a double-edge sword; what warms may burn, what gives power may also consume, what gives life may take it away just as easily.*[170]

That inherent duality in the usage of fire cuts through our entire civilization, if not our entire human nature.

Many philosophers have examined the dilemma of human existence and note an almost existential flaw or inherent contradiction within us. We contain vying for attention and dominance within us both the mortal and the immortal, both the spiritual and the material, both good and evil. We have two minds, one ruled by selfish desire and the other by unselfish love.

Our soul is like a light covered in darkness, the infinite trapped in the finite. We want to break out and expand back into the limitless light. Yet, at the same time, we glorify our prison and are afraid of the unknown beyond it. On one hand, we seek the higher light of freedom; on the other hand, we cling desperately to the darkness as our home.

In spite of all the advances brought about through our emergence as a species, we humans are not happy creatures and have not yet produced a really harmonious society. An internal battle — a clash between two fires — rages within us. We are fighting an internal war between the spiritual fire of evolutionary intelligence and the material fire of desire that we have taken from the animal kingdom but artificially stimulated by the human ego. There is an upward moving flame of consciousness and a downward moving flame of ignorance competing for our minds and hearts.

This battle takes many names and forms in different mythological stories throughout time — the war between the angels and the demons of Biblical thought, the Devas and Asuras of Vedic thought, and the Gods and the Titans of the Greeks. Heaven as a solar realm of light, and hell or Hades as a sulfurous fire beneath the Earth, clearly reflect these two types of fires.

In the Vedic view, the *Devas* or gods are those that regard consciousness as the supreme reality, while the *Asuras* or anti-gods are those who believe in the body and its outer fulfillment as the ultimate, making this a clash between the spiritual and materialistic side of our minds.[171] Our consumer culture can easily fall into Asuric or dark tendencies as it exaggerates our material desires and stimulates our aggressive propensities for gain and profit.

Our minds have the capacity not only to open up to the higher light, they can artificially augment the drives and passions of our lower nature, rekindling elemental forces that should be beneath our evolutionary striving. We can access the Divine fires of love and understanding but also magnify the undivine fires of division and deception. We can incarnate the fires of light that burn with purity and peace or the dark fires that burn with smoke and conflict.

Our real purpose as a species is to unite the earthly and

heavenly fires — to link the fire at the center of the Earth with that in center of the Sun, our bodily fire with the fire of the higher mind. But this requires finding the Divine light hidden in matter, not simply glorifying material enjoyment as the goal of life. It means making our world into a world of light. To reach this goal, we must continue our upward movement into the light of awareness and resist the inertia to return to the dark and heavy forces pulling on us from the obscure beginnings of the world.

Today we have gone much further than any previous civilization in harnessing the material fires of nature through science and technology. But we have forgotten to cultivate the necessary spiritual fires to go along with them. We are artificially stimulating our bodily fires and choking the spiritual fires necessary to keep them in balance. We are devoted to the anti-Gods, the undivine or material powers, seeking outer conquest, control and acquisition as the goal of our endeavors. We have little regard for the spiritual principles of renunciation, self-sacrifice and self-transcendence. Instead of using the powers of fire to purify ourselves, we use them to dominate, if not destroy others.

Will we build a new realm of light on our planet or turn it into a smoldering realm of darkness? Will we be destroyed by the fire power we have released upon the world or will we discover a light of truth that can control it? All this depends upon whether we once more learn to cultivate the sacred fire bequeathed to us by our spiritual ancestors.

The Dark Fires of Our Species

Ours appears to be a young species that has yet to manifest its real potential and develop the higher aspects of its intelligence. A lower animal fire still burns strongly within us, but without the grace of nature that animals have to keep it in harmony with life. We have cultivated this artificial animal fire through our consumerist life-style and outward sensate view of life.

We take on a karma of violence from the animals that we unnecessarily and often cruelly kill for food. Presently in the United States alone around fifteen billion animals are slaughtered yearly, largely raised under cruel and inhumane methods of factory farming. This stands in contrast to the animals sacredly killed by native peoples and used with care and discretion, or even older farming methods in which the animals at least had a life in the sun before being used as food.

We are under no environmental dictate, like that of non-agrarian cultures, to require such a massive meat industry. We can at least treat the animals as living beings instead of as only mere commodities. Such unsacred meat increases negative emotions of fear and anger within us. The animal souls that we have harmed leave us with a legacy of hurt and betrayal, with their lives cut short by the very species that should be their guardians and protectors. As animals represent the fruit of entire ecosystems, we must remember that by protecting animals we are protecting our entire natural environment.

I have been a vegetarian for over thirty years and find that it is both perfectly healthy as well as ecologically beneficial for the planet. As an Ayurvedic doctor, I often recommend a vegetarian diet to patients for health purposes, as vegetarians generally suffer less from cancer, heart disease, obesity, allergies and arthritis — the most common, most difficult and hard to treat conditions that afflict us today.

Such a vegetarian diet requires seeds, nuts, grains and beans, and sometimes dairy products. It is not limited to raw food, juices or salads, which many people find insufficient for their energy requirements. But there is no health necessity for meat in our diets, regardless of your body type, in spite of what the meat industry would like us to believe. Not only is a vegetarian diet better for the planet and its creatures, it is also good for our bodies, minds and souls as well. Yet there is no excuse for abusing animals as we do, even if we take a meat diet. If we do take meat, we should at least insist upon humane treatment of the animals whose vitality we take into our own.

We take on additional karma of insensitivity from the stimulants, intoxicants and drugs that so many of us are habituated to. Our culture not only encourages the use of mild stimulants like alcohol, tobacco and coffee, recreational drugs from cocaine to ecstasy are trendy as well. Such drugs artificially boost the fires of the mind and the nervous system making us feel temporarily elevated or content. But they can also increase negative fiery emotions of anger and violence, and in the long term cause darkness and depression in the mind.

The usage of medicinal drugs has gone up rapidly as well, whether anti-depressants, weight-reducing pills, sleeping pills or antibiotics. These also have many side-effects for both body and mind which can bring their therapeutic benefits into question.

When we add our diet of fast food and junk food to this plethora of drugs, it means that there is little left of our natural chemistry in our own nervous systems! There is little in our body that is ours! Many of us have totally forgotten what it feels like to have a bloodstream free of chemicals. Since the body cannot process these inorganic drugs or eliminate them properly, they accumulate in our tissues, causing various diseases and dulling our minds. Such drug-enkindled fires can put out the natural fires of the senses and block any higher perception from developing within us.

Sexuality — one of the most sacred aspects of our nature and the very basis of our physical existence — has also been turned into another form of indulgence, escape and domination. Sex has become the basis of social manipulation, advertising and the promotion of every sort of artificial want. We have cultivated an exaggerated sexual desire, which covers over our natural love and poisons it. The fire of such unsacred sex creates an unsanctified progeny, born with no real place in life, merely an unwanted by-product of selfish pleasure. Children born of such a legacy naturally find it hard to either love or be loved.

Our civilizational wealth and glory resides in great shopping malls, sports arenas and multi-story business complexes — what could be called 'temples to the unsacred fires'. We are so caught in our material pursuits that we no longer have adequate time to care of ourselves, much less our family, and certainly not our world.

We must remember that society always serves to create a certain type of human being depending upon its values, practices and institutions. The question is what type of human being are we breeding today? Instead of using our intelligence to create a kinder and wiser human type, we are breeding a human being defined neither by nature nor by God, but by corporations and their need for perpetual profit. We have created a species that seems to be against both nature and the spirit, trapped in a world of artificial intelligence and contrived cravings it does not understand and which have no natural basis that can allow them to be satisfied.

The most visible fire that we have cultivated is the 'fire of war'. We have learned to harness the destructives power of fire from nitroglycerine to the very atom itself. We have the greatest 'fire power' of any previous civilization but perhaps the least 'fire wisdom'. We have created sophisticated weapons of mass destruction, with arsenals capable of wiping out all life on the planet, but have forgotten how to light up the hearts of even our own children. Yet we are still developing subtle new weapons of social control; we are still looking to outer domination rather than to self-control as the means of advancing our civilizational aims.

Our main energy source is the 'fire of oil' — a dark fire from the ground that consumes the remains of previous life on Earth. This impure fire releases an ugly smoke of pollution that is the main factor of environmental degradation today. It also feeds a fire of greed on a psychic level that leads to conflict and oppression. Oil has become the main drug of our civilization to which we are collectively addicted, regardless of its many and growing side-effects. Not surprisingly, the energy created by oil only serves to drive our outer ambitions further and cannot give us peace. In fact, it is becoming the main cause of war in the world.

A Call for a New Sacred Fire

The result of our indiscretions is that the human being, who should be the crowning glory of nature and the protector of the Earth, is trampling upon the very animals, plants and rocks that have nurtured it. One is reminded of a verse from the *I Ching:*

> *The legs of the* ting *(the sacred fire vessel) are broken.*
> *The prince's meal is spilled.*
> *And his person is soiled.*
> *Misfortune.*[172]

We have lost touch with our heart, our origin and our goal. Instead of promoting the Divine light, we have lit a false fire of ego assertion and unleashed it like a plague upon the world. In little more than a century, our species has devastated the beautiful planet that gave it birth, scarcely noticing the inexcusable nature of what it has done.

It is crucial, therefore, that we replace these dark fires of destruction with the visionary flame of a new creation. For this we must return to our origins in the world of nature and honor our ancient spiritual heritage in all of its forms. We must create a new *evolutionary fire of consciousness* to carry us forward. There is no other real solution to the current growing world crisis. Other efforts will either be incomplete or fail owing to the lack of vision behind them. To increase this spiritual fire we ourselves — our minds and hearts are the greatest offerings. If even one person offers himself or herself into the sacred fire, such action can counter manifold darkness, just as a single flame can illuminate an entire room.

We need a new spirituality that starts with the Earth —

that reclaims our true evolutionary heritage as carriers of the sacred fire of consciousness. We need new fire gurus, teachers whose inner eyes are open and can see the oneness of all life. We need those who can speak with the voice of the Earth and the sacred fire within her. This is our true salvation, not more mere human creeds, ideologies, utopias or Brave New Worlds.

We must enkindle within ourselves a fire of planetary consciousness, remembering both the fire in the Earth and the fire in our souls as the keys to the process. We must bring a new light out of the depths both of the Earth and our hearts. We need to retrace the journey of our soul through the kingdoms of nature and restore our connections with the planet as a whole.

We must return to the mineral fire and embrace the rocks, stones and mountains as the greater foundation of our lives. We must return to the plant fire and commune with the trees, herbs and grasses as our greater home and place of dwelling. We must honor the animal fire and learn to communicate with wild and domesticated animals as our fellow creatures. And we need to reclaim our own sacred fires as a species — the spiritual heritage in our religions, yogic paths, native traditions, poetry and philosophy — as our true culture.

Such a new sacred fire will gather together our spiritual aspiration in all the forms that it has taken, rejecting nothing of the light. For this, we must particularly listen to the messages of indigenous and native traditions, especially to the elders who represent the transmission of their flame. We must look to our pagan roots as our ancient European ancestors from Ireland to Russia were also keepers of the flame, intimately connected to the world of nature around them, seeing the spirit in every hill and vale.

We must look to the religions of the East as belonging to us as well, including Hinduism — Sanatana Dharma or the 'Eternal Dharma' — which, in spite of the passage of the long centuries and many ups and downs, has maintained the continuity of its flame perhaps more so than any other tradition, showing how fire represents our true Self and Being.

One of the largest modern movements in Hindu Dharma, the *Arya Samaj*, founded by Swami Dayananda Saraswati in the nineteenth century, was based upon a return to the *Vedas* and reestablished the worship of the sacred fire. It uses Vedic fire rituals and mantras as the basis of all its practices. Many other modern Hindu movements are following this same trend. The entire Yoga-Vedanta tradition, which has spread worldwide since the time of Swami Vivekananda at the end of the nineteenth century, is such a return to Vedic wisdom.

Iran's Zoroastrian tradition of fire worship must also be recognized and revered as one of the great religions of the world. Yet we should note that Zoroaster was not the founder of this religion — whose correct name is the Mazdyean tradition or Mazda-Yasna — but only its renovator. It roots go back to the same ancient fire traditions as the Vedic.[173] The Zoroastrian religion had a strong influence on Judaism, early Christianity and on ancient Greece and Rome. The medieval mysticism of Europe looked back to it for its emphasis on the higher light.

We must also look to the spiritual fire behind the Judeo-Christian tradition — not simply the words of Moses but the burning bush through which God spoke to him, not only to the sacred heart of Jesus but to the sacred fire of the soul that is the real sacred heart of all. We must remember the many great mystics like Meister Eckhart or Hildegard of Bingen, who had their own direct experiences of the Divine beyond the dogmas and edicts of any church or organization.

Above all — if we really want to contact the Divine through any path — we must learn to experience the spiritual fire within ourselves, a flaming presence that transcends all forms and institutions. Its embers that have fallen and cooled off over time cannot save us any more than the ashes of a fire can warm our house or cook our food.

By reclaiming the sacred fires behind these great traditions we are reclaiming the Earth not merely as a material globe but as an evolutionary manifestation of the spirit. We are restoring our greater spiritual humanity transcending all divisions of creed, culture and dogma — the legacy of the great seers, sages and yogis from the beginning of civilization before any institutions had come into being to control us.

To create such a new sacred fire, we must gather together spiritual teachers, artists, thinkers and visionaries of all types and persuasions, if not in body at least in our hearts. We must offer our knowledge and creativity, both spiritual and scientific, into the seeking for a new planetary light. We should sacrifice all our human differences, whether by sex, race, religion or nationality to create a new dawn within us. Then we can transcend our current evolutionary crisis and enter into a new age of consciousness — a renaissance of the heart far greater than our recent rapid but spiritually vacant era of technological advances.

CHAPTER FOURTEEN

Healing the Planetary Soul:
Towards a Yogic Ecology

The planet is the field of experience for the soul. We could say that the planet is our greater body, while our soul is part of its indwelling planetary intelligence. Our soul may have a focus within our body, but it pervades our entire environment, stretching far beyond both our physical and mental boundaries in time and space. The soul has grown up along with the planet as its inner being. The soul is the self-creating planet's self-awareness.

All true healing powers lie within the soul, which is the very spirit of life. The soul has an inner connection with the forces of immortal life, the waters of eternity that can bring wholeness to all things. The soul has the power to heal the planet. Once we awaken at the level of the soul, which is the level of our planetary being, we can act to save our world and to save ourselves. This is the challenge facing the coming generation, which has taken birth in a species out of harmony with life and has inherited a wounded planet. Without such a spiritual awakening, our efforts to save the planet and its natural resources will lack depth and determination and easily become subverted by vested interests.

In ancient stories, the king (the soul) and the land (nature) mirrored one another. Note the legend of King Arthur and the Holy Grail, the myth of the sick king who caused the very land to wither and decay. To heal the king is to heal the world. The king we must heal is our own soul. Ancient mythology from the Egyptians to the Mayas required that the king shed his blood in order to make the land fruitful. A few special drops of his blood were put into the first plowing of the ground in order to make it fertile. This symbolizes the soul's self-sacrifice to the universe, which is necessary to make the creation flourish.

It is not the sacrifice of an external savior that heals our world but the offering of our own soul, our own individual fire, into the cosmic fire. By offering the blood of the soul, which is the blood of light, we can create a better world for generations to come. In this regard we must remember that one cannot know God without first becoming the Earth. One cannot reach the sky without first becoming firmly rooted in the ground. Our soul is always present at the root in order to lead us to the summit.

With all our technology we have forgotten how to use the forces of nature in a humane manner. We may know how to harness fire in industry but we are ignorant of how to harness the spiritual fire within our own hearts. We have forgotten how to communicate with the very Earth and the multitude of creatures that inhabit the planet along with us. Most of us do not even know the names of the plants or rocks around our own house or in our local environment. We have forgotten how to listen to what the waters are saying as they flow. We may be able to use wind power, but we have forgotten how to let our spirit soar on the breath. We have missed the beauty and magic of the sacred universe — and for what? For bigger movie screens, more hectic office lives, urban sprawl and hopes of more money? We are alienated from the very planet that has given us our bones and our blood.

And if we are successful in life, what do we do to reward ourselves? We return to nature. We go fishing, hunting or camping or take up other recreational sports in the outdoors. We organize even longer returns to nature when we retire at the end of our work years. We get into our motor homes and visit the national parks, striving to connect with the beauty of nature as perhaps the last phase of our existence. The instinct to return to our home in nature is so strong that even with all our machines and affluence we cannot forget it.

In other words, as our special reward, we do what so-called primitive people do every day. We set aside our careers, bank accounts and cell phones and enjoy just being in the wild, without any social baggage or demands. The question arises, therefore, why we can't find a better way to integrate such natural living into our ordinary lives, so that we can live the life of the soul first, instead of just attending to it at in the end when all else has been dealt with first?

To restore wholeness to our lives, we must recall our soul's evolutionary journey through all the kingdoms of nature. We must remember the healing rocks, waters and plants. We must honor the healing wisdom that the animals possess and that is carried by the wind. We must recognize that all nature is a park, a monument, a retreat and a temple.

Everything in nature contains its own medicine just as the Native Americans understood long ago. When we recognize this, then all things can heal us and we can heal all things, not by any personal effort but by the very power of existence.

The Diseased State of the Planet

Today our planet appears like a patient coming down with a great disease. The symptoms are everywhere, with the global environmental degradation that increases dramatically on a yearly basis. The Earth as an organism has clear signs of disease with its soil, waters, air and ecosystems contaminated or compromised. Anyone trained in any natural system of medicine cannot ignore these obvious symptoms of an organism that is disrupted.

As an Ayurvedic doctor, the signs of energy imbalance, toxicity and growth of unhealthy tissues are easy for me to recognize in our civilization. I have noticed such symptoms in individuals and traced their long term consequences as the precursors of major diseases. On a bodily level, such toxicity lead to fevers and infections, nervous system disorders, immune system breakdown or even cancer — to an entire set of deep-seated, complicated and hard to treat conditions.

And yet we are continuing the destructive activities that only insure such a pathogenesis will occur on our planet. We ignore the disease symptoms because time moves slower at a collective level than at the individual level in which we personally live. Like a patient in the early stages of a disease, we can still deny that the disease is happening to us or that we have caused it. The full blown symptoms of our planetary disorder are not yet painfully evident to all of us, particularly those of us in positions of power and affluence. How long can we continue in such a state of denial?

The Mineral Soul of the Planet

The damage has perhaps been the least to the mineral kingdom, the oldest and firmest of nature's dominions. But even here, it is not hard to find. We continue to dig up the Earth for mineral and energy resources and often leave devastation in our wake, turning beautiful landscapes into piles of barren rubble or toxic waste dumps, whether in fertile valleys or in high mountains.

We have damaged the soils that hold the main nutrients for life. Much of our topsoil has washed away. What remains has been polluted by every sort of chemical fertilizer and pesticide. The fire of life cannot endure in such unsacred ground, and healthy seeds cannot take root in it. Instead we are creating our own manmade unsacred seeds developed not by the evolutionary fire of nature but by laboratories funded by the global agribusiness, the new God of the Earth and new lord of our soils.

We have damaged our waters even more severely. Most of our rivers are dammed or obstructed in their flow. Some no longer reach the sea, including great rivers in North America like the once mighty Colorado. In natural healing systems like Ayurvedic medicine, one of the main causes of disease is 'blockage of the channels', meaning obstruction in the flow of blood, nutrients and energy (Prana) throughout the body. Such blockage results in pain, bleeding, tremors, arthritis and the growth of tumors. Damming up of our rivers is like damming our own blood vessels and expecting to remain healthy. We no longer even let the waters flow! This is indicative of how we are resisting the very movement of life.

We have polluted the rivers, turning them into sewers for our urban and industrial wastes, damaging the very lifeblood of the planet. We let our toxic waste flow into the sea as our offering to the waters in which life originated. Now as water is fast becoming a diminishing resource, we are already fighting to control as much of it as we can for the future, as if water were a commodity like oil to be owned and dispensed by corporations! Soon all the water on the planet will be owned by someone and taxed by the government!

The air we breathe has been polluted from automobile exhausts, industrial smoke and emissions from power plants. This weakens the atmosphere's ability to hold the life-fire. What we breathe is not the spirit in nature but a stagnant air, heavy with hidden toxins. Meanwhile we are filling the air waves with the noise of our mass communication and entertainment industries that is saturated with violence and sensation. We are not even allowing the atmosphere its sacred space of silence.

Our land, water and air globally contain residues of poisons and heavy metals, reaching even to the polar ice. These toxins can cause significant damage even in small amounts, interfering with the genetic code in creatures.

Such poisonous chemicals are slow to break down and will remain on our planet for centuries as the bitter legacy of our careless civilization. The mineral soul of the planet is under siege by our deviant culture that fails to honor the sacred ground from which it has arisen.

The Plant Soul of the Planet

The plant soul of the planet is suffering in a yet more visible way, particularly the great forests that are the lords of the plant kingdom. Most have been cut down and at best have only second or third growth trees. Many are being destroyed altogether, particularly the great rainforests of the tropics, and the rate of their elimination continues to increase. As trees are the human beings of the plant kingdom, their destruction is a kind of genocide. It removes the botanical support for our soul and its spiritual striving.

Though in the United States we may have set aside many National Forests, we haven't even protected these from the forces of development and their wood and mineral resources remain open to exploitation. There is an unprecedented dying off of trees in our forests from the pines of the West to the maples of the East.[174] We are no longer talking about a distant environmental problem. It is in our own backyards.

Wandering through the Rockies here in New Mexico, I find it easy to spot hillsides with numerous Pinyon pines that have died this year alone from drought and insect infestations.[175] One can also find Aspen stands and extensive Fir and Spruce forests weakened by insects, with many dead trees scattered among the living. Elsewhere one can find hillsides denuded of all vegetation by recent forest fires. The landscape in many areas has turned from a scene of beauty to one of decimation. The same scenes can be found over much of our nation and throughout much of the world. While we humans may not be entirely to blame, we are certainly the main culprit in this growing environmental catastrophe that is just beginning.

Charles E. Little notes in his *The Dying of the Trees*:[176]

I have learned things I wish I had not learned. I have learned that the trees are dying. And that the more trees die, the more will die. I have learned that we have crossed the threshold. And I simply do not know how we can get back safely to the other side.

The threshold that we have crossed is the demise of many other creatures. Many ecosystems have been marginalized or destroyed from the tropical to arctic regions, with the most sensitive being the first to go. We haven't even spared the deserts, which now have sprawling urban developments where people were never meant to live in great numbers. We have scarred the desert with trails for racing motorcycles as if these great domains of light had no purpose of their own but to be trampled over.

Not even the grass is allowed its day in the sun without interference. The great grasslands of the world, which provide nourishment for so many animals, have almost disappeared in our effort to exploit their rich soils, which we replaced by farmlands instead. Yet even the family farm, the organic basis of our human economy, is now perishing, replaced in turn by a corporate agribusiness devoid of any human touch or individual connection with the living ground. The plant soul of the planet has been struck at its roots, though we continue to depend upon its fruits to feed our families.

The Animal Soul of the Planet

Today we are also witnessing an unprecedented dying off of animal species. This cuts across the entire animal kingdom, with smaller species like insects and birds suffering the greatest damage. It affects all ecosystems, particularly remote, jungle, mountain and desert regions previously too harsh for humans to penetrate. Even animals in the remote wilderness areas cannot hide from human interference, if not depredation. It is not only the buffalo that has disappeared; the majority of animal species in the world have lost their habitats of merely a century ago.

One must ask whether we can live without our animal companions, not only domestic but also wild. While we may create zoos or animal parks instead, can we really separate the animal from the land and expect either to flourish? While we may set aside a few nature preserves and wilderness areas, these remain but isolated islands in a great continent of life that we have broken up into small pieces. The animal soul of the planet is losing its home. Without it the spirit of the wild, the great vital energy reserve of the planet, is disappearing, replaced by sterile and artificial urban deserts. The animal soul of the planet is being sacrificed, as it were, for the demigod of human greed and carelessness.

The Soul in Humanity

The soul in human beings is probably the foremost casualty of our destructive civilization. We may have more people alive today and more material affluence, but is there a greater soul force among us? Is character, wisdom, creativity or spirituality on the increase? Do we find such qualities in our leaders? Most of the great art, philosophy, religion and spirituality that we admire derives from previous centuries. For all that we are producing today in our hightech world, there seems little of lasting value in it.

Our growing personal and social problems mirror our wrong relationship with nature. Our medical system is not only failing to make us well; it is becoming a great burden on our resources, increasing the cost of living more dramatically than improving our health. Just as we are failing to heal the planet, our own medical system is also failing to heal us. Just as we are destroying the biosphere, which could be called the immune system of the planet, our own energy sphere or immune system is breaking down in new diseases like AIDS. Our overpopulation of the planet is mirrored in a rise of cancer, an over proliferation of unhealthy cells in our own bodies. Without a strong life-force on the planet itself, can any drugs or genetic alterations save us? Can we flourish if the life around us does not flourish?

Yet it is at the level of the heart where we have the greatest suffering. Those of us living in the developed world have a great deal of psychological pain even in the absence of any notable physical afflictions. Even those who are highly educated, including doctors and psychologists, seem lacking in any real peace of mind. Depression like an epidemic is perhaps the most urgent health complaint in America today. We have created an entire new set of anti-depression drugs to deal with this problem, yet these have extensive side-effects. Isn't depression just another symptom of being out of harmony with life? Can it be solved apart from restoring our balance with nature and with our deeper Self?

Our religions, whose purpose should be to awaken the soul within us, have often lost their own souls, functioning more as competing belief systems than as means of personal or social integration — as if spirituality were a mere business to accumulate followers. Instead of true inner spirituality arising to counter the materialism of our times, we often see a regressive fundamentalism fed by a fire of intolerance creating only more conflict and violence. There is little of nature in our religions and even less of any higher consciousness. Yet the state of nature is also the state of our soul or natural being. Without restoring the nature around us, it is not possible to raise our souls either.

The Planetary Organism

Each aspect of nature is like an organ of the Earth's body. The soils are like the skin of the Earth. The rocks and mountains are like her bones. The rivers and ocean are her blood and vital fluids. The plants are like her lungs and the animals are like her heart. We humans should serve as the nerve tissue of the Earth and as her brain. This body of nature is suffering on all levels from the excesses of our civilization. Can we survive as a species if our world body is damaged or dismembered?

The ancients worshipped the Earth as our mother, recognizing an organic connection between themselves and the planet. In India, the Earth was honored as a Divine Cow dispensing bounty to all her creatures that are like her calves. The Greek term Gaia, which is now used for the Gaia principle or idea of the Earth as an organism, also originally meant a cow. We can compare it to the Vedic term Gau, which means both a cow and the Earth.[177]

We human beings are meant to milk nature and the Earth like a cow — to cultivate and protect her with love and respect — skimming off her abundance, not reducing her to scarcity. Unfortunately, today it seems that we are trying to slaughter her instead. Though our natural resources continue to diminish from our over-consumption, we as yet have no long term plan to protect them.

Each ecosystem as a part of a Divine nature has its own soul, its own spirits, Gods and Goddesses. When we destroy plants, animals and ecosystems we are also removing the Divine forces that they carry from the Earth. We are casting out the Gods from our world, which means that we are creating a space for ungodly forces to take root and make their home.

Planetary Civilization

Our current global crisis mirrors a 'civilizational' disorder – a diseased civilization founded on wrong values and practices. The main disease of our civilization is that we lack unity, both with other human beings and with the greater universe. Unaware of the unity of life, we promote our own special interests over the greater good of all, which results in conflict.

Today we need a new planetary civilization in which we are citizens of the entire conscious universe. For this we must break down the barriers that separate human civilization from other species and manmade from cosmic intelligence. It requires recognizing consciousness as a universal power, not merely as a force that is evolving but as the power behind all evolution. For this to occur, we must redefine the planet as ourselves.

We are the planet. We are composed of its elements and are the products of its development on all levels. We are the result of a planetary intelligence whose first imperative is preserving and maintaining its planetary field of being. We must recognize this 'planetary imperative' within us to protect our world. We must look at the Earth as our greater body and its many species as our greater society.

Our law code should reflect the laws of the universe, starting with the law of karma itself. What we do to others — not merely to human beings but to all creatures — we do to ourselves. What we do to our world, we do to our own bodies and minds and create as our own future.

We need a planetary ethics, not merely a social set of laws, edicts or customs. This means that we must recognize not only the rights of human beings, but also the rights of all species, both animal and plant, and the rights of the planet itself, including the rights of different ecosystems to exist without our interference.

Our social order should follow an organic structure like the human body — a single entity with many different orans and systems working together for the good of the whole. Yet our social organism should be linked with all the communities of nature and to the Cosmic Person or consciousness principle as its ultimate support. We must recognize that human unity is not possible apart from unity with all beings. Otherwise just as we are divided from the rest of the world, we must be fragmented among ourselves as well. There can be no world peace unless we as a species are at peace with our environment, which means that we must honor all life as sacred and not to be interfered with.

The Need for a New Sacred or Yogic Ecology

A new ecology is needed to heal the planet, a sacred or 'yogic ecology' that honors the consciousness both in nature and in ourselves. This is not the ecology of science, business or even religion but that of the sacred fire arising from the Earth itself.

The organic unity of life, such as ecology proposes, lies in the higher consciousness that pervades the universe. This unity is not a mere construct of interlocking parts, much less a blind by-product of evolution, but the reflection of a single spirit that creates and sustains all things from within. This spirit, in turn, is not a mere theological belief but the very ground of existence.

To discover this unitary essence, it is not enough to work to save various habitats and ecosystems, however important that is. It requires honoring the Divine forces behind nature and opening up to them at the level of the heart. It requires sacred action, what one could call ritual, both externally and internally to restore our organic connection to all life. It requires a yogic process of reintegration with the greater universe of body and mind.

A truly spiritual ecology requires that we ourselves become spiritual beings, that we discover our own higher nature in the world nature. Only a spiritually focused or dedicated humanity can solve the current planetary dilemma. This requires that we as a species awaken at the level of the soul. We must no longer define ourselves according to a social or species-centric vision. We must recognize our immortal being that takes many births through all the kingdoms of nature as a portion of cosmic consciousness.

Is it possible for us to act from the level of the soul, aware of the organic unity of the entire universe? Certainly many people have reached this in states of inspiration, through meditation or through selfless service. It is the foundation of any real spiritual path. Can we as a species reformulate our civilization so that our very way of life becomes a spiritual path? This is what is needed today and it is not without some precedent at least in certain spiritual communities. However, it necessitates a change in our civilizational values and in our educational system, a movement away from the pursuit of personal achievement to the seeking of the sacred, in which we ourselves become an offering or a prayer.

To accomplish this, we must cease to define ourselves on a personal or egoic level with our own private fulfillment is the main góal of life. We must recognize our greater soul that exists for nature's evolutionary development of consciousness. We must act from the eternal and universal aspect of our being, which is our global conscience that will not sell itself out at any price.

If we look at ours not as a separate species but as an integral part of the conscious universe, then we can become a conduit for all the healing forces of nature. For this we must go beyond any commercial or ideological definition of who we are. We must return to both the soil and to the stars as an unbroken continuum of light.

Fortunately, we still possess tremendous resources that we can draw upon in this labor. Our ancient spiritual heritage remains alive in much of the world and among many individuals, scattered though they may be. Experiential spiritual traditions like Yoga, Buddhism and Taoism are rapidly growing in popularity on all continents. Even belief-oriented faiths are looking more towards an inner experience or practice of meditation to afford them more depth. Our indigenous cultures, in spite of all the efforts to eradicate them, have managed to preserve much Earth wisdom that we can access. Our natural healing traditions are arising once more with many new dietary, herbal and body-work practices as well as energetic, vibratory and spiritual healing methods. A new deep ecology is arising that is aware of our connection with the planet and with the greater universe beyond.

However, we still have very far to go — a long journey that may take decades and face many apparently insurmountable obstacles. We must take these transformative movements from the periphery to the center of our culture for the decisive change to occur. We must create an ecological revolution in society in order to overcome the many dangers that lie ahead for our species. Yet for this to be truly possible, there must first be a greater revolution, a new spiritual fire within our own hearts.[178]

CHAPTER FIFTEEN

Sacred Relationship and Our Collective Flame

Fire is the basic entity around which, in one form or another, we all come together. Our human society grew up around fire and today remains a fire community, a gathering around the light. As fire beings, our human interactions are another form of fire. We transmit different forms of fire to one another, both in order to sustain our individual existence and to build up greater collective orders.

Our coming together creates both constructive and destructive fires. We seek warmth in human contact but avoid heat. We enjoy the security of being with others but do not want to be consumed by them. Like a fire we must tend to our associations carefully, aware of both the benefits and dangers that they pose.

All social gatherings generate a certain warmth, heat and passion. They generally center on some shared 'fire' function like eating food, watching some entertainment, having a discussion or listening to a talk. As we come together our fires intermingle and grow, often taking on proportions far beyond their individual constituents, just as cells come together to form a larger body.

Ancient people gathered around the community or tribal fire for ritual, dance, storytelling and conversation. Today we have divided up these functions into churches, theatres, sports arenas, libraries and other forms of congregation. Our main enjoyments since antiquity have been spectacles of light and color, up to our high tech special effects in movies. The modern human watching a television at night is really no different than the caveman watching his fire. However vastly the appearance has changed from our organic roots, we are still performing the same type of ritual. The main difference is that the uplifting sacred fire that connects us to the greater universe has been replaced by a commercial fire that only breeds wasteful desires and exploitation of the Earth.

Communities, our Circles of Fire

Fire is our leader, the light that carries us forward in our endeavors. Whoever becomes the leader of a social group becomes, as it were, its flame or guiding light. Our leaders are the chief fires that motivate us, whether in the political, financial, intellectual or political spheres. They are the center of our community fires and usually the one who lights them as well.

Our social gatherings create a 'circle of fire' that defines a particular community, serving as a boundary or a barrier for those who dwell outside of it. Our social orders are defined by such 'circles of fire', with our proximity to the center or leader of the fire usually marking our place in the hierarchy. Such groups become families, clans, tribes, friends or associations that share a common bond between them. They provide nourishment for the members of the group and also afford protection against enemies or predators.

The heat such association generates can create love and harmony or become a suspicion and intolerance if directed against other groups. Mass-generated group emotions can generate the most destructive fires. They give rise to mob actions, riots and even war. We must make sure that our gatherings are made sacred so that the energy they inevitably create has only an uplifting effect. Our sacred circle should not exclude other beings but only exclude what is unsacred.

Our Role in the Social Fire

All our human roles have a basis in the sacred, starting with family roles of father and mother, brother and sister, son and daughter, grandfather and grandmother. These become the models for other human associations such as friends who are like a father or a brother to us. Male and female, young and old, guest and neighbor all have their place in the sacred order of life. We are each compelled to play different roles depending upon our age and station in life, sometimes quickly moving from one to another as we change masks in the ever-shifting drama of human interaction.

Throughout all these roles we are really tending to the soul in one form or another. We should realize that whatever person we are caring for is another form of the sacred fire that also dwells within us. Then whatever role we may play will be helpful and our own inner fires will be nourished as well. A fully developed human being is capable of performing all the roles of life because he or she understands the beauty of the entire play.

The most basic fire of human relationship is that of the family, from which we derive our birth. The family is based upon the fire of the blood, which is a primal and instinctual force. Sharing the family fire is the linkage of a son to his father's aspiration in life, or of a daughter to her mother's. It can carry a family wish, work or business over many generations.

The family tie connects us to greater kinship groupings, to the extended family or tribe and its older and broader ancestral fires. The tribe in turn links us to a community that lives in a particular locale, reflecting the bond of the land. It should link us to our greater community in nature, as part of the greater world of creatures around us.

Yet kinship is not only a physical phenomenon, we also belong to spiritual or soul families. These are groups of kindred spirits who come together for a special work in life. Spiritual families are connected to spiritual tribes or communities of souls. The ties of this greater soul community can extend beyond death and spread across many streams of time.

The Need for a New Sacred Community

Our kinship is not only with other humans but with all living beings. Among native people, tribes define themselves according to a totem or tribal spirit, a sacred animal that reflects their deeper life connections. The totem is a means of linking human communities with the greater communities of nature. Tribes are defined as fire people, sun people, bear clans, eagle clans or other power animals or nature symbols that indicate their particular quality and energy. Some of these tribal images remain in our flags or have become national symbols like the American eagle. The individual has a special identity within the tribe that is played out in rituals. This may involve taking on the role of an animal or a god, as the tribal force lifts the individual into a greater mythic existence and cosmic expression through which his soul or spirit can come forth.

Today we are trying to change human life according to 'inorganic factors' — political agendas, dogmatic religious beliefs and manipulative marketing strategies. I believe that all ideologies, political or religious, are dangerous and ultimately destructive because they are not rooted in the land. They do not come from nature or her indwelling spirit but from human cunning, if not prejudice. They seek to impose an artificial human standard upon life that overflows all attempts to control and define it. The Earth has no ideology. The Sun and stars have no belief or creed that they must follow. Any social orders created or run by an ideology must eventually fail because they are contrary to the intricacy of the living universe. They have no organic structure through which they can develop naturally but, like our modern cities, must proliferate an artificial and wasteful existence. They must break down over time and leave us rootless.

While we may recognize the importance of 'human' rights, we have forgotten the rights of other creatures, along with their feelings. Even human rights have largely been reduced to only 'individual rights', forgetting the rights of the family, community and ecosystem without which the individual has no meaning. True universal rights are the rights (and rites) of the universe, not the selfish demands of our single species.

Today we have eliminated our greater ties to both humanity and the world of nature. We have become isolated individuals, each seeking his or her private fulfillment through career, money, status or pleasure. If we are successful, we are left with no one to share our success with. If we fail, there is no one to console us or to inspire us to try again. No matter how much we gain, we still feel empty. This is because our evolutionary heritage conditions us to find happiness only as part a greater community that cannot be separated from the whole of life.

Today we need a new sense of community — a 'new spiritual tribalism' as it were — to restore our organic link with the conscious universe. We need a new 'sacred community' not based upon the interests of one segment of society against another, but upon our ultimate ancestry with the Cosmic Person or Purusha. We must restore our link in the chain of life, placing ourselves in the network of souls that forms the necklace of God. We must forge a new *sangha* or spiritual fellowship, much like the Vedic communities of old, led by seers and yogis, rather than by politicians, preachers or businessmen.[179]

We need a community that includes not only our fellow

human beings but all of nature. We must have a relationship with the rocks, plants and animals that also inhabit our world, and with the Earth, atmosphere, sky, Sun, Moon and stars that form it. Such a relationship should be one of unity, as one manifestation of consciousness to another, not based on our superiority over other creatures, much less our exploitation of them. *One of the reasons that our human relationships are in so much turmoil today is that we no longer have a real relationship with nature.* We cannot hope to have harmony in our society if our society does not recognize the consciousness that pervades the entire universe.

For such a new sacred society, we need a new collective fire. We need new social identities forged in that common fire. We need new rituals that link us with the greater communities of life, honoring our ties to the rock, plant, animal and god. Out of this new fire we can create new culture of life and consciousness, with organic forms of art, science, medicine, philosophy and religion that unite us with all worlds and all creatures.

If we don't create a new spiritual sense of community, then a darker form of tribalism must arise within our societies. Denying any sacred community, the energy of our collective urge to ritual must come out in distorted forms as gangs and cults of criminal and fanatical types. Nazi Germany was a country that came under the grip of a destructive tribalism that arose to fill such a spiritual vacuum. Even communism was largely a non-spiritual cult, with politics elevated to a religious fervor. We cannot have a tribeless society any more than we can have a classless society, but we can replace artificial social orders with those that follow the rhythms of the soul and place us in harmony with the universal life.

The Human as a Sacred Species

We have always regarded our species as special. Our species is special, but not in the way of domination, which is only an assertion of crude animal impulses. Our species has the ability to embody cosmic intelligence, which is its real contribution to the evolutionary process.

To regain the sacred in our species, we must look at our society in a new light. There is a way for our culture to be spiritual, peaceful and tolerant, aware of the sacred nature of all life, without falling into superstition, dogmatism or fundamentalism.

We must look to the Divine not only in nature but also in ourselves. We are all archetypal entities. The great forces of the universe work within our own flesh and blood. The great Gods and Goddesses and the Supreme Divine of which all time and space is but a manifestation are part of our own deeper nature. If we but remove the veil of the mind and open our hearts, we will discover that we are the sacred universe and never need to be apart from it, even in our sleep.

Woman as the Sacred Fire: The Goddess

The female embodies the fire of creation, having the ability to create new life from her own body and blood. On her rests the development of the species through the education of the young. She is the first guru or teacher of the child, responsible for the foundation of our lives.

In traditional societies, the woman tends the household fires, the fires of the home that provide the main sustenance for life. Food is the main sacred offering our life depends upon, and woman is the high priestess of this offering. Modern society may provide other means of fulfillment for women — which are certainly necessary — but this role in the home should still be honored. The woman is the sacred fire of the family that the husband and children should make their offerings to.

The Fire Goddess is the great world mother who provides all beings with food, shelter, warmth and love. This Divine Mother takes many forms in different cultures, whether as a maiden of pure light, the queen of the world, or the matrix from which even the light is born. Such a dynamic Shakti is essential to any action in the universe, upholding the powers of creation, preservation and transformation. Of course, the Goddess is more than fire as an element or material power. She is the creative force behind all nature that provides the impetus for all spiritual growth as well.

Many religions have not afforded the Goddess or feminine aspect of Divinity her proper place and sometimes deny her altogether. This is one of the main spiritual causes of the current global crisis. Without recognizing the feminine or receptive power of the Divine in nature, in the Earth and in our own souls, we miss the real grace of life and our sense of God becomes rigid, artificial or even violent. We must once more honor the Goddess, not simply as a religious image but as the transformative power of life itself that is rooted in peace and selflessness.

The Fire of the Goddess

I first discovered the Goddess as the muse that arose as part of my youthful poetic inspirations before I had even heard of the path of Yoga or studied any eastern spiritual traditions. The muse is the intimation of beauty and mystery who guides us along our path beyond the world of necessity to the heart of creation. She is a form of the Goddess highly honored by the ancient Greeks and Romans and never completely lost to western culture unlike so many others.

Many western poets have lauded her from the medieval poet Dante to the modern French poet Yves Bonnefoy whose works I found particularly inspiring. Most poignant is Bonnefoy's discovery of the muse of the Earth, the stone and shadow who carries the secret light that allows us to go beyond death and suffering. This is a power that we need to recognize once more today for a creative renewal to occur within us:

Oh with your wing of earth and shadows wake us
Angel vast as the earth, and bear us here
To the same part of the mortal earth
For a beginning. May the ancient fruits
Be our thirst and hunger now assuaged.
The fire be our fire...[180]

The muse is the secret voice and presence of nature as the guide of the soul. Through her the forms of nature become transparent as symbols and metaphors for our own deeper strivings and aspirations. She is the beauty of nature personified as a spiritual force.

In the yogic traditions of India, I discovered that this feminine power of inspiration had never been reduced to a mere poetic device but remains as a spiritual reality, the very power of consciousness itself. In Vedic thought, the Goddess herself is the Divine Word, called *Vak* — the Word Goddess who like the Logos creates the entire universe. In the yogic view, in the beginning was the Word but the Word was the Goddess. Her main form is called Sarasvati, which means 'she of the flowing movement of inspiration'.

The Goddess represents the Divine creative force, which is only natural as it is the mother who gives birth to and nourishes the child. In Yoga she is a living force of inner transformation that one can contact within one's own heart. She is the very power of Yoga or Yoga Shakti that provides the energy and grace to carry us along the ascending path to Self-realization.

Yet the Goddess is not simply an ethereal form but is embodied through great female gurus like Anandamayi Ma (1895-1982), the 'bliss-permeated' mother of Bengal. Anandamayi Ma was generally regarded as the foremost woman saint of India of the last century, the Great Mother for many yogis, sadhus and pandits, comparable only to Ramana Maharshi as the Great Father.[181] I corresponded with Ma for several years in my twenties through Atmananda, one of her western female disciples. She guided me in my early Yoga practices and aided in my discovery of the *Vedas*.[182] She gave me the confidence to proceed in my esoteric quest, at a time in which I had no other real support. For her devotees, Anandamayi Ma was the Goddess as a human being.

Another such living form of the Goddess is Mata Amritanandamayi of Kerala, also called Ammachi, who has many centers in the West and frequently visits the United States. Nearly a million people from all over the world recently came to India for her fiftieth birthday celebration. Several other such great mothers or female gurus now visit the West regularly as well.

The Goddess is an essential part of any real work with the sacred fire, which is her means of manifestation. All the main Hindu Goddesses, including Lakshmi, who rules over beauty, love and prosperity, and Kali, who governs suffering, death and transformation, originally arose from the sacred fire.[183] In my study of Vedic and Tantric Yogas, I discovered many forms of the Goddess that we can approach through ritual, mantra and meditation — notably the Dasha Mahavidya or Ten Great Wisdom Powers of the Goddess, on which I have written.[184] Her powers and manifestations occur on all levels of existence from the Absolute to the very ground on which we stand. The entire universe is her flowering, but fire is perhaps her most essential form.

We can all feel the presence of the Goddess in nature, particularly in displays of beauty and light. I came to sense her in the feminine forms of nature through the waters, valleys, plants, clouds and stars. As the mountain Goddess and wife of Shiva, the mountain God, I could feel her as much in the Rocky Mountains of this country as in the Himalayas of India. She communicates to us through nature wherever we may be, as the spirit of the land on which we live.

As I took on a more social activist role relative to environmental issues and the preservation of native cultures, I found her again as the warrior-goddess Durga, who leads the Divine army. [185] All those who strive to take the light of truth forward in humanity, we could say, become part of

Durga's army. To those whom she specially blesses, she grants her many weapons to destroy the powers of darkness, the foremost of which is her sword that represents the power of discrimination. Certainly we need the help of Durga in order to overcome the many difficulties that lie before our species. A famous hymn to Durga states:

> *She who has the color of fire, blazing with ascetic power, resplendent, sought in achieving the fruits of our labors,*
> *For our deliverance, we take refuge in the Goddess Durga, who takes us across to the other shore.*[186]

Visit to Kamakhya, the Home of the Goddess: The Tantric Fire

Throughout India there are many sacred sites to the Goddess. For example, the Goddess Kali, who represents the Divine power that transcends death and suffering, has her main temple in Calcutta where the great Hindu saint Ramakrishna lived.[187] Yet perhaps the most sacred and mysterious site to the Goddess is Kamakhya in Assam in the northeast of India, which represents her generative organs that symbolize the powers of universal creation.

Kamakhya is one of the most important centers of Tantric Hinduism, where regular Tantric rituals and worship of the Goddess have gone on for thousands of years. While Tantra is often reduced to sex in the West, it is really a comprehensive system of working with the primal powers of the living universe, turning even our ordinary biological drives, including sexuality, into forces of inner transformation. Tantra is not concerned with sex as a mere human drive but with the entire creative energy of nature that works behind our impulses and can also afford us the power to master them. Such a transformative Tantric approach to life, in which we connect our personal nature with the universal nature and supreme consciousness, is important for any higher evolutionary change within us. Its concern is with turning all aspects of our lives into yogic rituals of inner transformation, yogic fire practices.

Some scholars, usually coming from an academic rather than experiential background, like to separate Vedic and Tantric approaches, as if the two are very different, failing to note their obvious connections. Both Vedic and Tantric practices are rooted in the forces of nature as powers of consciousness and both use the sacred fire as their primary tool and metaphor. Most Tantric rituals are based on older Vedic rituals using fire, water, special plants and, above all, on special Vedic and Sanskrit mantras like OM and HREEM.

Tantric Yoga has its roots in internal Vedic rituals of pranayama, mantra and meditation. It takes the female principle of fire (Agni) in the root chakra upward to unite with the male principle of ambrosia (Soma) in the head, uniting the Shiva and Shakti or Divine feminine and masculine forces within us. The great Vedic deities of fire (Agni), water or the Moon (Soma), air or wind (Vayu), and the Sun (Surya), are also the prime factors of Tantric practices.

I visited Kamakhya in early 2002 as part of a tour of the northeast of the country working with the tribal peoples. The temple is located on a small hill on the bank of the Brahmaputra River, one of the largest rivers in the world, considerably larger than the more famous Ganges into which it flows. Kamakhya carries the energy of this great stream that is the result of five great rivers that cascade with great fury down the slopes of the eastern Himalayas, which is the wettest place on Earth.[187] The river's name Brahmaputra, or 'the child of God', suggests its magnificence. This region of great floods is a natural place for the Goddess, whose main form is water, to be honored.

As one drives up the small hill to the main shrine, one observes the ancient temples and pilgrims in traditional dress and feels a humid and hot air thick with the energy of the Goddess. In the main temple near the top of the hill a special small spring of water arises, which represents the generative fluid of the Goddess and is famous for its great healing and spiritual powers. Kamakhya represents the ultimate creative power of the Goddess that arises out of the corpse of Shiva, the cosmic masculine force in its state of complete rest. She is the supreme transformative power that arises out of the state of total stillness.

As I visited the temple I felt the Goddess as if she were riding in a helicopter spinning her powerful energies above Shiva like the unmoving ground below. I saw this image many times in my mind and wondered what it meant. I was scheduled to take a special two hour helicopter ride across the Brahmaputra valley to the town of Itinagar in the nearby state of Arunachal Pradesh in the Himalayan foothills. Such old helicopters in India are not always safe and recently an important Indian political leader had perished in such a crash. So I wondered if I was going to the abode of Shiva myself!

When I got into the helicopter a few days later, sure enough the vehicle was old and shook badly as it took off. The old pilot himself, with a handlebar mustache, looked like a figure from a World War II movie, which didn't inspire much confidence either. Then a few minutes after we ascended in altitude I looked down below and to my surprise saw the Kamakhya hill below. I could see the great temple and shrine of the Goddess from a point directly above it. Suddenly I was in the whirlpool of the Goddess' own energy at the center of her world. Time seemed to stand still at that moment and space opened up like a lotus. One was simultaneously at the center and at the periphery, at once a point of pure focus and a boundless expansion through all possibilities.

I received a 'helicopter darshan' (vision) of the Goddess, both outwardly and inwardly as it were. Her energy is much like a whirling helicopter, a spiraling power of transformation rooted in the supreme silence. It is the highest form of fire that dwells within the void or emptiness of pure consciousness. There the fire burns on itself, with its own flames as its fuel.

This experience taught me how silence and energy, stillness and movement, inaction and the highest transformation, Shakti and Shiva always go together. The highest transformation arises from Being itself. When we rest in the center of our own being, we are dwelling at the heart of all creation. Then through all events we can enter into eternity. Through all places we can touch the infinite.

Afterwards I was involved in an exhausting speaking tour of the area, traveling to remote villages in the hills, but whenever I started to feel fatigued, I remembered the energy of Kamakhya Devi and accomplished my work without exhaustion.[189] To save our planet today we need such immutable stillness on the inside along with the greatest dynamic action and effort on the outside. We need the creative powers of the Goddess rooted in fire, water and the Earth that carry the blessings of the God of infinite space.

Man as the Sacred Fire: The Fire God

Fire is rightfully regarded as a masculine and aggressive force. We could say that the destructive force of fire is masculine, while its constructive form is feminine. The male embodies more the protective fire, the female more the nurturing fire, though the two are as interrelated as the sexes. The male was traditionally the warrior, hunter, gatherer, farmer and provider. He provided the fuel and the food for the fire in the home that the woman tended. He also built the great collective fires for various holidays and feast days.

The Fire God is the main primal form of God. He is the great world father, the ancient of days, the perpetual flame that guides, corrects and watches over us with both sternness and compassion. He takes on many forms as the king, law giver, magician, priest and seer. From Moses to Merlin and Lao-Tzu his cultural forms are many but similar — the long white beard, the eyes of fire and the secret wisdom. We also need to rediscover the Fire God, the being of light and consciousness behind these ancestral images. He is the role model for the male spiritual force and power of enlightenment needed to restore the male to his proper role.

This great Fire God is also Lord Shiva, the original Yoga guru and guide on the spiritual path. One of his most important forms is Nataraj, the Lord of the Dance, who spins the dance of fire at the end of the cosmic cycle through which the entire universe is consumed back into the Divine light that is its origin. This supreme Fire God holds the keys to all the powers of consciousness and to the Existence beyond all time and space in which is the highest liberation.

The problem with our current society is not simply its dominance by male energy or the patriarchy as some feminists propose, but its dominance by a regressive and unspiritual male (and female) energy. The solution is not to emasculate men but to spiritualize masculinity. This requires awakening the Fire God as an archetype of self-discipline, self-mastery and self-realization within us.[190] The true male energy manifests that inner fire as a self-transforming force. It does not burn others. It gives light to all through offering itself.

Restoring the Sacred Balance

The cosmic feminine is worshipped in many forms as the river, valley, flower, ring-stone, sacred circle or Shakti power. The cosmic masculine force is worshipped in many forms as the flame, mountain, tree, standing stone or Shiva force. These two powers are not simply human but universal forces. In fact the human male and female are but manifestations of these greater cosmic forces.

Freudian psychology errs in regarding human sexuality as the root of the human psyche. Rather it is cosmic sexuality that is the root of the human psyche, not as a reproductive urge but as a universal creative force. Human sexuality is a manifestation of deeper powers that go beyond the merely human and pervade all of nature. The real way to deal with our sexuality is to honor the cosmic mascu-

line and feminine forces as the powers of nature and consciousness behind the world. This is the view of Yoga psychology.

By honoring both cosmic masculine and feminine powers, we can make our sexuality sacred. We can unite the
God and Goddess both within ourselves and within our
world and restore the balance of nature that leads to new
creation in consciousness.

The Divine Fire Child

Our soul itself is the Divine Fire Child that is born in the
sacred space of the heart. He is the savior that takes us
across the ocean of ignorance from darkness to light, from
mortality to immortality. This Divine child of immortality
takes many forms like the baby Krishna or the baby Jesus.
It sometimes takes the form of the warrior child who over-
comes the powers of darkness, like Horus among the Egyptians or the Hindu God Skanda (son of Shiva and his wife
Parvati). The Divine Child is not only male but also female
as the maiden or virgin Goddess, like the youthful form of
Durga (Kumari), or the Dawn (Ushas), the daughter of
Heaven of Vedic thought.

The Divine Child of soul is the real inner child that we
must heal and who has the power to heal us, once we return our minds to their original natural state. This Divine
child carries our original face before we were born, to use a
Zen metaphor, which is the face of fire or the presence of
transforming light. It is the pure and innocent awareness
that existed before our ego was formed, whose power can
purify all things. Children embody this innocence of the
soul and if we care for them as Divine children they can
maintain it for the rest of their lives.

The Meaning of 'Namaste'

Our main sacred role in relationship is to embody the cosmic masculine and feminine forces and recognize the soul
both within and around us. This is to mirror the Divine

back to each person that we meet and each being that we see. This is to perceive the Purusha or Cosmic Person in all creation. A simple way to do this is with the Hindu greeting of 'Namaste' meaning "I bow to the Divine in you", which is made along with raising one's hands together in the gesture of prayer. This gesture reflects raising our inner flame to welcome the same flame in others, uniting the light with the light. It is also an integral part of the Yoga of devotion, in which we honor the Divine presence in all life.

We live in a 'user friendly' conscious universe that will respond to our every sincere call for help, support or guidance. We have nothing to fear but our own unwillingness to open up to life. Whatever we approach with consciousness must respond to us in kind, not only other human beings but even the rocks! If we offer our respect, our greeting of Namaste to everything, even the wind, each thing in nature will communicate to us in its own way and give us its blessing.

Everything in the universe is our friend and well-wisher. All creatures are part of our own greater family with whom we have eternal and unbreakable ties. Even the forces of nature are powers of our own greater Self and spirit. *Remember to greet the God in all, and God will come to you through everything. Offer your greeting of Namaste to all. Anything else is a squandered opportunity that can only leave us in isolation and sorrow.*

V

Planetary Yoga and the Planetary Flame

CHAPTER SIXTEEN

Planetary Fire Yoga

An old Vedic prayer to the Earth, the *Bhumi Sukta*, portrays the Earth as the formation of a spiritual force and as carrying a spiritual destiny. It speaks of the planet not merely as a material globe but as a power of divine creation arising from the highest consciousness:

> *Truth, vastness, energy, initiation, asceticism, prayer and sacrifice uphold the Earth.*
>
> *May she, the queen of what was and what will be, create a wide realm for us.*
>
> *Who existed at first in the waters of the sea, who the sages found by their magic wisdom power;*
>
> *Whose heart is in the Supreme Ether, immortal and covered in truth;*
>
> *May the Earth grant us strength and splendor in the highest kingdom.*[191]

This inner Earth of the soul is the true Earth of our birth and our destiny. We need to recover such a spiritual sense of the Earth today, but this requires a seer vision in order to bring it forth. The seer Agastya, the founder of the yogic traditions of South India, has a prayer in the *Rig Veda* which reflects such a vision of a spiritual Earth linked to the sacred fire:

Again for our sacred journey, oh Divine and Sacred Fire
(Agni), be for us an Earth with all the immortals.[192]

The idea of the Earth as a spiritual force may seem strange
to our scientific vision and to our ordinary religious views
which place God in some Heaven beyond. Yet the Earth
with all of its beauty remains a force of spiritual enlightenment for humanity. Being in nature elevates our souls, as
great poets, mystics and yogis have so often proclaimed. In
fact, one could argue that the Earth is a more spiritual
planet than our humanity is a spiritual species. Unfortunately, we are destroying nature and replacing it with an
artificial environment of metal, glass and cement more
suitable to our less spiritual urges.

This vision of a spiritual Earth that can uplift us was a
theme of one of my early poems and remains one of the
most important aspirations behind my work.

Earth of our dreams awaken us
Lift us to the hidden heights
Where you lay humble and alone

To reach the heavens, we must become one with the
Earth. The outer planet is a manifestation of the inner
Earth of our soul's creative vision.

Yoga goes back to such a higher vision of the Earth and
our human destiny. Yoga, properly understood, is a means
of furthering the evolution of consciousness on the planet.
It is not limited to the concerns of one species, much less
to those of the individual. It addresses all aspects of our
nature from body to spirit and all aspects of nature from
matter to pure consciousness.

Yoga goes back to the first human being or Manu. The
intelligence of Yoga is part of the very light that comes to
us from the Sun. It is part of the fire that burns in the center of the Earth. It is an expression of the flame of the soul
behind our own minds and hearts. Yoga is central to our
planetary being and is the essence and the methodology of
our planetary journey and pilgrimage through all of nature.

Our tendency today is to define Yoga mainly as a personal practice but Yoga is not merely about personal integration, it shows us how to reintegrate ourselves with all of nature. *The Self that Yoga aims at realizing is this cosmic or 'natural' Self — the Self of the universe. This means that Yoga in the true sense is always 'planetary'.*

A true Yogi is an awakened being who aids the evolution of consciousness in the universe from a higher awareness within. He or she is not simply an asana expert who can move the physical body with ease, but one in whom the soul fire stands at the forefront of all that they do. A true Yogi knows all the healing and evolutionary fires of nature and how to energize them. He or she can work with the powers of the rocks, plants, animals, human beings and all the great forces of nature as aspects of the conscious universe.

An Ecological Approach to Yoga

Each aspect of Yoga relates to a particular 'loka', meaning a layer of world-experience on the many levels of this multi-strata universe. Each aspect of Yoga connects us to a corresponding realm of consciousness relative to that loka.

- Yoga postures are about becoming one with the Earth — connecting our body with the forces of the mineral kingdom and its inherent strength and stability. Our spine itself is the Earth or bedrock of our being.
- Yogic breathing practices are about becoming one with the Atmosphere — connecting our breath with the great power of the wind and the bio-electrical forces of nature. Our own breath is also our atmosphere or energy of our being.
- Yogic meditation is about becoming one with the Heavens — having a mind as vast as the sky, which can illumine the world like the Sun. Our own mind is the light of our inner world.

Yoga practices use the forces of nature on an internal level as the powers of fire (speech), wind (breath), water (feeling), earth (body) and space (the empty or silent mind). Yoga also works with the deities (powers of the universal soul or Cosmic Person) behind these elements, linking us to Nature's inner intelligence. Yoga practices constitute an inner technology of consciousness, the main purpose of which is evolutionary. They show us how to systematically develop the higher potentials latent within our deeper minds and hearts.

One of the problems with modern Yoga in the West is that it has largely become a commercial urban yoga done in gyms, as an enhancement or as a compensation for our hectic life-styles out of harmony with nature. While this may at times be necessary given our current culture, we should remember that true Yoga as part of nature is usually done in nature, in a room without walls. It was originally taught in 'forest academies' as part of a way of simple natural living and detachment from human affairs.

Real Yoga requires that we unite ourselves with our natural environment from the soil to the stars. The great elements of earth, water, fire, air and ether that make up the universe are but different expressions of our own cosmic body, our body of Yoga. We must reclaim our universal form of which our physical body is just a material representative.

To really implement the integrative approach of Yoga requires that we think ecologically about all that we do. Starting at a physical level, we must consider not only whether the food that we eat is appropriate for our well-being but also how it affects the planet and the feelings of other creatures. On a psychological level, we must consider whether our communication fosters harmony with all creatures, not just whether it works to promote our own self-interests.

We must consider whether our career is elevating not only to our own consciousness but also to that of the entire planet, or if it is just a means of making money at the expense of other creatures. We must consider how we are

living overall. Are we functioning in a yogic way to integrate our world and its competing forces into a greater harmony; or are we acting in a non-yogic way to increase the
entropy in the world toward fragmentation, isolation and
division? If we haven't asked such questions, how can we
claim that we have really practiced Yoga?

Our yogic journey is not just to better bodily flexibility.
It is not just a transition from a troubled psychology to a
peaceful state of mind. It is the soul's journey through the
entire realm of nature back to the Godhead that is our real
home, bringing all the creative potentials of the natural
world along with us. The liberation of the individual soul
is part of the liberation of all life.

All nature will help us in this greater yogic quest if we
sincerely take it up. The very stars and rocks will be our
gurus, passing on the insights of the primeval intelligence
that envisioned this world long before any creature existed.
The clouds and rivers will provide us with the energy to
propel us along our yogic path that goes everywhere. To
achieve this, we must embrace the evolution of all life as
our own growth and progress. We must care for the world
of nature as the garden of our soul. We must realize that
the entire universe dwells in the space within our hearts
for us to cherish and to foster. This inner recognition of the
All within us has always been the goal of true Yoga.

The Work of Sri Aurobindo: Yoga's Seer of a New Humanity

Such an evolutionary approach to Yoga is probably most
obvious in the work of the great modern Yogi and Rishi Sri
Aurobindo.[193] Aurobindo (1872-1950) began his career as an
intellectual and political activist in India around the turn
of the twentieth century. He was a great writer, thinker
and poet educated in England, who returned to India to
help liberate his country from the oppressive British colo-
nial rule. Aurobindo's political and journalistic work
achieved great prominence in a short time, and he was

soon in a position to become the very head of the Indian independence movement. At one point he was put in jail by the British and scheduled to be executed for sedition but was saved by a last minute reprieve.

After a profound inner experience that occurred while he was jailed by the British, Aurobindo decided to renounce politics for Yoga and never again returned to the political arena. It was only some years after Aurobindo left the political scene that Mahatma Gandhi arrived from South Africa and became the new leader of the movement.[194] Aurobindo felt that Yoga had a greater power to effect a real and lasting change in humanity than any outer activities, for those who could take on the real yogic force. However, he continued to support India's independence movement in his writings and helped guide it from the distance, interacting with many of its leaders, like Rabindranath Tagore, who looked up to him for inspiration.[195] Many people still look upon Aurobindo, rather than Gandhi, as the real father of modern India.

Sri Aurobindo created a new evolutionary approach to Yoga for developing a higher humanity – what he called a 'supramental' being beyond the ego-based human mind and its genetic and karmic limitations. He stressed bringing down the Supermind, the solar intelligence of the Godhead, for taking not only the individual but also the planet itself from darkness to light.

Aurobindo stressed an 'integral yoga', a term he first invented to describe combining the yogas of knowledge, devotion and works, providing appropriate teachings and practices for all aspects of our nature. His Yoga aims not simply at individual realization but at world transformation, at a change in the very Earth consciousness itself from a mere force of ignorance to a Divine energy.

For his inspiration Aurobindo went all the way back to the ancient *Vedas*, whose yogic value, hidden behind archaic symbols like the fire ritual, had all but been forgotten for centuries, and which western translators and interpreters starting with Max Mueller had failed to understand.

Aurobindo's main focus was the *Rig Veda,* the oldest Vedic text, on which he wrote extensively, particularly its Agni or fire hymns, which he translated into English.[196] In the *Vedas* Aurobindo found an organic and evolutionary approach to Yoga working with the body, the Earth and the forces of nature to bring about a higher creation in the world. He used these ancient and eternal Vedic insights as the foundation to build his own futuristic planetary Yoga. He relied on the *Vedas* probably more than any other great modern guru in India.

Most important for Aurobindo's Integral Yoga is the role of Agni or the sacred fire as the representative of the Divine Will within us, what he calls the 'psychic being' or essence of our spiritual striving as a soul. He emphasized awakening Agni as the first step in our spiritual development, as the very inner wakefulness necessary for all higher practices to be effective. According to him, only those whose inner fire is awake can really practice Yoga and understand its methods. He writes:

> *To what gods shall the sacrifice be offered? Who shall be invoked to manifest and protect in the human being this increasing Godhead?*
>
> *Agni first, for without him the sacrificial flame cannot burn on the altar of the soul. That flame of Agni is the seven-tongued power of the Will, a force of God instinct with knowledge. This conscious and forceful will is the immortal guest in our mortality, a pure priest and a divine worker, the mediator between earth and heaven. It carries what we offer to the higher Powers and brings back in return their force and delight and joy into our humanity.[197]*

Aurobindo's insight, his social, political and artistic vision as well as his yogic realization — especially his ability to bring the Vedic Rishi culture back to the modern world — make his work essential for the development of any Planetary Yoga. He was also a great devotee of the Goddess and emphasized her role as the world-transforming Divine Shakti.

His main disciple and co-guru was a French woman, mystic and occultist named Mira, often simply called 'the Mother'. Sri Aurobindo saw in her the advent of the Divine will-power or Shakti necessary for such a Planetary Yoga to occur. The Mother's presence, which I have also felt on many occasions, remains in the world to facilitate this process, just as Sri Aurobindo remains close by the Earth plane to oversee it. Her force can be felt as much in the West as in the East, particularly in the flowers that she was so fond of, like the jasmine and lotus, which are reminders of our soul's aspiration in life. Yet it remains strongest in Pondicherry at the Aurobindo Ashram from which emanates a pillar of light to guide the planet.

Aurobindo left as perhaps his greatest work, the epic poem *Savitri*, perhaps the longest poem in the English language, to describe his world-transforming Yoga. Savitri is the woman of Yoga, the woman of the Divine Sun, who embodies the Shakti necessary to take the planet from darkness to light.[198] His poem outlines her journey throughout all the worlds and planes of existence in order to bring about a transformation at the deepest and darkest core of matter within us.

The Role of India in Planetary Transformation

According to Aurobindo, India is the Divine Mother incarnate among the nations of the world. India's soul or purpose as a nation is to serve as the spiritual guide and guru of nations to lead humanity forward into a truly planetary age. If any nation can lead the world spiritually, it is probably India, which has never lost its ancient spiritual and yogic roots.

Today there is a new movement in India — based considerably the inspiration of great yogis like Sri Aurobindo and Swami Vivekananda — to reclaim this higher spiritual destiny of the land. Unfortunately, few in the West, even those who practice Yoga, know of this movement, much less are part of it. If we hear about it at all, it is generally labeled as backward or fundamentalist because it does not cater to western commercial or political values. Yet this Vedic revival is becoming a powerful force in India, not only among the spiritually minded but also among scientists and businessmen, who recognize that such yogic knowledge is not simply a relic from the past but a key to the future. India's real place in the world is not in becoming another materialistic nation like those of the West but of showing the way to a civilization based on spiritual freedom and oneness with both Nature and God.[199]

I have been very much involved in this movement for reawakening India to its spiritual purpose — working with social, intellectual and spiritual groups in the country over the past fifteen years. I have written several books on. this topic that have addressed it in some detail.[200] This work centers on redefining the Hindu tradition or Sanatana Dharma, humanity's oldest of the major world religions, in the planetary age. It includes promoting Vedic knowledge through Yoga, Ayurveda, Vedic Astrology and Vedanta, as universal forms of wisdom. It emphasizes a new view of ancient India and the *Vedas*, reflecting recent archaeological discoveries that show the great antiquity of Vedic culture in India as even possibly the true cradle of civilization.

Whether India can function as the real guru of nations remains to be seen, but it is doubtful whether there can be any real spiritual awakening in humanity if it does not first occur in India, which has always carried so much of our planet's spiritual aspiration. Those looking to a planetary transformation should not forget the place of India as an important catalyst for this process or regard what happens there as unimportant. They should visit the country and dialogue with the great teachers of the region, whose voices need to be heard all over the world.

The Fire of Yoga and Higher Human Evolution

Throughout our evolutionary journey, the same fire of the soul has been capable of diverse transformations, creating new powers out of itself from the density of the mineral realm to the intelligence of human beings. It contains yet another great transformation, a secret God seed that can prepare our way to a higher state of consciousness beyond the current limitations of our species.

Latent within us is another fire that can bring about a radical change of awareness from the individual to the universal. This is as monumental an evolutionary step as the one that initially developed human beings out of the animal kingdom . Our species is meant to be the matrix of this new 'fire of consciousness' that is at this moment only flickering dimly within us.

We must prepare a new birth of the sacred fire that leads beyond the human to the Divine. Not all human beings may be called to this task, but those who earnestly seek the spiritual life must take this mission upon themselves if they want to go far in their inner quest. As our current human consciousness appears inadequate to guide the evolutionary process on our planet, or even to protect the planet today, it is imperative that at least a few of succeed in embodying this higher force in our lives.

We must become mothers, as it were, of the soul fire within us; we must gestate it and deliver it forth into a higher birth. In this process it is we ourselves who die and are reborn; much like the Phoenix bird that resurrects itself from the fire. This yogic fire alchemy can be found behind the many paths and branches of Yoga.

Kundalini: The Serpent Fire of Yoga

The fire of consciousness is best known in yogic thought as the *Kundalini* or the 'Serpent Fire', said to be coiled like a serpent at the base of the spine. Kundalini represents a very subtle yet extremely powerful bioelectrical force, with a lightning-like action to unfold higher states of consciousness and perception. It is said to be composed of primal sound and mantra that constitute the energy of consciousness.[201] It contains the secret evolutionary power of nature within us, motivating us towards a higher consciousness and Self-realization.[202]

According to great yogis, the Kundalini is the root energy of the soul and carries its power.[203] It is the ultimate transformative power of the soul's fire. When the Kundalini awakens, it rises through the spine and opens the seven chakras that are the seats of higher consciousness placed along it. Once it reaches the head or crown chakra, our consciousness is liberated from time and space and we realize the universal Self, becoming one with the cosmic being or infinite light. Kundalini is the fire of the soul that is the basis of all evolutionary transformations. Its yogic awakening helps unfold our species potential to realize God.[204]

Kundalini Yoga is part of many Yoga paths. Different forms of Kundalini Yoga teach us how to access this power through various practices of asana, pranayama, mantra, visualization and meditation. The term 'Kundalini Yoga' has been popularized in the West mainly through Yogi Bhajan and the western Sikh community,[205] which uses the name for its White Tantric Yoga practices. However, in India, Kundalini Yoga is more commonly a Hindu practice, relating to various Tantric traditions of which there are many throughout the country from Tamil Nadu in the south to Kashmir in the north.

Unfortunately, Tantric Yoga and Kundalini are often wrongly equated today with mere sexual practices, when they are really a means of developing our internal energy to transcend our bodily urges. Kundalini Yoga is not about sexual enjoyment but about redirecting the essence of our vitality to unite with the great powers of the conscious universe.[206] Most of the sexual Kundalini Yoga practices

that are emphasized today have little to do with the higher
Tantric traditions. Some are even modern inventions.

A form of Yoga now common in the West that is also
connected to both the Vedic Rishi tradition and later
Kundalini approaches is the 'Kriya Yoga' tradition, which
Paramahamsa Yogananda first brought from India to the
United States in the nineteen twenties.[207] Yogananda, the
author of the classic book *Autobiography of a Yogi*, has been
perhaps the most significant figure in the Yoga tradition in
America over the past century. Kriya Yoga emphasizes special pranayama techniques along with meditation and devotional practices, and is a comprehensive, yet practical integral Yoga for arousing the Kundalini and opening the
chakras. It reflects the ancient Vedic fire Yoga, as
Yogananda himself notes:

> *The real or inner fire ceremony is the uniting of life with
> the greater Life, by the practice of pranayama or Kriya
> Yoga, the technique of life-control.*
>
> *When through the astral fire-rite the pranic current
> withdraws into the subtle centers of the spine and brain,
> then instead of wasting its energies in reforming matter-
> bound cells, the freed reinforced prana awakens those cells
> with divine life by baptizing them with the light of
> Spirit.*[208]

Yogananda himself mentioned the need for India and the
United States to come together for the future evolution of
humanity. He saw the combination of the yogic spirituality of India with the scientific humanism of America as the
two complementary powers necessary to lead civilization
forward to its higher purpose. Much of his work in America
was aimed in that direction.

Babaji — the supreme guru behind the Kriya Yoga tradition — who was said to have achieved physical immortality through its practice, is perhaps the ultimate guide for
this planetary transformation needed today. He may be one
of the old Vedic Rishis who has remained with us through
the centuries, as many Rishis, particularly Vasishta and

Agastya, were not only great yogis but the very founders of the Yoga tradition.

Personally, I practice a Vedic form of Kundalini and Mantra Yoga based on the teachings of Ganapati Muni, the chief disciple of Ramana Maharshi, which has much in common with Yogananda's Kriya Yoga. It uses pranayama, mantra and meditation as tools of Self-inquiry, emphasizing the sacred fire of awareness in the spiritual heart. It also follows an integral approach, using practices from both the Yoga of devotion and the Yoga of knowledge, including surrender to the Divine along with formless meditation methods.

Following an older Vedic vision, it works with the three great powers of Fire, Wind and Sun (Agni, Vayu and Surya) as universal principles of consciousness that comprehend the entire movement of life both inwardly and outwardly. In this present book, I have mainly discussed the fire or Agni aspect of this great Vedic teaching, but the other Vedic deities have their principles and practices as well, which are just as complex and profound.

The Hindu God Ganesha, the elephant-headed God, is the master deity who oversees the Kundalini force in the Yoga Tradition, dwelling in the root chakra from which the Kundalini rises. To safely and effectively arouse the Kundalini, one should first meditate upon Ganesha in this chakra. It is quite fitting that this elephant image — the largest yet wisest, most caring and gentle of animals — represents the natural intelligence behind our own higher evolutionary process. To control this powerful Kundalini force we must be as grounded as an elephant, possessing its giant strength and enduring power.

Kundalini and the Spiritual Heart

Yet as representing the power of the soul, Kundalini has its base in the spiritual heart. Though working through the chakras from below, the Kundalini is rooted in the spiritual heart at the core of our being.

In this regard, we must recognize that the spiritual

heart, the seat of the soul, is not the same as the physical or emotional heart. The spiritual heart can be identified with the entire channel at the center of the spine, called the *Sushumna* in yogic thought, through which the Kundalini arises. Opening the Sushumna, therefore, is also opening the spiritual heart. The spiritual heart is not simply the center of our being but surrounds us on all sides as the greater field of awareness in which we live.

Many Yogis speak of an additional subtle channel, the immortal or *Amrita Nadi*, which runs from the crown chakra down to the spiritual heart, as the ultimate goal of all practice. This is another way that we can experience the movement of the Kundalini back to the heart.

In this regard there are two primary yogic approaches. The first is the movement of the Kundalini up the spine or the ascent of the fire of consciousness that takes us through all the levels of creation to the supreme light. The second is its movement back and within, a withdrawal into the fire of consciousness in the spiritual heart that is behind all creation. The first approach can be called 'ascending path'; the second the 'path within'.

Both ascending and internalizing approaches are complementary. When we reach the highest light, we also discover that it is the deepest flame within us. When we dive into our deepest light, we also discover that it is the highest flame behind the entire universe.

One can go directly to the fire of the spiritual heart either through the power of Divine love in the Yoga of devotion (Bhakti Yoga) or through the power of deep meditation in the Yoga of knowledge (Jnana Yoga). Each of these Yogas also has its specific and clearly delineated methods, practices and attitudes.

The merging of the mind in the heart through the process of Self-inquiry is the main method of the Yoga of knowledge, such as taught by Ramana Maharshi,[209] and the essence of non-dualistic or Advaita Vedanta.[210] Many Buddhist and Taoist meditational approaches are similar. Through it we reach our higher nature of pure awareness that is the Absolute reality beyond all manifestation. As the *Upanishads* tell us:

> To the extent that the mind is absorbed or gone to rest in the heart, that is true knowledge and liberation. Anything else is just a lot of useless words.[211]

Bhakti Yoga, the yogic path of devotion, works to merge our minds into the deity in the heart, however we may wish to formulate it as the Divine Father, Divine Mother, the Beloved or as formless in nature — a process that can be called 'becoming one with God'.[212] It uses many different forms and figures like Krishna, Shiva, Rama, Hanuman or the Goddess. Much of Christian mysticism, focusing on the sacred heart of Jesus or the compassion of Mother Mary has a similar devotional approach. Judaic and Sufi mysticism is also often of this type.

Besides accessing the Kundalini force from below, one can call down the Divine grace or Shakti from above. The Divine consciousness can descend into us and aid us in our ascent, accompanying us as our inner guide as we move upward in consciousness. This is the way of Sri Aurobindo's Integral Yoga in which a higher force, the supreme grace of the Mother — her white light — guides the entire process, making it both safe and certain.

The approach of Yoga must be as many-sided as we are. There is no single path of Yoga that is meant to be imposed upon everyone like a creed or dogma, much less to be mass-produced or turned into a franchise! Yet all yogic approaches involve setting in motion a higher evolutionary force or Kundalini power in one form or another. As creating a new birth of our souls, they involve energizing the Divine Mother or Goddess energy within us. Her Divine grace is the ultimate power. The tools, methods and processes we employ are but aids for what the Divine will and energy decides. What is essential is to awaken the fire within ourselves in a way that is true to our own being and its specific karma in life. The fire is the guide and knows the way to the light, of which it is also the seed.

Generating a Planetary Fire of Consciousness

Just as there is a higher evolutionary power hidden within each person, a similar power is hidden deep within the planet. There is what we could call a 'global Kundalini' or 'planetary yogic fire', the power of the planet's soul. It is coiled like a serpent around the Earth's core sustaining its primary electrical, pranic and consciousness forces. The soul of the planet, the planetary Purusha, carries this power as its means of expression and development.

The same is true of the universe as a whole. There is a universal Kundalini or serpent power upholding all the worlds, represented by Lord Sesha, the serpent on which Lord Vishnu, the supreme Person dwells while dreaming the dream of the universe. In this regard, we should remember that Patanjali, the great rishi who compiled the *Yoga Sutras*, the guidebook of classical Yoga, was said to be an incarnation of Lord Sesha.

The fire at the center of the Earth has a spiritual basis, a will and purpose hidden behind its metallic and mineral heat and density. Only a small portion of its energy is accessible to us ordinarily — as we work only with the material resources of the planet, not its spiritual treasures, to which our species is generally blind. Yet if enough individuals cultivate the fire of Yoga with a consciousness of its roots in the Earth, then this global force of transformation can be aroused to help develop a planetary consciousness in humanity.

The planet has its own soul and sacred fire which contains the blueprint and the power for all its potential evolution. This planetary sacred fire is the carrier flame for our own higher evolution as a species. The aspiration of the planetary soul is the basis of our own individual spiritual striving. The Earth is seeking God through us — developing life, senses, mind and heart in order to merge into the Infinite.

We must learn to energize this planetary power of consciousness not only individually but also collectively. This is the real purpose behind spiritual gatherings, collective rituals or meditation retreats. When individuals come together for inner practices — whether physically or only mentally — they can generate a power that grows geometrically according to the degree to which their hearts are attuned and unified. They can create a powerful psychic energy in the collective mind that can neutralize even the darkest karmas that haunt our species. This is the purpose of *satsangas* or gatherings of spiritual seekers in the name or in the presence of the guru.

Even individuals working alone can help increase this planetary force, if they access the consciousness in nature or connect to the greater spiritual heritage of the planet. We do have the power to change our world, not from the outside but from within. From the fire in our hearts we can access the planetary fire and through it the Sun, the stars and the supreme cosmic light of awareness.

To do this we must attune our minds to the center of the Earth and the center of the Sun and allow the currents of light, life and love to flow freely between the two. We must honor the soul of the planet in all of its forms from its metallic core to our own higher intelligence. We must make our life into a ritual, prayer and meditation to carry the spiritual aspiration of all creatures and all the ages. Remember when you pray or meditate to first honor the Earth on which you sit, not as a mere support but as the very fountain of Divine energy that you are seeking.

The Ascension of the Sacred Fire

However one may define the ascension of the sacred fire, we must enter into its movement in order to really grow in life. It is not the name or form of what we do that matters but the quality of the flame we energize through it. We must awaken the soul individually, collectively and on the planet as a whole, not simply as a religious belief or a personal urge but through a cosmic sense of unity. We must link our inner fires with the fires of all people, all nature on the planet and the energies of the greater universe beyond. We must unite the light within us with the light around us, merging consciousness into consciousness that has no limits.

The call of the sacred fire takes us to spiritual practice, meditation or Yoga in one form or another. We must heed that call, arousing our soul's memories to its eternal striving. Our evolutionary journey as a species has just begun. At this point, we are lost in its backwaters and must now make a radical change of course in order to really go forward again.

We are all fire beings, with the eyes of the Sun and the intelligence of the stars. We contain the rocks in our bones and the rivers in our veins. We are made of this universe, which lives within us on all levels of our being. We are the universe awakening to itself, discovering its secret soul and hidden spirit, reclaiming its greater destiny as a single Being of light.

We are Nature and all of Nature moves through us. We cannot be apart even if we try. We overflow into all Being, which ever arises within us through our very blood and breath. Our true civilization is that of the cosmos, not that of one nation or one species only. Our current alienation from the conscious universe is a dangerous detour from our real evolutionary path, which we must not let continue.

We must once again embrace nature within and around us, not merely as body but also as spirit. We must reclaim our secret world soul. We must live our sacred fire, even if it consumes us. We can burn up all darkness, fear and attachment into a new radiance of joy. Our true being will not be lost in the process but will emerge glittering and transformed like pure gold extracted from crude ore.

We must strive to transform our planet into a harmonious world that appears like a jewel of love in the greater universe of light. We must fulfill the legacy of our souls, our ancestors and our spiritual guides. We cannot abandon either ourselves or the world that we are part of. Otherwise, whatever we may do is a rejection of our inner life, a separation from our deeper being that will keep us in sorrow, cut off both from our hearts and all other creatures. We can only become the entire universe. That is our ultimate, primary and enduring destiny. It is the only way beyond death and sorrow.

Our Future as a Species

There is an entire higher evolution available to our species. There is a natural force and intelligence within us that we can activate in order to catalyze this process. The potential is there, should we be ready and willing to pursue it.

This higher spiritual evolution is our true future as a species. Our true progress does not consist of a devastated planet overpopulated by a greedy and selfish humanity. It is a planet in which consciousness and nature unite in a supernature, through an enlightened humanity in harmony with its world and aware of its cosmic purpose. This is an evolution not into time but beyond time and into eternity, where we move beyond history to immortality.

We can take the forces of our own nature — our food, breath, impressions, emotions and thoughts — and use them as building blocks for a new vision of both Self and world. All the tools of Divinity are hidden within us in the very natural rhythms of our lives. We need only energize them on a daily basis and in time they will, quite unexpectedly, yield a magical transformation beyond our greatest dreams. If we cultivate our internal fires with love and attention, all the light in the universe must eventually come to us, unraveling the deepest secrets of existence.

As we return to the circle of the sacred fire, it will expand beyond all boundaries, at the same time bringing us back to our spiritual home in the heart that is the real goal of our journey — fire to Fire, light to Light, and consciousness to Consciousness!

CHAPTER SEVENTEEN

Our Five Internal Fires

The following chapter contains a table of the five main fires (Agnis) of our nature — body, breath, emotion, mind and soul[213] — and the five states in which they may be burning. This classification allows us to recognize the condition of our internal fires and determine how harmoniously they are working:

The Five States of Fire

1. Excess or burning too high.
2. Deficient or burning too low.
3. Variable or inconsistent.
4. Creating smoke or burning impurely.
5. Burning with clarity, light and balance.

Fire has five states both externally in the outer world and within us.[214] While we can easily recognize their differences externally, we can also apply the same model to understand them relative to our internal fires:

- In the excess state, fire becomes destructive. Instead of providing warmth, light and nourishment, it becomes too hot and makes us overheated, burning us up in one manner or another. This condition is more common in people of a hot, fiery or willful (Pitta) temperament.

- In the deficient state, fire fails to create the proper warmth and energy and leaves us cold, weak, constricted and unable to function in the right manner. This condition is usually caused by the fuel or food for the fire being wet and is more common in people of a watery or emotional (Kapha) temperament.

- In the variable state, fire is unpredictable and can either burn too high or too low, shifting suddenly from one condition to the other, disrupting our organic equilibrium and leading to various extremes. This is usually caused by too much wind on the fire and is more common in people of an airy or nervous (Vata) temperament.

- In its smoky state, fire becomes toxic, breeding various distorted conditions of body and mind. This is usually caused by a wrong fuel and occurs more commonly in people who have a lot of toxins in their systems (Ama) owing to wrong living practices.

- In its balanced state, fire provides warmth, light, energy and nourishment in a consistent and harmonious manner. This condition can be achieved by any person who is able to create internal balance through conscious living and right management of food, nourishment, expression and behavior.

Observe whether your five fires of the physical, vital, emotional, mental and spiritual aspects of your nature are burning properly, as indicated below. Learn to monitor your internal fires according to their signs and symptoms.

1. Physical Body - Digestive Fire

1. Excess or burning too high	Excessive appetite, abnormally high hunger and thirst, high or fast metabolism, excessive body heat, quick metabolism and fast elimination
2. Deficient or burning too low	Poor appetite, dislike of food, low or slow metabolism, excessive weight gain, low body heat, sluggish elimination
3. Variable or inconsistent	Variable or nervous digestion and elimination, irregular appetite, irregular body heat
4. Creating smoke or burning impurely	Toxic indigestion and elimination, unhealthy metabolism, skin rashes, discolorations or infections
5. Burning with clarity, light and balance	Healthy but moderate appetite, balanced metabolism, good digestion and elimination, good complexion

2. Energy Body - Pranic or Breath Fire

1. Excess or burning too high	Aggressive energy, excessive movement, lack of self-control, impulsiveness, too much heat in the breath
2. Deficient or burning too low	Low energy, lack of movement, sedentary nature, lack of motivation, weakness or shortness of breath
3. Variable or inconsistent	Erratic or changeable energy levels and movement, erratic breathing patterns, hyperactivity followed by exhaustion
4. Creating smoke or burning impurely	Toxic energy, intoxication, delirium, impurities or toxins in the lungs and in the blood
5. Burning with clarity, light and balance	Balanced, calm and consistent energy and movement, steady, deep breathing

3. Emotional Body - Emotional Fire

1. Excess or burning too high	Anger, jealousy, lust, hot temper, prone to argument, conflict or violence
2. Deficient or burning too low	Depression, grief, fear, bitterness, deep-seated attachments, caught in emotional lethargy or resignation
3. Variable or inconsistent	Moodiness, emotional instability, changeability and agitation, anxiety, hypersensitivity
4. Creating smoke or burning impurely	Emotional delusion, suspicion, paranoia, hatred and turbulence
5. Burning with clarity, light and balance	Love, joy, forgiveness, contentment, fearlessness, emotional sense of ease and well-being

4. Mental Body - Mental Fire

1. Excess or burning too high	Overly critical mind, judgmental, self-righteousness, opinionated, argumentative
2. Deficient or burning too low	Dull or slow mind, weak reasoning ability, poor perception, bad judgment, poor learning skills
3. Variable or inconsistent	Confusion, indecisiveness, doubt, inability to concentrate, unstable beliefs or shifting values
4. Creating smoke or burning impurely	Mental delusion, wrong values, destructive beliefs, wrong perceptions, disturbed imagination
5. Burning with clarity, light and balance	Clarity of mind, balanced judgment, wisdom, discrimination, insight

5. Soul - Spiritual Fire

1. Excess or burning too high	Religious fanaticism, intolerance or fundamentalism, intolerance of other beliefs or spiritual practices
2. Deficient or burning too low	Lack of faith or spiritual aspiration, attachment to the material world, spiritual darkness
3. Variable or inconsistent	Inconsistent faith, erratic aspiration, unsteady practices, lack of peace or spiritual equilibrium
4. Creating smoke or burning impurely	Religious or spiritual delusions and self-aggrandizement, Kundalini or medita-tional disorders, disturbed altered states of consciousness
5. Burning with clarity, light and balance	Soul awareness, enlightened conscious-ness, internal peace, beatitude, bliss, oneness with God or the higher Self

Observe the conditions of your own internal fires and whether they are too high, too low, variable, burning impurely or properly balanced on these five different levels. Through these you can determine whether you are a 'high fire' type person, a 'low fire' type person, a 'variable fire' type person, or a 'balanced fire' type person and whether you are suffering from toxic fire, and on each of the five levels of body, energy, emotion, mind and soul. See what kind of fire you are contributing to the universal flame, whether you are sustaining the higher light or promoting smoke or darkness. Note how your different fires are inter-related and how they change over time.

We should strive to keep our internal fires in a balanced or clear state.

The key to this is to provide each fire with its proper fuel. These are:

- Natural and organic vegetarian food, herbs and spices for the physical fire,[215] particularly spices like ginger, cinnamon, basil, turmeric, saffron and cardamom, with cayenne, black pepper and mustard for very low fire conditions.

- Good quality air and Prana for the vital fire, such as derived from deep breathing practices (pranayama), calming exercises like Yoga asanas, walking, gardening or hiking in nature. Living in a natural environment with many positive life-energies and activities. For low Pranic fire, the fuel of strong Prana through strong pranayama practices like Bhastrika, Kapalabhati or right-nostril breathing (Surya Bhedana).

- For the emotional fire: positive, supportive and loving emotions from an emotionally healthy environment and associations with like-minded spiritual people. Directing one's emotions to the Divine in Bhakti Yoga (the Yoga of Devotion), particularly the use of mantra, prayer and Divine Names. For low emotional fire, taking refuge in forms of God like Shiva, Rama or Durga that grant us fearlessness and protection.

- For the mind's fire: higher spiritual teachings and insights from great books, gurus or spiritual friends, along with practices like contemplation, concentration, mantra and meditation. Following the Yoga of Knowledge (Jnana Yoga) and higher philosophies of Yoga and Vedanta. For low mental fire, the practice of concentration on light, fire, the Sun or illuminating spiritual insights.

- For the core fire of the soul: proper spiritual sources of nourishment through an internal connection to great gurus, teachers, forms of the Divine and the Divine presence in the universe. Awareness of God and the higher Self. Cultivation of meditation and samadhi (mergence into the flame of love and awareness in the heart). For low spiritual fire, coming into physical proximity to great living teachers or holy places.

Tend to your soul's fires as you would tend to a fire in your fireplace on a cold winter night. Remember that your true happiness dwells in your inner fire, along with your connection to all beings, with whom you share a common home and hearth. Your inner being remains ever present around that fire of the heart, though your outer mind and body may wander far away.

CHAPTER EIGHTEEN

Yogic Fire Practices

The ancient Vedic Fire Yoga provides many methods to work with the sacred powers of the universe. The following are a few that you can use to contact your inner fire and experience its different energies.

I. Meditation on the Witnessing Flame

The soul within our hearts is the immutable witness of all that we do — the eternal and inextinguishable flame within us. Our soul is the seer of all time and space, encompassing all our experiences, desires and aspirations in life. Returning to this core flame of the witnessing consciousness allows us to transcend all external disturbances and difficulties, to step out of all material and bodily limitations into a pure unbounded existence and peace.

One of the most important meditation practices is to dwell in this witnessing consciousness within the heart and to strive to return to it whenever we may lose our center or fall into conflict or confusion. To enter into this meditation practice, simply recognize your true Self as the witnessing awareness behind both body and mind, which is not tainted or limited by any of their activities, good or bad, happy or sad.[216]

We can all easily sense this witnessing awareness if we simply look within. It is that part of ourselves which remains unaffected by any external changes, gain and loss, pleasure or pain. Whenever you get agitated in life remember that all-seeing flame within you that is your true soul. Offer whatever afflicts you into this fire of the witness for purification and transformation.[217] You are the silent witness of all that is, a fountain of peace and contentment.

II. Meditation on the Spiritual Heart from the Upanishads

Meditating on the fire of consciousness in the heart is the central practice of the ancient Vedic fire yoga. It can also be used along with other spiritual methods.[218] *However, we should note that the lotus of the spiritual heart, in which the flame of the soul is located, is not the ordinary heart chakra, the fourth of the seven usual chakras of the subtle body, but the spiritual heart center behind all the chakras.* Its eight petals include the other seven chakras and their different lotuses, with itself as the eighth.

1. In the center of your heart, visualize a lotus with eight petals, dark blue in color, representing the eight directions of space. In the small space at its center the entire universe and all creatures can be found, including everyone that you have ever known or loved and all that you have ever been or ever could wish to be.

2. In the middle of this heart lotus visualize a flame the size of a thumb, golden in color, taking the shape of your own bodily image. This is the Agni Purusha or fire being within you. It represents your subtle body that energizes your physical body from within.

The spiritual flame in the heart is the source of all light and life within you. It takes in all your experiences as food for the soul. Projecting its energy downward from the heart and out through the navel, it heats your entire body from the feet to the head, enkindling all the other fires of the body, breath and mind.

3. At the crest of this flame of the heart, visualize your own soul, the essence of your being, atomic in size, flashing forth like a radiant streak of golden lightning in a dark blue cloud, illuminating the entire fire.

Your soul is the point of light that energizes your life flame. It carries the essence of all your experiences throughout your many births. It flashes golden as the subtlest of all forms. Its electrical currents pervade your entire being and energize every moment of your life, lighting up your mind, heart, brain and nervous system.

4. In the middle of this lightning flash of the soul, smaller than the smallest point, recognize the Supreme Self, the universal Spirit or God, greater than the great, infinite in size, as the pure light of the Sun beyond all darkness.

The unbounded light of consciousness is hidden deep within you, yet even more subtle and radiant than the powerful light of the soul. That smallest of points is the doorway to the vast expanse of pure existence. That point of pure light at the core of your being is the Creator (Brahma), Preserver (Vishnu) and Destroyer (Shiva) of the entire universe, the imperishable reality and the highest truth beyond all sorrow and limitation. Using the lightning ray of your soul as the means of entry, cross the threshold into that supernal Sun of pure consciousness that lies behind the entire universe, illumining all things with the clear light of awareness. There is nothing else in life that you need to do. This meditation is the ultimate fulfillment of the soul, the return to the highest light.

The lotus of the heart is closed and turned downward in the ordinary state of human consciousness defined by time, space, karma and ego. The flame of the soul is suppressed and its consciousness is trapped inside the boundaries of the body and the senses, like a bird in a cage. Through the practice of Yoga and meditation, the lotus of the heart turns upward and blooms. It opens inwardly into infinity and eternity, releasing all sorrow and discontent into bliss. The soul becomes free to travel throughout the entire universe as its own Self, free from the bondage of time and space as an essence of light and love.

Learn to dive deep into your spiritual heart with either the power of devotion (Bhakti) or the force of concentration (Jnana). Recognize the heart as the source of all that you are and all that are meant to be. Returning to the spiritual heart is the supreme Yoga.

III. The Seven Yogic Fire Offerings

There are various yogic fire offerings — internal rituals or Yajnas in Sanskrit — in which we offer various aspects of our being into the sacred fire of awareness for purification and transformation. Such Yogic Yajnas are sacrifices of the personal self or ego, through which we can realize our higher or Divine Self beyond separation. Through these we can learn to develop all our inner fires.

1. The Body Offering

Visualize your entire body seated in the lotus posture, dwelling like a flame within the lotus of your heart. Your body is sustained by and assumes the form of this flame in which it is purified, energized and transformed.

Offer your body consciousness into this internal flame or fire body. Along with it offer all your physical pain, disease, discomforts and inadequacies for it to transform as needed or simply to render irrelevant in its purer light.

Let your body arise radiant from the fire, full of lightness, joy and energy, itself a spiritual flame in physical manifestation, an embodiment of the light, no longer tied to the density and inertia of physical matter. Let your body feel like a flame of light that no darkness can limit.

2. The Breath Offering

Inhale deeply and slowly, directing the energy of your

breath* downward and inward to its source in the fire of the heart. Offer our all your vital energies, instincts, urges and desires, all the movements of the life-force within you, into this core life-fire of the heart that is ever full, happy, radiant and content.

Exhale, directing your transformed vitality as a force of health, creativity and energy to your entire body, filling every limb, joint and organ with renewed strength, vigor and capacity.

Remember always to breathe with the light, making your every breath an offering of the light to the light. Let your breath be a sharing of your internal light with the light of all creation that is the life of all.

3. The Speech Offering

Take any mantra or prayer that you like, such as OM or HREEM (the heart mantra),[219] and repeat or chant it softly at least one hundred times. Direct its energy downward from your throat to the heart. Let the flame in the heart repeat the mantra for you, carrying your wishes deep into the subconscious mind and into all your life experience to transform your karma.

Let the flame in the heart speak the mantra back to you, bringing along with it the guidance that you are seeking from your higher Self. Learn to speak from the flame in the heart, to echo its voice of silence, and to articulate that flame of knowing within you as your true voice. It is the Divine Word within you that holds the key to all wisdom and grace.

4. The Mind Offering

Offer your entire mind — all your thoughts, feelings, emotions and sensations — into the fire of the heart. Merge your restless mind into the deep and boundless silence of the ocean of the heart. Sink the mind in the heart's flame, and let all of your worries, doubts and anxieties be consumed.

Keep your awareness centered in the heart, and let all

your wandering thoughts dissolve back into it like flames from a fire or waves on the sea. Whenever you are confused or disturbed, simply return your mind to the heart in which there is neither dilemma nor duality, where no thought or worry can enter. Let your mind itself be an offering to the light within you. Let the flame be the knower, seer and thinker within you, where the mind is no mind and memory is only of the presence of light.

5. The Self-consecration

Offer your human self, your self-image, your ego, your pride and ambition into the spiritual flame, the true Self within your heart. Let the flame consume all your karmas, attachments, fears and desires, from this or previous lives. Recognize that only what you have voluntarily given up can become permanently yours, not as your possession but as a gift of God. Your true Self is no thing and no body, but only that pure light within you.

Let your purified self come forth from the inner fire with a new mission of consciousness and enlightenment for the entire world. Learn to be your Self of light and radiate that Self in all that you do. Welcome all other selves as different aspects of the light that is your true nature.

6. The Planetary Offering

Visualize the great Earth with her lands, mountains, seas and clouds and all the varied people and creatures that inhabit her. Offer your vision of the Earth as a gift to the sacred fire at the center of the Earth for the fire to transform for its own higher purpose. Recognize the planet and all that lives on it as an offering to the universal life that is the heart of the Earth.

Out of this flame visualize a new Earth purified of all environmental damage and destruction, with a new spiritual humanity in harmony with all creatures leading the planet forward into the light of truth and divinity. Learn to radiate this inner spiritual vision of the planet as you walk on the Earth, bringing light with your every step, touching the light on the ground on which you walk.

7. The Universal Offering

Visualize the entire universe with all of its planets, stars and galaxies, all of its worlds, creatures and deities, blooming like a giant lotus of light in the sea of space. Offer that flower into the flame of the Cosmic Fire which itself is also that same flower of light.

Recognize this universal flower of the Cosmic Fire as the deepest core of your being, as the flame within the lotus of your own heart. See all things as an offering of the One to the One, the infinite to the infinite, in which unity and boundlessness are ever preserved and ever renewed. Let your light pervade all the directions, with the entire universe at home within you. See all things as a play of the light of consciousness that can encompass all of space outside of you and the essence of your being within.

IV. Meditations on Fire in Nature

We have discussed the development of the universe through the cosmic fire, the fire in the Sun, the atmospheric fire (lightning) and the fire at the core of the Earth. We have explored our sacred journey as souls through the natural kingdoms on Earth as fire in the rocks, the waters, plants, animals and humans. We should remember and contemplate these fires on a regular basis as we observe the world around us. All these apparently different forms of light are really only different aspects of who we are and carry the secret force of what our life is really meant to be. We are these many fires of both nature and the spirit. Contemplating these fires of the universe is another important path of meditation and perhaps the ultimate form of science as well.

Fire also governs the cycle of time. The fire of time creates, ripens and destroys all things by its power. Traditional fire rituals, like Vedic fire sacrifices, follow daily rhythms with practices at sunrise, noon and sunset — the high points of the transformation of the light during the day. Try to light a flame like a candle or ghee lamp, or burn incense at sunrise or sunset to honor the movement of the light during the day. Perform a Vedic fire offering if you can. Such daily offerings are called *Agnihotra* and can be done with a copper vessel, cow dung, wood, ghee and rice.[220]

Traditional fire rituals also have their monthly rhythms with special fires for the new, half and full moons — the points of the transformation of the light during the month. Try to light a flame or burn incense to honor the full moon, or at least meditate upon the Moon as the reflective light of the mind within you.

Seasonal rituals occur according to the spring and autumn equinoxes and the winter and summer solstices — the points of the transformation of the light during the year. Remember at these special times to offer some form of light, whether externally with a fire or candle or internally as a visualization or meditation, particularly at the winter solstice, which is the time of the year at which the light returns and gets renewed. Be aware of the cycles of the Sun as the light of lights and lord of time and as the perceptive power of consciousness within you. Eclipses of the Sun and Moon are additional special times of the transformation of the light during the year, with two sets of eclipses happening every year. Learn to honor these with some form of light.

All such transitional points of the day, month or year are important times for practicing meditation, our inner fire ritual. They are special junctures at which times our energy can be transformed, making pranayama good during these times as well.

Our own personal life cycle should be sanctified with rituals for birth, growth, maturation, retirement and death. Special events like starting school, marriage, entering a new house or starting a new career also have their important fires. Whatever we wish to achieve in life, we should also light a special flame for. We can use the methods of Vedic astrology and its special rituals and meditations for the stars and planets to sanctify such events, as well as to determine the most auspicious time for them.[221]

In addition, our society needs its collective sacred fires to promote harmony and understanding between people and to harmonize society with nature and with God. Public fire rituals are a great way to do this, whether small communal events, festivals or greater societal gatherings. These can be done in temples or outdoors along with prayer, mantra and meditation for universal peace and well-being. Vedic prayers for peace and peace-offerings can be a good model to follow in this regard. The Divine flame can purify and transform all things, but we must enkindle it along with the movement of our lives on all levels. As all life is a naturally movement of the light, this can be done simply and easily by following not only the visible and tangible rhythms of nature but also by following the subtle rhythms (rituals) of the soul, which are linked together.

V. OM and the Sacred Fire

The Divine Word OM is said to be the sound or mantra of Agni or the sacred fire. OM is composed of three letters, A, U, M. Its chanting is like lighting a fire.

- First, draw up the A-sound (pronounced long like the 'a' in father) from the base of the spine to the navel as if one were starting a great fire.

- Second, extend the A-sound into the U-sound (pronounced like 'oo' as in food), drawing the energy up from the navel into the heart as if one were making the fire grow and expand.

- Third, extend the U-sound into the M-sound (as in mmm), drawing the energy up from the heart into the head and finally out through the top of the head, making the fire into a crest that ascends into the infinite space of awareness beyond all time and manifestation.

Chanting OM in this way, one awakens one's own inner fire for the ascension to the Godhead within. Learn to ride your inner flame upward out of the body and into the entire universe of pure consciousness, all of which belongs to you as an immortal soul.

OM is part of a longer chant, the Gayatri, the most famous Vedic mantra, which beautifully reflects our soul's aspiration to the light of truth. Gayatri refers to the 'means of travel' and provides the power to propel our soul in its cosmic journey through the universe. It is has been the most commonly recited prayer in India for thousands of years and is still popular throughout the land.[222] It is repeated along with daily and seasonal rituals and also used for pranayama and meditation. The Gayatri mantra is a good prayer and aspiration to remember, connecting us up with all the forces of both nature and the spirit:[223]

> OM! Reverence to the Earth, the Atmosphere and Heaven.
> OM! We meditate upon the supreme flame of the Divine Creative Sun that he may inspire our souls.[224]

Uniting OM and HREEM: The Sound of the Infinite and the Sound of the Heart

After raising one's energy upward on inhalation to the top of the head with the mantra OM, a second step can be added to the practice. After the ascent through OM, bring your energy back down from the top of the head through the throat and into the spiritual heart on exhalation with the seed mantra HREEM. Return to the power of the infinite at the core of the soul within you. In this way you can combine the ascension of the spiritual fire through OM with its internalization through HREEM, the mantra of Divine grace and of the Divine descent into man.

HREEM is the mantra of the spiritual heart (Hridaya). It opens the small space within the heart in which the entire universe dwells. It is the source of the Divine Word, the unstruck sound that creates all things starting with space itself.[225] HREEM represents the golden light of the Sun of truth as it shines within us, carrying all creative, magic and wisdom powers within itself.

HREEM is also the prime mantra of the Goddess or Divine Mother and brings us all of her creative and transformative powers. You can use it to contact the Supreme Goddess in the heart; however you may wish to view Her.

The joint use of the two mantras OM and HREEM is the union of Shiva and Shakti, the cosmic masculine and feminine forces. You can use these two mantras together in order to unite the God and Goddess in your own heart as well as to contact their energy in the world around you.

This union of the infinite with the heart is the central teaching of the Vedic Fire Yoga. The unity of the sacred soul fire in the heart with the supreme light of consciousness is the essence of all knowledge. We should never to forget this great truth, even for a moment. It is our very heartbeat on both physical and spiritual levels. Remembering its power, there is nothing we cannot overcome — and our current planetary crisis can be dealt with directly and solved completely for the good of all.

VI
Appendices

1. List of Fires Mentioned in the Book

Below are the main sacred fires or Agnis mentioned in the book. The Rishis or seers of fire were able to yogically discern all these fires and determine their properties, including their healing and spiritual influences that we can access.

COSMIC

Universal - cosmic fire behind the entire universe

Galactic - fire behind the galaxy

Solar - fire in the stars

EARTH

Core - metallic fire at the Earth's core

Mantle - mineral fire in the Earth's mantle

Crust - magma fire erupting to the surface of the Earth

EVOLUTIONARY

Mineral - fire in the mineral kingdom

Plant - fire of photosynthesis in plants

Animal - digestive fire in animals

Human - fire of intelligence

COMMUNITY FIRES

Fire of the Family

Fire of the Tribe

Fire of the Community

Fire of Society

INTERNAL

Digestive Fire

Fire of the Breath

The Fires of the Senses

The Fire of the Mind, including emotion, will, intellect and intelligence

Fire of Consciousness

Fire of Healing

SPIRITUAL

Fire of the Soul or Individual Self - central flame in the heart

Fire of God or the Creator

Fire of the Supreme Self

YOGIC FIRES

The Fire of Asana

The Fire of Pranayama

The Fire of Internalization

The Fire of Concentration

The Fire of Meditation

The Fire of Bliss

The Fire of Divine Love

The Fire of Spiritual Knowledge

The Kundalini Fire

2. Glossary of Terms

Advaita - non-dualistic form of Vedanta, which teaches the absolute unity of all

Agni - inner or spiritual fire

Asana - yoga postures

Atman - higher Self

Ayur - life as a manifestation of the life-fire

Ayurveda - Vedic mind-body medicine

Bhakti Yoga - Yoga of devotion

Bhasma - Ashes from the sacred fire; also special Ayurvedic mineral preparations

Brahman - Absolute or supreme existence

Chakras - subtle energy centers

Devas - Divine powers of the conscious universe (the Gods)

Dharma - natural or universal law

Dhyana - meditation

Doshas - biological humors

Durga - Divine Mother in her protective and saving role

Ganesha - elephant-headed God and symbol of higher intelligence

Hanuman - monkey God and symbol of Prana

Jatharagni - digestive fire or fire in the belly

Jiva - life-essence of soul

Jivatman - individual soul

Jyoti - light

Jyotish - Vedic astrology as the science of light

Kapha dosha - biological water humor

Karma - effect of our actions in this and previous lives

Krishna - great avatar, yoga guru, teacher of Bhagavad Gita

Kundalini - serpent fire or energy of consciousness

Mahat - natural or cosmic intelligence responsible for the order that we see in the world of nature

Mantra - spiritually energized words and sounds

Nakshatras - lunar constellations, important karmic indicators

Paramatman - supreme or transcendent soul

Pitta dosha - biological fire humor

Prakriti - nature, particularly in terms of the practical power behind its action

Prana - vital force

Pranagni - life fire or fire of the breath

Pranayama - yogic breathing exercises

Pratyahara - yogic stage of interiorization of the mind and senses

Purusha - higher Self or Cosmic Person, Atman

Rama - the seventh incarnation or avatar of Vishnu as the Dharma king

Rig Veda - oldest Vedic text, consisting of the mantras of the ancient Rishis

Rishis - ancient Himalayan seers and sages

Shakti - Cosmic feminine force and Goddess energy as the primal power of the universe

Shiva - Cosmic masculine force and deity of supreme awareness

Skanda - Divine child and yogic fire God

Upanishads - ancient scriptures of Vedanta

Vata dosha - biological air humor

Vedanta - Vedic philosophy of Self-realization

Vedas - core yogic or mantric teachings of ancient India

Yoga - the science of Self-realization working with body, mind, prana and soul

Yoga Sutras - prime text of Yoga compiled by the sage Patanjali

3. Bibliography

A. Books by the Author

Astrology of the Seers: A Guide to Vedic/Hindu Astrology. Twin Lakes, WI: Lotus Press, 1991, 2000.

Awaken Bharata: A Call for India's Rebirth.

Ayurveda and Marma Therapy (with Ranade and Lele). Twin Lakes, WI: Lotus Press, 2003.

Ayurveda and the Mind: The Healing of Consciousness. Twin Lakes, WI: Lotus Press, 1997.

Ayurveda, Nature's Medicine (with Subhash Ranade). Twin Lakes, WI: Lotus Press, 2001.

Ayurvedic Healing: A Comprehensive Guide. Twin Lakes, WI: Lotus Press, 1989, 2001.

From the River of Heaven: Hindu and Vedic Knowledge for the Modern Age. Twin Lakes, WI: Lotus Press, 1990, 2000.

Gods, Sages and Kings: Vedic Secrets of Ancient Civilization. Twin Lakes, WI: Lotus Press, 1991, 2000.

Hinduism and the Clash of Civilizations. New Delhi, India: Voice of India, 2001.

In Search of the Cradle of Civilization (with Georg Feuerstein and Subhash Kak). Wheaton, IL: Quest Books, 1995, 2001.

The Oracle of Rama. Twin Lakes, WI: Lotus Press, 1997, 2000.

Rig Veda and the History of India. New Delhi, India: Aditya Prakashan, 2001.

Tantric Yoga and the Wisdom Goddesses: Spiritual Secrets of Ayurveda. Twin Lakes, WI: Lotus Press, 1994, 2003.

Vedantic Meditation: Lighting the Flame of Awareness. Berkeley, CA: North Atlantic Books, 2000.

Wisdom of the Ancient Seers: Selected Mantras from the Rig Veda. Twin Lakes, WI: Lotus Press, 1993, 2000.

Yoga and Ayurveda: Self-healing and Self-realization. Twin Lakes, WI: Lotus Press, 1999.

Yoga of Herbs (with Vasant Lad). Twin Lakes, WI: Lotus Press, 1986, 2001.

Yoga for Your Type: An Ayurvedic Approach to Your Asana Practice (with Sandra Kozak). Twin Lakes, WI: Lotus Press, 2001.

B. Bibliography

Aurobindo. *Hymns to the Mystic Fire*. Twin Lakes, WI: Lotus Press, 2001.

Aurobindo, Sri. *The Life Divine*. Twin Lakes, WI: Lotus Press, 2001.

Aurobindo, Sri. *Savitri*. Twin Lakes, WI: Lotus Press, 2001.

Aurobindo, Sri. *The Secret of the Veda*. Twin Lakes, WI: Lotus Press, 2001.

Bhagavad Gita of Sri Krishna (several versions available).

Chopra, Deepak. *Perfect Health*. New York City: Harmony Books, 1995.

Feuerstein, Georg. *The Yoga Tradition*. Prescott, AZ: Hohm Press, 1998.

Hancock, Graham. *Underworld, Flooded Kingdoms of the Ice Age*. London, U.K.: Penguin Books, 2002.

Lad, Vasant. *Ayurveda, the Science of Self-Healing*. Twin Lakes, WI: Lotus Press, 1984.

Maharshi, Ramana. *Ramana Gita*. Tiruvannamalai, India: Sri Ramanasramam, 1998.

Maharshi, Ramana. *Saddarshana*. Tiruvannamalai, India: Sri Ramanasramam, 1990.

Maharshi, Ramana. *Talks with Sri Ramana Maharshi*. Tiruvannamalai, India: Sri Ramanasramam, 1990.

Maharshi, Ramana. *Upadesha Saram*. Tiruvannamalai, India: Sri Ramanasramam, 1990.

Nikhilananda, Swami, Translation. *The Gospel of Sri Ramakrishna*. New York City: Ramakrishna-Vivekananda Center, 1942.

Ramayana of Tulsidas (several versions available).

Ramayana of Valmiki (several versions available).

Rig Veda (several versions available).

Simon, Dr. David. *Vital Energy*. New York City: John Wiley and Sons, 2000.

Upanishads (several versions available).

Yoga Sutras of Patanjali (several versions available).

Yogananda, Paramahansa. *Autobiography of a Yogi*. Los Angeles, CA: Self-Realization Fellowship, 1985.

Yogananda, Paramahansa. *The Bhagavad Gita: God Talks With Arjuna*. Los Angeles, CA: Self-Realization Fellowship, 1995.

4. Footnotes, References and Comments

Prologue

[1] Books like *Gods, Sages and Kings* (Frawley) discuss these issues in detail.

[2] Note *Underworld, Flooded Kingdoms of the Ice Age* by Graham Hancock for a recent discussion of the possibility of such older civilizations including Vedic India. In the view of the great Yogis of India, our current materialistic type of civilization that began around 3100 BCE was preceded by more spiritual but less technologically advanced cultures. The Mayas also recognize a similar development from 3100 BCE, which they see ending around 2012.

[3] Note author's books *Wisdom of the Ancient Seers* and *Gods, Sages and Kings* for translations from the *Vedas* and a discussion of their historical and cultural background.

[4] The Rishis were called Angirasas, or powers of Agni, a term closely connected to the English word angel which is cognate with Greek Angelos.

[5] The Chinese identified these seven sages with the stars of the Big Dipper just as the Hindus did. For the Sumerian account note *Underworld, Flooded Kingdoms of the Ice Age* by Graham Hancock, pg. 40. For the Indian account, see the same book pages 140-141.

[6] M.P. Pandit once wrote, "Frawley is superb when he discusses in what sense the world is a creation of the Word. His note on the Vedic Mantra is as chiseled as the Vedic Mantra itself."

[7] These Sri Aurobindo journals included *World Union*, *Sri Aurobindo's Action* and *the Advent*.

[8] Pandit is a term for one knowledgeable in the Shastras or the Vedic spiritual teachings, which was certainly the case with M.P. Pandit. In the case of M.P. Pandit, however, it was also a family name.

[9] Most of the early yoga teachers who came to the West from India, starting with Swami Vivekananda, were great Vedantins. Unfortunately, in recent years, the asana side of Yoga has become more prominent and the Vedantic essence of Yoga, its emphasis on Self-realization, has become obscured.

[0] *Rig Veda* I.164.46.

Shvetasvatara Upanishad 2. 16-17.

Part One - Chapter 1

[12] The *Brihat Yogi Yajnavalkya Smriti IX.5*, an ancient yogic text, identifies the soul in the heart with Agni or fire and God in the heart with Vayu or air. The mergence of our soul flame with the cosmic air is liberation from embodied existence.

[13] Poems of Wordsworth, the World is Too Much With Us.

[14] A common statement in *Brahmanas* and *Upanishads* (*Aitareya Upanishad* III.4).

[15] The sages require special initiations to prepare students to receive their teachings, just as a farmer prepares the ground before sowing the seed. This is called diksha in Sanskrit.

[16] We associate the idea of sacrifice with offerings in which animals were ritually killed, which did occur at times in the ancient world. But the term sacrifice had a

much broader meaning as worship or even Yoga – spiritual practices to unite us with God. The Vedic term for sacrifice, Yajna, also stood for the sacred nature of reality.

[17] Note books like *In Search of the Cradle of Civilization* (Feuerstein, Kak and Frawley) and *Gods, Sages and Kings* (Frawley) for recent geological discoveries of the Vedic Sarasvati River, which dried up in India about four thousand years ago.

[18] *Rig Veda* I.1.1, 2, 7.

[19] *Rig Veda* II.1.1.

[20] *Rig Veda* VI.48.5-6.

[21] *Atharva Veda* XIII.1.19-20.

[22] My main teacher of this deeper understanding of Hinduism was Ram Swarup, whom the magazine *Hinduism Today* has praised as perhaps the greatest teacher of Hindu Dharma in the past few decades.

[23] *Zend Avesta*, Yasna XXV, 7. Sacred Books of the East Vol. 31.

[24] Communicated to the author from Hector Currie, Professor Emeritus of the University of Cincinnati, from his own research.

[25] *Song of Amairgen*, v. 15 -16, communicated to author by friend and Celtic scholar Boutios (Michel Boutet) of Canada. There are deep connections between Druidic and Vedic thought on many subjects including karma, rebirth and the immortality of the soul.

[26] Note *Of Gods and Holidays, The Baltic Heritage*, edited by Jonas Trinkunas, one of the main leaders of this neo-pagan movement, whom I was fortunate enough to meet at a recent conference.

[27] *Egyptian Book of the Dead*, E.A. Wallis Budge translation, pg. 317.

[28] I studied the *I Ching* and Taoist philosophy for several years and learned the system of Chinese herbal medicine as well. The Taoist tradition helped me a great deal in understanding the cosmic symbolism of fire and the religion of nature.

[29] *I Ching*, Wilhelm-Baynes translation, pg. 119.

[30] *I Ching*, Wilhelm-Baynes translation, pg. 194.

[31] According to S.D. Youngwolf, a Cherokee leader, the Cherokees recognize four great fires – that of the Sun, the Earth, the cooking fire and the life fire within us. These are very much like the different fires recognized in Vedic thought, of which three are most important (the Earth fire or Agni, the life fire or Jatavedas and the solar/cosmic fire or Vaishvanara).

[32] Graham Hancock, *Underworld: Flooded Kingdoms of the Ice Age*, pg. 196.

[33] Yogananda's, *God Talks With Arjuna: The Bhagavad Gita*, Introduction xviii-xix.

[34] Poems of Wordsworth, Ode, Intimations of Immortality.

Chapter 2

[35] *Brihadaranyaka Upanishad* I.3.28. Darkness is tamas, the quality of inertia in nature, not simply an absence of physical light. Light itself is sattva, the quality of clarity in nature.

[36] The science of Yoga rests upon the five element theory from Samkhya philosophy, one of the six Vedic philosophical schools. The Samkhya system in turn reflects older Vedantic models in the *Upanishads* going back to the *Rig Veda*.

[37] Such nature spirits, Gods and Goddesses are worshipped systematically in the Hindu tradition, through different rituals, prayers, mantras and meditations that link us with the greater powers of consciousness in the world.

[38] As in Jung's series of books on Psychology and Alchemy.

Chapter 3

[39] *Yoga Sutras of Patanjali* I.3.

[40] Yoga philosophy, based upon Patanjali's *Yoga Sutras*, is one of the six schools of Vedic philosophy that accepts the authority and insights of the *Vedas*, *Upanishads* and *Bhagavad Gita*.

[41] The philosophy that the Self is the supreme reality is called 'Vedanta' and is the culmination of Vedic thought. There are many modern and ancient books on this teaching from the *Vedas* to the works of modern sages like Vivekananda or Ramana Maharshi.

[42] *Rig Veda* X.90, 2, 12, 14.

[43] This point is discussed in the ancient *Aitareya Aranyaka* II.3.1, connected to the *Upanishad* of the same name.

[44] *Aitareya Upanishad* I.1.1; III.11, 12, 13.

[45] *Isha Upanishad* 6, 7.

[46] *Katha Upanishad* 4.13.

[47] *Isha Upanishad* 6-7.

Chapter 4

[48] David Suzuki, *The Sacred Balance*, pg. 112.

[49] *Mundaka Upanishad* II.1.1.

[50] The cosmic form of Fire is identified with Lord Shiva in yogic thought, particularly as Rudra, who represents the fire of eternity. The entire universe is the fire dance of Lord Shiva.

[51] The Pleiades is called Krittika Nakshatra in Vedic astrology. It includes the point in the zodiac (03 Taurus) in which the Moon, the planet of the Divine Mother, is exalted.

[52] Mars, on the other hand, is at the outside of this solar ring of fire, and so is too cold and too small to hold life. Venus, though similar in size to the Earth, by its closer proximity to the Sun is mainly a volcanic realm where no life can survive.

[53] David Suzuki, *The Sacred Balance*, pg. 114.

Part Two - Chapter 5

[54] *Chandogya Upanishad* VI.1.

[55] *Shukla Yajur Veda* XI.57.

[56] The rock cycle of geology begins with igneous or fiery rocks, which then weather into sedimentary rocks that in turn get reformed as metamorphic rocks. Igneous rocks, therefore, form the first phase of all rocks.

[57] These are the plutonic or extrusive igneous rocks and regional metamorphic rocks of geology.

[58] In the Vedic system of astrology called 'Jyotish', such gemstones are used to transmit positive planetary influences to improve our lives. Note authors' *Astrology of the Seers*.

[59] These stones are commonly found in the Narmada River of central India.

[60] Vastu is also called 'Sthapatya Veda' or Vedic architectural science and remains the basis of temple construction in India.

Chapter 6

[61] A wonderful Vedic chant called Apam Pushpam or the flower of the waters

expresses this connection.

[63] David Suzuki, *The Sacred Balance*, pg. 113.

[63] Jehovah was originally a God of Gods or King of the Gods ruling the atmosphere. These many Gods are not separate deities but different forms and functions of the One God or Truth that is pure light and pure consciousness.

[64] The Apam Napat or Son of the Waters of the *Vedas*.

[65] *The Druids*, Peter Ellis, pps. 118-119.

[66] *Shvetasvatara Upanishad* 6.15.

Chapter 7

[67] Bacteria are almost an entire level of evolution itself. We could say that they represent the raw material of life out of which the mineral kingdom gets transformed into plants and animals.

[68] David Suzuki, *The Sacred Balance*, pg. 116.

[69] *Chandogya Upanishad* I.1.

[70] Fiery plant derivatives include spices, oils, resins, salts and alkaloids. In Ayurveda, spicy, sour and salty tastes are considered to be fiery or heating in nature.

[71] Vedic texts mention a number of Soma like plants including various orchid, reed and lilaceous plants, as well as nervine herbs like ephedra and cannabis.

[72] *Katha Upanishad* VI.1.

[73] The Ashwattha and Shami trees were mainly used for this purpose. The Ashwattha or sacred fig tree was the main wood used for the sacred fire.

[74] *Rig Veda* VI.16.13.

[75] Note author's *Tantric Yoga and the Wisdom Goddesses*, pps. 86-95.

[76] Pujas are of different types, but all involve offering flowers, incense, light, food and fragrant oils to a representational form of the deity.

[77] Plants used for this purpose in India include durva, kusha and shara.

[78] In Ayurveda, honey and ghee are not used in equal proportions, which is regarded as harmful. A good proportion is two parts honey to one part ghee.

[79] Note the *Mahabharata,* the great epic in which the *Bhagavad Gita* occurs, for a discussion of the five senses and consciousness in plants, *Moksha Dharma Parva* 184 10-17 (in some editions 185; for example K. M. Ganguli translation Vol. III, *Santi Parva* Part II pg. 26).

[80] In Ayurveda such sacred house plants include holy basil (tulsi), aloe and hibiscus.

Chapter 8

[81] Darwin's theory of evolution and the survival of the fittest arose mainly through an observation of the animal kingdom and has its greatest validity on that level. Unfortunately, it tries to use the animal model for all possible evolution, which prevents it from understanding any higher evolution of consciousness.

[82] The Jatharagni of Ayurvedic medicine, which we humans also have.

[83] The fire of the blood is called 'Ranjaka Pitta' in Ayurvedic medicine.

[84] The old Sanskrit *Ramayana* is by Valmiki. William Buck has offered a good English translation. A sixteenth century Hindi *Ramayana* by Tulsidas is very popular in India.

[85] *Rig Veda* VIII. 100.11.

[86] There are about twenty *Puranas*, which are vast encyclopedic works dealing with cosmology, history, philosophy, geography, arts and social customs according to a

view that God takes many forms and functions throughout our entire existence. Unfortunately, they are one of the most neglected aspects of the vast spiritual literature of India.

[86] Her story is related in the *Devi Mahatmya*. She is honored by the great autumn Durga festival in India that runs for ten days and is most popular in the state of Bengal.

[88] *Chandogya Upanishad* IV.4-14.

[89] From *Brihat Stotra Ratnakara*, a collection of Hindu chants and hymns to various deities.

[90] This was part of a visit to the Hinduism Today monastery, which has enshrined of the largest crystals in the world. Its temple is an important conduit of spiritual energy into the planet.

[91] Animals can stand for our lower or uncontrolled emotions like anger or lust, just as they can indicate.

Part Three - Chapter 9

[92] Manu is a progenitor like the Biblical Adam, but not subject to any fall. He is portrayed as a Self-realized yogi. He is also a flood figure like Noah, who took the seeds of all living creatures into his boat, which settled on a Himalayan peak after the flood waters receded. Note Graham Hancock, *Underworld: Flooded Kingdoms of the Ice Age*, pg. 132-136.

[93] *Rig Veda* V.21.1.

[94] The digestive fire or Jatharagni is the root fire for our physical existence.

[95] This fire of the breath, called 'Pranagni' (Prana-agni) in Sanskrit, is the subject of many yoga teachings.

[96] Agni or fire at a psychological level in Vedic thought correlates to Vak or speech.

[97] In the *Upanishads* (*Mundaka Upanishad* I.2.4) the sacred fire has seven tongues or seven flames, the foremost of which is Kali who is also the Goddess of time.

[98] The Sanskrit language is said to be a manifestation of this primal fire or light language.

[99] Ayurveda recognizes a special fire or Agni in the skin called 'Bhrajaka Pitta', which is responsible for the luster and warmth of the skin.

[100] It is called 'Kamagni' or Kama-Agni, the fire of desire, and connects to the root desires of the soul.

[101] Note the practice of Brahmacharya in the Yoga tradition, which is not simply celibacy but directing our creative fire towards inner transformation.

[102] In Vedic thought, fire or Agni is called Grihapati or the lord of the house.

[103] For example, in terms of profession the artist has his particular fire, the scientist another, the soldier yet another, even the cook another. Most of our vocations can be defined by fire, which is the power of work and inspiration.

[104] Hindu Brahmins and Zoroastrian Magi were such orders of fire priests.

[105] The worship of fire is often criticized by monotheistic traditions as a form of idolatry, nature worship or polytheism, but this is a superficial reading of its real meaning that goes much deeper.

[106] The angushta-matra Purusha of various *Upanishads* like the *Katha*.

[107] He taught the Yoga of the *Katha Upanishad*, which he had rediscovered.

[108] *Shvetasvatara Upanishad* 4.3; 2. 16-17.

Chapter 10

[109] Prakriti is said to be composed of three prime qualities called gunas (sattva or harmony, rajas or energy, and tamas or inertia) and the five elements. It works to unfold the powers of the mind, sense organs, motor organs and Prana on individual, collective and cosmic levels. Prakriti is not a mere blind material force but a power of intelligence that works to create the bodies through which the Purusha or pure consciousness can realize itself. It works through the reflection of the light and consciousness of the Purusha.

[110] This cosmic intelligence, 'Mahat' in Sanskrit, can be called the 'mind of God'. It contains all the seeds and laws, the dharmas from which the universe develops.

[111] Satchitananda in Sanskrit.

[112] Krishna, *Bhagavad Gita* IV.1.

[113] *Matsya Purana*, an ancient Hindu text, I.13 describes Manu, originating from the Malaya hills of Kerala, as having achieved the highest Yoga (yogam uttamam). It states (II.17-19) that Manu was able to take the seeds of all living beings into his ship because of his yogic powers. Note Graham Hancock, *Underworld: Flooded Kingdoms of the Ice Age*, pps. 132-136.

[114] Note author's *Rig Veda and the History of India*, pp. 235-239.

[15] Hiranyagarbha is the founder of Yoga in the *Puranas* and classical Yogic texts. There is no tradition which attributes the origins of Yoga to Patanjali, who was only the compiler of a much older tradition.

[16] Hiranyagarbha represents the universal subtle body or Pranic force. As the golden embryo, it refers to the subtle body that is like a golden fire egg within the heart.

[17] *Mahabharata, Moksha Dharma Parva* 308.45. In some editions 309; for example K. M. Ganguli translation Vol. IV, *Santi Parva* Part III, pg. 31. There is also a famous Yoga text attributed to Vasishta, the *Vasishta Samhita*, reflecting this connection.

[18] Vedic martial arts or Dhanur Veda uses yoga postures and movements in order to aid in physical strength and flexibility. Most of these traditions go back to the great warrior-rishi Vishwamitra, who was also a great yogi and the seer of the Gayatri mantra. A Vishwamitra taught the martial arts to Lord Rama.

[19] Indian dance traditions use yoga asanas to give the dancers greater flexibility. Dance movements, postures and gestures also reflect yoga asanas and mudras. Lord Shiva, the lord of the dance, is the great lord of the yogis. His dance postures are important asanas.

[20] *Shvetasvatara Upanishad* II.1.

[121] According to yogic thought, before souls took birth as physical creatures they inhabited the atmosphere and the surface of the Earth in subtle physical bodies composed of energy. These subtle energy bodies underlie our physical body. This means that the soul has been present on Earth for eons, both within and behind nature's various forms. When our physical body is withdrawn during sleep or death we can experience these energy bodies again.

[122] As the lord of the dance, the cosmic fire dancer, Shiva is called 'Nataraj'.

[123] *Shvetasvatara Upanishad* II.12.

[124] *Yoga Sutras* I.2-3.

[125] The building of the sacred fire altar was called Agni chayana. It is an elaborate subject in Vedic texts like the *Satapatha Brahmana*, in which the fire altar is identified with both the Self and the entire universe. This fire altar can be made externally with bricks or envisioned internally as a form of meditation.

[126] *Yoga Sutras* of Patanjali II.29. These eight limbs are much older than Patanjali and

are common to many yogic texts and teachings including the *Mahabharata, Puranas* and *Upanishads.*

[127] We could say that Yama and Niyama create the fire of Dharma necessary to purify ourselves in order for any yogic practices to truly work.

[128] In Sanskrit, ahimsa, satya, Brahmacharya, asteya, aparigraha, *Yoga Sutras* II.30.

[129] This yogic principle of aparigraha is very hard to translate into English. It refers to non-possessiveness, simplicity and non-clinging. It means not holding to things in our minds, hence non-coveting. However, it refers to not keeping any unnecessary possessions and was a term for monastic vows to give up all outer belongings in life. But it is the giving up of the inner possessions of the ego that is its real goal.

[130] Ahimsa is said to be the highest or supreme dharma. Yet it is important not to confuse ahimsa with a mere absence of overt violence. True ahimsa involves actively working to reduce the amount of harm going on in the world. Traditionally it does not necessarily exclude self-defense either. Great yogic teachings like the *Gita* explain the place of a dharmic war, though only as a last resort to prevent greater harm from occurring.

[31] In Sanskrit, tapas, svadhyaya, Ishvara pranidhana, saucha, santosha, *Yoga Sutras* II.30.

[32] Tapas, which I have called self-discipline, literally means 'creating heat'. Agni or the cosmic fire is said to dwell in Tapo-Loka, the world or plane of Tapas, which is also the realm of pure consciousness.

[33] Note *Yoga for Your Type* (Frawley and Kozak) for a discussion of asana practice relative to Ayurvedic medicine and such concepts as Agni.

[34] Kripalu Yoga and Amrit Yoga, invented by Yogi Amrit Desai, are of this type. I have witnessed a number of Desai's demonstrations in which he allows the Prana to guide his asanas in an effortless flow.

[35] *Bhagavad Gita* IV.36.

[36] There are various biographical accounts of his life.

[37] Ramana Maharshi, *Five Verses in Praise of Arunachala* (Sri Arunachala Pancharatnam), v.2.

[38] Note also Graham Hancock, *Underworld: Flooded Kingdoms of the Ice Age*, pg. 227.

[39] Paul Brunton, *Search in Secret India.*

[40] Ganapati Muni, *Forty Verses in Praise of Sri Ramana*, v. 30.

[41] This story can be found in various *Puranas* and is the subject of a great poem called *Kumara Sambhava* by Kalidasa, the great classical Sanskrit poet said to be the Shakespeare of India, who lived about two thousand years ago.

[42] Note *Tantric Yoga and the Wisdom Goddesses* (Frawley) that is based upon the work of Ganapati Muni.

[43] Ganapati's other main disciple was Kapali Shastri, who later joined the Sri Aurobindo Ashram. M.P. Pandit, who initially inspired the author in his Vedic writings, was himself a disciple of Kapali.

[44] *Chandodarshana*, pp 18-19. Brahmarshi Daivarata (the book, published by Bharatiya Vidya Bhavan, is long out of print).

Chapter 11

[45] My main Ayurvedic teacher, Dr. B.L. Vashta of Mumbai, India, emphasized this Vedic basis of Ayurveda in my studies with him. But it is commonly mentioned in Ayurvedic literature with Vedic deities like Indra and the Ashvins or Vedic Rishis as the first teachers of Ayurveda.

[46] Note *Perfect Health* by Dr. Deepak Chopra for a good contemporary introduction into Ayurveda and the *Ayurveda, the Science of Self-Healing* by Dr. Vasant Lad for a good practical guide to the subject.

[47] Even ancient classical texts of Ayurveda like *Charaka Samhita* and *Sushruta Samhita* refer to pollution of the environment as a major cause of disease and of social collapse. In particular, note *Charaka Samhita* Vimanasthana III.

[48] *Rig Veda* I.31.11.

[49] Note *Yoga and Ayurveda* (Frawley) pp. 105-118, for a discussion of Ayurveda and Yoga, including the different forms of fire used within them.

[50] *Taittiriya Upanishad* II.2.

[51] Agni lives in an ocean of ghee (Rig Veda II.3.11). Ghee also symbolizes the waters of space that have the power to nourish the light.

[52] Ghee is regarded as cooling in energy in Ayurveda, while most other edible oils are heating.

[53] Ayurvedic medicine has a complex pharmaceutical industry that employs many different forms of heat or Agni to bring out herbal properties, cooking both herbs and minerals in various ways.

[54] Note *Yoga of Herbs* (Frawley and Lad) for a materia medica of herbs from an Ayurvedic perspective.

[55] Sweating (Swedana) therapy is an integral part of Pancha Karma, Ayurveda' radical detoxification therapy.

[56] There are a few special yogic forms of mouth breathing which ally the power of speech with that of the breath, but if we do these we must make sure to keep our nostrils clear and the breath in the nose strong.

[57] A common yogic method for this is called the *breath of fire* (Bhastrika). Kapalabhati is another very heating form of pranayama.

[58] These practices are called 'Surya Bhedana' and 'Chandra Bhedana' in Sanskrit.

[59] This is yogic sleep or Yoga nidra.

[60] Ayurveda has an entire rejuvenation therapy called 'Rasayana Chikitsa'. Besides special foods and herbs it relies heavily on various Yoga practices and periods of retreat in nature.

[61] There are many rejuvenative (Rasayana) herbs and formulas in Ayurveda like the famous herbal jelly Chyavan prash or the formula Brahma Rasayana.

[162] Examine *Yoga of Herbs* for more details on such rejuvenative herbs.

[163] Pancha Karma uses methods like purgation, emesis or enemas along with special oil massage and sweating methods to clear deep-seated toxins from the body and make it fit for rejuvenation.

Chapter 12

[64] Note *Ayurveda and the Mind: the Healing of Consciousness* (Frawley) pp. 169-186, for more information on these topics and for an examination of yogic and Ayurvedic psychology.

[65] The practice of silence or non-speaking is called 'mauna' in Sanskrit and is an important yogic discipline.

[66] Such methods of mental fasting are generally part of Pratyahara, the fifth limb of classical Yoga, which involves turning the senses inward.

[67] Called 'Smarana' or the practice of remembrance in Sanskrit.

[68] *Isha Upanishad* 17, 18.

Part Three - Chapter 13

[169] The traditional name for Hinduism is 'Sanatana Dharma' or the Eternal Dharma. Buddhism calls itself 'Buddha Dharma'. Jainism is called 'Jain Dharma'. Such dharmic traditions are closely connected, sharing the idea that dharma or universal law is the supreme principle.

[170] David Suzuki, *The Sacred Balance*, pg. 120.

[171] Note *Chandogya Upanishad* VIII.8-12 for the story of Indra and Virochana.

[172] *I Ching*, Wilhelm-Baynes translation, pg. 196.

[173] Note the work of Subhash Kak, notably his article *The Indian Religion in Ancient Iran and Zarathustra*, in which he draws such important correlations.

Chapter 14

[174] *The Dying of the Trees* by Charles E. Little addresses this in both an informed and poignant manner.

[175] That remark was written in 2002. In 2003 the die back of Pinyons in the Southwest, particularly in the Santa Fe area, has increased rapidly, with whole hillsides lost. With a seven year drought, the problem may get even worse – truly an ecological disaster that should warn us of things to come if we don't change our life-styles.

[176] Ibid. pg. 234.

[177] The Sanskrit language, called the language of the Gods, reflects such cosmic wisdom in its root sounds. For example, the root 'ga' behind such terms as 'gau' means to go, to count, to speak, to sing, to measure, a word, the earth, a sense organ, and a ray of light.

[178] According to Hindu thought, the dark materialistic age of Kali Yuga began around 3100 BCE when the stars Aldeberan in Taurus and Antares in Scorpio (called Rohini and Jyeshta in Vedic astronomy) marked the vernal equinox. This ushered in a materialistic culture that has reached its culmination in our current high tech civilization. The Mayans have similar views. Now we have the opportunity to transcend this materialistic way of life or be destroyed by it. The decisive change has yet to be made. It is doubtful that we can survive the coming century without a major change of how we live, which reincorporates a respect for the older pre-technological spiritual basis of our species.

Chapter 15

[179] A new group of this type is the Vedic Friends Association (VFA), which is seeking to create a broad and non-sectarian Vedic fellowship in the West.

[180] *Selected Poems of Yves Bonnefoy* (Anthony Rudolf translation), the Dialogue of Anguish and Desire.

[18] There is a wonderful reference to her in Yogananda's *Autobiography of a Yogi*, recounting his visit with her in India in 1935.

[182] This was the period between 1976 and 1982, starting before I met MP Pandit.

[183] Note the famous Sri Sukta of the Vedas, the main hymn for worshipping Lakshmi, which asks the sacred fire or Agni to bring Lakshmi to us.

[184] *Tantric Yoga and the Wisdom Goddesses*.

[185] Mother India as a Goddess is generally portrayed in the form of Durga with her lion.

[186] Durga Sukta, *Taittiriya Aranyaka* 4.10.2.

[187] Note his biography, *The Gospel of Ramakrishna*.

[188] Cheripunji is perhaps the wettest place on Earth. The eastern Himalayan foothills

get more rain than any other ecosystem on Earth through a heavy monsoon that lasts two thirds of the year.

[189] Another related sacred site for the Goddess is Kamakshi in Kanchipuram near Chennai (Madras), which has a beautiful gold domed temple to the Goddess and is also the site of one of the great Shankaracharya Maths (centers). I have visited it and its great gurus several times. Kamakhya is the Assamese pronunciation of Kamakshi. Kamakhya is the Kamakshi of the north.

[190] This is the Yoga practice of tapas, one of the three main aspects of Kriya Yoga as taught in the *Yoga Sutras* II.1.

Part Five - Chapter 16

[191] Hymn to the Earth, *Atharva Veda* XII.1, 8.

[92] *Rig Veda* I.189.3.

[93] Note particularly his *Life Divine*, which discusses his view of human and cosmic evolution.

[94] Aurobindo disagreed with Gandhi on several policies and felt that Gandhi's extreme ahimsa was not always the right policy. He encouraged Gandhi to support the British in the war against Hitler, though Gandhi declined.

[95] Note various biographies of Aurobindo like *Sri Aurobindo and the Mind of Light* by Satprem.

[96] His *Hymns to the Mystic Fire* contains translations of the hymns to Agni from the *Rig Veda* along with explanatory notes.

[97] Sri Aurobindo, *Hymns to the Mystic Fire* pg. 30.

[98] Sri Aurobindo. *Savitri*.

[99] The social and political situation in India is very complex, perhaps more so than that of the United States; so what I have said here is only general. Besides more spiritual trends, commercial, Marxist and fundamentalist trends also exist in the country and are vying for influence.

[200] Like the author's books *Arise Arjuna* and *Awaken Bharata*.

[20] Kundalini is the power of the Divine Word, the awakened Prana, the power of consciousness and the Yoga Shakti. It can be symbolized by various deities like Kali with her garland of skulls, Shiva with his garland of snakes or Vishnu who rests upon a serpent. Many mythological stories of the dragon or serpent relate to it. The arousing of the Kundalini is sometimes regarded as the slaying of the serpent.

[202] Note the work of Gopi Krishna that explains his own direct experience of the Kundalini.

[203] This was the view of Ganapati Muni, the chief disciple of Ramana Maharshi.

[204] There is a great deal of New Age speculation about Kundalini and the chakras, much of it insightful but much of it inaccurate. It often shows an inability to discriminate between the yogic and ordinary levels of chakra functioning. The account here is from a yogic perspective and should not be simply equated with New Age views.

[205] Yogi Har Bhajan Singh and this 3HO organization. I have had the good fortune to meet with Yogiji, as he is called, a number of times, as he lives not far from me in New Mexico

[206] This topic is discussed in the author's *Tantric Yoga and the Wisdom Goddesses*.

[207] Note Yogananda's *Autobiography of a Yogi*, for his amazing life story.

[208] *The Bhagavad Gita, God Talks with Arjuna*, Paramahamsa Yogananda. This is one of the best books available on the real teachings of Yoga.

[209] Note Ramana Maharshi's works like *Ramana Gita, Upadesha Saram* and

Saddarshana. English versions are available through the Ramanashram.

[210] Non-dualistic or 'Advaita Vedanta' is perhaps the highest teaching of the Vedic tradition, showing us how to directly realize the Supreme Self or the Divine I am as our true nature.

[211] *Maitrayani Upanishad* VI.34. .

[212] The *Bhakti Sutras* of Narada is the prime text on this yogic path.

Chapter 17

[213] These five fires follow the five koshas or sheaths of Yogic thought as taught in the *Taittiriya Upanishad* (1. Annamaya kosha or food sheath, 2. Pranamaya kosha or breath sheath, 3. Manomaya kosha or sheath of the outer mind, 4. Vijnanamaya kosha or sheath of the inner mind, 5. Anandamaya kosha or bliss sheath). See also *Yoga and Ayurveda* pp.110-112.

Postscript

[214] Ayurvedic medicine recognizes four states of Agni or fire as too high, too low, variable and balanced. I have added its smoky condition as the fifth in order to bring additional clarity to its functioning.

[215] Books on Ayurveda like *Ayurvedic Healing* (Frawley) and the *Ayurvedic Cookbook* (Morningstar) discuss diets to increase Agni and balance the doshas.

Chapter 18

[216] This practice is called 'Sakshi-bhava' in Sanskrit.

[217] An important principle of Vedantic meditation is that the seer transcends the limitations of whatever it sees. This means that the seer of time is not of time but of eternity. In your true nature as consciousness awareness you transcend all time, space and karma.

[218] *Mahanarayana Upanishad* IV.13, Narayana Sukta, on which this information is based.

[219] Hreem is a good mantra for both awakening and controlling the Kundalini.

[220] A number of groups teach the Agnihotra including the Arya Samaj, the Fivefold Path and the Gayatri Pariwar.

[221] This practice of choosing an auspicious moment is called Muhurta in Vedic astrology. It rests on the Panchanga or fivefold Vedic calendar.

[222] The modern Hindu sect, the Arya Samaj, has emphasized the Gayatri as a mantra for everyone and is responsible for much of its modern popularity. So has the Gayatri Pariwar. Many Yoga students also know it.

[223] While the Gayatri mantra derives from the *Rig Veda*, a more extensive form of its recitation is found in the *Mahanarayana Upanishad*.

[224] *Rig Veda* III.62.10.

[225] This small space is called the 'dahara akasha'. The unstruck sound or 'anahata nada' is the source of all energy and movement in the universe, the vibration of universal space.

Biodata

Dr. David Frawley (Pandit Vamadeva Shastri) is one of the few westerners ever recognized in India as a Vedacharya or teacher of the ancient wisdom and as a Pandit or Doctor of Vedic Science. His fields of study include Yoga, Ayurveda, Vedic Astrology, Tantra and Vedanta, with a special reference to the Vedas, the ancient root of India's healing and meditational traditions.

He is the author of over twenty books and many articles over the last twenty-five years and has taught and lectured worldwide.

Vamadeva is an unusual western born knowledge-holder in the Vedic tradition. He carries many special Vedic (vidyas) ways of knowledge, which he passes on to a variety of students. He has studied many traditional texts in the original Sanskrit with several great gurus but has cultivated a special intuitive insight as well, making his work both classically grounded and relevant to the modern context. He sees his role as helping to revive Vedic knowledge in an interdisciplinary approach for the planetary age.

Currently, Dr. Frawley is the director of the American Institute of Vedic Studies and an advisor to many Vedic groups and organizations worldwide including the National Association of Ayurvedic Medicine (NAMA), the American College of Vedic Astrology (ACVA), the California College of Ayurveda (CCA), the European Institute of Vedic Studies, the Chopra Center for Well-Being, and the World Association of Vedic Studies (WAVES).

American Institute of Vedic Studies

The American Institute of Vedic Studies is an educational center devoted to the greater systems of Vedic and Yogic knowledge. It teaches various Vedic Sciences including Ayurveda, Vedic Astrology, Yoga, Tantra and Vedanta with special reference to their background in the *Vedas*. The Institute is also engaged in several educational projects in the greater field of Hindu Dharma including:

- Translations and interpretations of the *Vedas,* particularly the *Rig Veda*, and an explication of the original Vedic Yoga.
- Vedic History: The history of India and of the world from a Vedic perspective and also as reflecting latest archaeological work in India.
- Vedic Europe: Explaining the connections between the Vedic and ancient European cultures and religions.
- Projection of Vedic and Hindu knowledge in a modern context for the coming millennium.

The Institute also has two important Distant Learning Programs outlined below as well as special tutorial programs.

Ayurvedic Healing
Distance Learning Program

This comprehensive practical program covers all the main aspects of Ayurvedic theory, diagnosis and practice, with special emphasis on herbal medicine and dietary therapy. It also goes in detail into Yoga philosophy and Ayurvedic psychology, following an integral mind-body approach. It contains most of the material covered in longer two-year Ayurvedic programs.

The course is designed for health care professionals as well as serious students to provide the foundation for becoming an Ayurvedic practitioner. Over the last fifteen years around five thousand people have taken this course, which is one of the best of its kind available.

Astrology of the Seers
Distance Learning Program

This comprehensive homestudy course explains Vedic Astrology in clear and modern terms, providing practical insights on how to use and adapt the system for our needs today.

The goal of the course is to provide the foundation for the student to become a professional Vedic astrologer. Its orientation is twofold: To teach the language, approach and way of thinking of Vedic Astrology; and to teach the Astrology of Healing of the Vedic system, or Ayurvedic Astrology. It trains the students not only how to read Vedic charts but how to understand their Ayurvedic and Yogic implications as well. It is one of the oldest and most popular courses in its field.

Yoga and Ayurveda
Distance Learning Progam

As of fall of 2004, the institute will be introducing a Yoga and Ayurveda course, similar in format to the Ayurvedic Healing course. It will consist of two levels, the first for students who are not knowledgeable of Ayurveda and the second for those who are. It will also reflect the ideas and views in this book, *Yoga and the Sacred Fire*.

American Institute of Vedic Studies
PO Box 8357, Santa Fe NM 87504-8357
Ph: 505-983-9385, Fax: 505-982-5807
Dr. David Frawley (Pandit Vamadeva Shastri), Director
Web: www.vedanet.com, Email: vedicinst@aol.com

Index

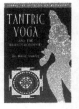